A Chosen Exile

A Chosen Exile

A History of Racial Passing in American Life

Allyson Hobbs

HARVARD UNIVERSITY PRESS
Cambridge, Massachusetts, and London, England
2014

Printed in the United States of America

First printing

Library of Congress Cataloging-in-Publication Data
is available from the Library of Congress

ISBN 978-0-674-36810-1

For my parents,
Al and Joyce Hobbs,
Who make everything possible

And in memory of my sister,
Sharon Rose Hobbs Bell,
The loveliest rose in the world
And the brightest star in the sky

Contents

On sunny summer Sunday afternoons in Harlem
when the air is one interminable ball game
and grandma cannot get her gospel hymns
from the Saints of God in Christ
on account of the Dodgers on the radio,
on sunny Sunday afternoons
when the kids look all new
and far too clean to stay that way,
and Harlem has its
washed-and-ironed-and-cleaned-best out,
the ones who've crossed the line
to live downtown
miss you,
Harlem of the bitter dream,
since their dream has
come true.

—*Langston Hughes*

A Chosen Exile

Prologue: To Live a Life Elsewhere

It's just as easy as falling off a log.
—MARY CHURCH TERRELL

On a sizzling summer morning in the late 1930s, a young girl waited on the curb of South Park Boulevard on Chicago's South Side for the Bud Billiken Parade to begin. The heat was relentless, but on the second Saturday in August, it made no difference to children who leapt from their beds in search of the best spot to view the parade. The young girl joined a crowd that numbered in the thousands, and she cheered as drum majors, baton twirlers, and celebrities in convertibles passed by. She ran out to the floats to touch the parade's anointed king and queen and caught the candy that the participants tossed to her. Beginning in 1929 as a celebration of the *Chicago Defender*'s newsboys, the Bud Billiken Parade later became a back-to-school celebration that honored all black children on the South Side. Known as the "god of things as the way they should be," Bud Billiken was a mythical character that showered black children with affection. The parade was a South Side institution. At a time when racial tensions ran

Figure P.1. Spectators enjoy the annual Bud Billiken Parade, a tradition on Chicago's South Side since 1929.

Photograph by Wayne F. Miller. Courtesy of Wayne F. Miller.

Figure P.2. Fans cheer at a Wendell Phillips-DuSable High School football game during the mid-1940s.
Photograph by Wayne F. Miller. Courtesy of Wayne F. Miller.

high, when black families squeezed into overcrowded kitchenettes, and when black children knew not to venture beyond the boundaries of the Black Belt, the Bud Billiken Parade evoked a deep sense of race pride, community, and togetherness. For one day a year, black children could imagine that the city of Chicago was all theirs.

The young girl could not have known that this would be her last time hearing the marching bands and the cheering crowds and following the parade to the picnic in Washington Park. Unlike many black parents, she would not share this experience with her children. She looked white, as did both of her parents. At the insistence of her mother, she would move far away from Chicago's South Side to Los Angeles to live the rest of her life as a white woman apart from her family. It was not her choice. She pleaded with her mother; she did not want to leave her family, her friends, and the only life she had ever known. But her mother was determined and the matter was decided.

Years later, after she married a white man and raised white children who knew nothing of her past, she received an inconvenient telephone call. It was her mother, and she called to tell her that her father was dying and she must come home immediately. Despite these dire circumstances, she would never return to Chicago's South Side. The young girl who had once sat on a curb in Chicago's most historic black neighborhood to watch America's largest black parade was a white woman now. There was simply no turning back.

This book is about loss. Racial passing is an exile, sometimes chosen, sometimes not. The story of the young girl at the Bud Billiken Parade in Chicago is one of my family's stories and one shared by thousands of other families. Between the late eighteenth and the mid-twentieth centuries, countless African Americans passed as white, leaving behind families, friends, and communities without any available avenue for return. Lives were lost only to be remembered in family stories. This book is an effort to recover those lives.

To pass as white was to make an anxious decision to turn one's back on a black racial identity and to claim to belong to a group to which one was not legally assigned. It was risky business. In today's multiracial society, the decision to pass may seem foolish, frivolous, or disloyal; it may be reminiscent of an unexpected plot twist in a novel or a film; or it may be understood as a desperate act compelled by the racial constraints of the bygone era of segregation and racial violence. Once one circumvented the law, fooled coworkers, deceived neighbors, tricked friends, and sometimes even duped children and spouses, there were enormous costs to pay. In each historical period, those who passed experienced personal and familial losses differently. Their experiences open a window onto the enduring problem of race in American society and onto the intimate meanings of race and racial identity for African Americans. The predicaments of those who could pass as white offer a lens to view the changing meanings of race in American history. From the late eighteenth century to the present, racially ambiguous men and women have wrestled with complex questions about the racial conditions of their times, and they have fashioned complex understandings about their places in the world.

Each era determined not only how racially ambiguous men and women lived, but also what they lost. In the antebellum period, enslaved men and women lived with a looming threat of loss, knowing that they could be bought, sold, and forever separated from their families if their master lost a card game or decided to present a slave as a wedding gift. To pass as white during this period was to escape—not necessarily from blackness, but from slavery—with the intention of recovering precious relationships and living under the more secure conditions of freedom. After emancipation, to pass as white was considered by many African Americans (and most famously by James Weldon Johnson in the 1912 novel *The Autobiography of an Ex-Colored Man*) to be "sell[ing] one's birthright for a mess of pottage."[1] In the short-lived but hopeful moment of Reconstruction and later, during the long years of Jim Crow, passing meant striking out on one's own and leaving behind a family and a people. Without a doubt, benefits accrued to these new white identities. But a more complete understanding of this practice requires a reckoning with the loss, alienation, and isolation that accompanied, and often outweighed, its rewards. As early as the 1940s and through the 1960s, personal testimonies began to declare that the losses were simply too much to bear; it was time to give up and "come home."

A study of passing uncovers a phenomenon that, by definition, was intended to be clandestine and hidden, to leave no trace. Conventional wisdom is that few sources exist because those who passed carefully covered their tracks and left no record of their transgression, and that writing about passing is an undertaking fit for novelists, poets, playwrights, and literary critics, but not historians. To reveal the history of passing, the historian must seek out unconventional sources that vary at different historical moments, both in the evidence presented and in the consequences of the act. The textured accounts of family histories cast the personal losses of passing in the starkest relief whereas other types of sources bring a blurred history into sharp focus.

In each era, Americans produced new sets of unexpected sources as well as new perceptions of, and possibilities for, the broader process of race-making: runaway slave advertisements and slave narratives in the antebellum period; the social gossip about the light-skinned wives of black elected officials during Reconstruction; the blurbs on the back of novels, the diary entries, and the letters of acclaimed light-skinned writers during the Harlem Renaissance; census data, newspaper reporting, and correspondence about laws designed to preserve racial integrity in Jim Crow; students' records at colleges and universities; reports about military enlistments; and Hollywood films, exchanges between actors and audiences, and celebratory mass-marketed articles in popular magazines about the success of racial integration in the early civil rights era. These cultural sources make plain that passing was a generally egalitarian practice: elites tended to have greater access to resources and opportunities to pass, but given the right circumstances, the poor could cross over too; men tended to enjoy greater mobility in American society, but under particular conditions, women passed almost effortlessly. Passing was not nearly as hidden as one may have believed, not in 1932 when it appeared on the front pages of both the mainstream *New York Times* and the black newspaper *Atlanta World,* not in the 1940s when it was featured in splashy photographs in *Life* magazine, and not in 1949 when it made regular appearances on the silver screen and was the subject of two of the *New York Times'* ten choices for the best films of the year. Sources on passing are abundant, but often found in unlikely places.

Literature is a critical artifact that provides powerful evidence of the salience of passing for many African Americans. Passing has been a dominant theme in African American fiction for the better part of a century. The particular ways that black writers represent passing and its dilemmas have much to tell us about the subjective experience, its social impact, and the eras in which these novels were produced. Still, the primary evidentiary base of this book is historical rather than literary. Viewed through a single type of source, the nature of passing remains occluded and hazy, but taken together, literary and historical sources illuminate the jagged and porous boundary along which racially ambiguous people lived.

The broader processes of race-making in the United States come into focus through an examination of racial passing and racial indeterminacy. Passing enables an interrogation of race by examining the act of denying race. The lived experience of passing—the act of negotiating the permeable border between black and white—reveals one way that everyday people have interacted with a racist society since the late eighteenth century. The constructed nature of race becomes evident when individuals changed their racial identity by changing location, clothing, speech, and life story, thus seemingly making themselves white. These individuals cast light on the historically contingent and processual nature of race-making and demonstrate that the concept of race can be specious but also utterly real, as the painful consequences of passing often demonstrated.

Racial indeterminacy lies at the core of passing; it is the precondition that made passing possible. Racial ambiguity is the inevitable consequence of racial mixture, and racial mixture has transpired whenever different groups of people encounter each other. But it is what one does with the ambiguity that may vex or unnerve the larger society. As the phenomenon of passing was reshaped in each historical period, the meaning and significance of passing also transformed. At times, passing was an act of rebellion against the racial regime; on other occasions, it was a challenge to African Americans' struggle to shape and to nurture group identities and communities.

The history of passing and racial indeterminacy offers multiple ways of looking at the color line. Passing reveals the bankruptcy of

Figure P.3. Portrait of Walter White, civil rights activist, journalist, and executive secretary of the NAACP from 1931 to 1955. *Photograph by Carl Van Vechten. Courtesy of the Van Vechten Trust. James Weldon Johnson Collection, Beinecke Rare Book and Manuscript Library, Yale University, New Haven, Connecticut.*

the race idea; it offers a searing critique of racism and it disarms racialized thinking. Walter White—the racially ambiguous executive secretary of the National Association for the Advancement of Colored People (NAACP), who also happened to be the great-grandson of President William Henry Harrison—made a practice of putting his blond hair and blue eyes to use to enter the South during the 1920s to investigate lynching.[2] White must have laughed nervously when he sat next to a white man on a train who bragged that he had special expertise in identifying a "yaller nigger." Taking White's hand into his and pointing at White's cuticles, the white man explained that if White "had nigger blood, it would show here on [his] half-moons," an antiquated belief about a telltale sign of black racial identity.[3]

The racial boundaries that defined America's social order were difficult to police, allowing the practice of passing to roil American courtrooms and mock racial conventions. The American racial regime overflowed with incongruities and folly. In a letter dated March 4, 1815, Thomas Jefferson relied on elaborate mathematical equations to answer the question, "What constitutes a mulatto by our law?" By the third cross, or the result of "*q*, (quarteroon) being ¼ negro blood crossed with $C-q/2+C/2=a/8+B/4+C/2$" was an *e* (eighth), and having only 1/8 of negro blood, was no longer a mulatto.[4] Charles Chesnutt, the racially ambiguous writer and the grandfather of the Harlem Renaissance, poked fun at the jumble of state laws that allowed a person to change his or her racial designation by walking across a state line in the 1889 essay "What Is a White Man?"[5] A brew of variables defined one's race. Skin color and physical appearance were usually the least reliable factors, whereas one's associations and relationships were more predictive. Drawing on this logic, a child in James Baldwin's novel *Tell Me How Long the Train's Been Gone* (1968) used his light-skinned mother's relationships to offer a compelling case that she was indisputably black: "Our mama is *almost* white . . . but that don't make her white. You got to be *all* white to be white. . . . You can tell she's a colored woman because she's married to a colored *man,* and she's got two colored *children.* Now, you know ain't no white lady going to do a thing like that."[6] This was the schema of racial identification that American society hewed to, regardless of its obvious paradoxes and puzzling contradictions.

Racial indeterminacy presented opportunities for "play" and made passing a subversive and theatrical practice. Convincing performances required gumption, resourcefulness, discipline, and no small measure of humor. The sheer joy of "getting over" and "fooling white folks," as Langston Hughes, one of the leading lights of the Harlem Renaissance, put it, made passing a means of poking fun at a racial system laden with absurdities about racial purity.[7]

Harry S. Murphy, who had a white complexion and wavy brown hair, said that he "really did not see what all the fuss was about" when he passed as white during his freshman year at the University of Mississippi in 1945 and 1946. This was no "cloak and dagger business"—Murphy had no intention to pass—but a military official checked the "W" box for white when Murphy enlisted in the Navy and unwittingly set Murphy on an entirely new path. At the same time that Ole Miss prided itself on 114 years as a lily-white institution, Murphy wore the college's colors as a member of the track team, made close friends with white students, danced with and dated white women, and ate at local restaurants without incident. Described by one classmate as "arrogant" and "a loud talker," Murphy was active on campus and even participated in a protest among a group of students who heckled Senator Theodore Bilbo, the fanatical segregationist, when he spoke at Ole Miss while Murphy was on campus.[8] In 1962, when James Meredith's attempt to integrate Ole Miss ignited widespread riots across the campus, Murphy observed, "right now they are fighting a battle that they don't know they lost years ago."[9]

As the old adage goes, "What you don't know won't hurt you." As long as race was invisible or unknown, it did not seem to matter. But once one's racial identity was known, the passage had to be hastily barricaded, the opening tightly sealed, and the color line swiftly redrawn.

Historians and literary scholars have paid far more attention to what was gained by passing as white than to what was lost by rejecting a black racial identity.[10] A white identity ensured easy access to countless benefits and privileges. Whiteness conferred economic, social, and political entitlements, as well as transformative psychological rewards. A white identity blunted the shame of low-status wage work and united white men, despite their inferior socioeconomic position, with their betters.[11] Almost all white women—even prostitutes—were remade into "ladies," a class that excluded even the wealthiest and most refined black women.[12] White ladies were to be protected—economically, physically, and sexually—at all costs, and in the Jim Crow South, daily reminders of white women's heightened status were visible on "white ladies only" signs on public bathroom doors. The "ladies car," or the first-class car, on trains excluded black men and black women unless a black caregiver accompanied a white child. No white child would be made to endure the indignities and the filth of the "smoking car," or the second-class car, to which all blacks, white drunks, and other undesirable passengers were assigned. Legal scholar Cheryl Harris has argued that whiteness is a form of property, a privilege that unfairly allocated economic, political, social, and institutional resources along the color line.

But in many places, the color line was fragile; sometimes it was so brittle that it could break easily. Homer Plessy, the one-eighth African American litigant in the landmark *Plessy v. Ferguson* case (1896), rode comfortably in the all-white first-class car until his legal team had no choice but to alert the conductors and the railroad company of his racial identity in order to launch a test case of Louisiana's Separate Car Act, passed in 1890. In 1896, Plessy's lawyer, Albion Tourgée, argued that Plessy had been denied his reputation or his "inheritance" as a white man; such a reputation had "an actual pecuniary value." Indeed, Tourgée claimed that it was "the most valuable sort of property, being the master-key that unlocks the golden door of opportunity."[13] The Fourteenth Amendment should protect a white man's reputation because most white persons, as Tourgée argued, "would prefer death to life in the United States as *colored* persons."[14] To be called black was to be defamed, insulted, and slandered. No injury was incurred when one was called white.

For African Americans, racial indeterminacy was a source of lighthearted humor coupled with profound anxiety. Passing was a potent weapon against racial discrimination, but it was also a potential threat to personal and community integrity. Just as passing exposed the contradictions of white racial thinking, it also revealed the tensions within African American communities about racial identity.

Passing is a deeply individualistic practice, but it is also a fundamentally social act with enormous social consequences. The iconic image of the heartbroken yet sympathetic black mother who must not speak a word nor lay eyes upon her white-looking child in public lays bare the painful consequences of this practice. A history of passing cannot be written without telling her story too. Passing was often an intentionally or involuntarily collaborative endeavor. Family members, friends, neighbors, and coworkers were often affected by and sometimes implicated in this practice. Those who were left behind describe the pain and the loss of this act just as keenly as those who passed.

The largely unexplored realms of African American family life reveal how everyday people made sense of their racial identities. A history of passing can be found in the private and innermost spaces of African American lives, in sources that were not organized or assembled around the theme of passing. Passing becomes an unintended and unmistakable subject throughout family histories, which offer firsthand accounts of the interruptions, gaps, and omissions that a relative's decision to pass created. Departing from narratives that portray passing as an individualistic and utilitarian enterprise or one reserved for a handful of black elites, family histories bring into focus the collective nature and communal politics of passing.[15]

Anchored by the experiences and the context of one's family and one's community, these choices reveal how race operates, not only as it is imposed from without but also as it is experienced from within. To pass as white meant to lose a sense of embeddedness in a community or a collectivity. Passing reveals that the essence of identity is not found in an individual's qualities, but rather in the ways that one recognizes oneself and is recognized as kindred. These forms of recognition may begin with superficial markers such as skin color, speech, and dress, but these are only indicators of associative relations, ways of being in the world, and an imagined sharing of a common origin and iconic experiences.

Passing works as a prism: it refracts different aspects of what we commonly think of as racial identity and reveals what is left once the veil of an ascribed status is stripped away. Behind that veil what we know as "race" is simply the lived experience of a people, expressed perhaps as an ache for family and interconnections or sometimes as a longing for music, humor, and food. Thus passing unmasks race as conventionally understood, revealing the intimate and personal meanings of a putative racial identity.

For many family members and friends of those who passed, racial identity came to mean much more than an individual's rejection of the race. It meant no longer belonging as a family member and no longer sharing experiences, stories, and memories of times past. The family, the "psychic rudder" and the formative site in the creation of an individual's identity, provides a rich and revealing terrain through which the salience of passing as a social practice can be fully explored and better understood.[16] To be sure, the experiences of African Americans who decided to pass as white varied widely and cannot be collapsed into a singular narrative. Family relationships were not always easy or harmonious, but the loss of kinship that resulted was equally acute for troubled or dysfunctional families as it was for stable ones. An exploration of black family life exposes the keen sense of loss and the painful familial ruptures that passing left in its wake.

This is not to suggest that every person who passed as white felt the same sense of loss. But it is human nature to make a decision and later wonder what could have been. Some writers, like Langston Hughes, would valorize a warm, welcoming, and romantic black community. Similarly, the legendary blues musician Rufus Thomas once gushed to a white man, "If you were black for one Saturday night on Beale Street, you would never want to be white again."[17] A journalist interviewed a man who was from his hometown of Louisville and who passed as white permanently. Afterward, the man visited the journalist regularly and spent several hours asking about the friends he had left behind. As the journalist explained, "None of his experiences as 'white,' it seemed, could rid him of the nostalgia he felt for the old scenes and the old friends."[18] These reminiscences offer only scattered parts of a much more complex whole. Undoubtedly, there were those who walked away from a black identity and never looked back. Fraught family relationships—conflicts between parents and children or brothers and sisters—may have driven some to "the other side," whereas others may have been unintentionally taken as white and seized the opportunity. Longing for a respite from daily indignities and racial cruelties, some may have decided that leaving family members behind was well worth the gamble. Once they arrived safely in the white world, some may not have felt any compunction about leaving a race that had constrained them, injured them, or meant little to them at all.

African American identities are often flattened, homogenized, and reduced to a form of shorthand or a taken-for-granted concept, such as "the black experience," "the black voice," "the black family," and "the black community." But no essentialized, immutable, or true "identity" is ever waiting to be found just below the surface. Rather, as Stuart Hall has argued, identities are conditional, contingent, elusive, and "always in process."[19] Indeed, passing illuminates the ways that African American identities function as an intangible space of imagination or a set of symbols to which people feel powerful attachments. Just as Americans might feel more self-conscious about their national identity in a foreign country, those who decided to pass described similar pangs of nostalgia for lost origins. To lose one's place in familial communities where much is instinctively understood and can go without saying; to miss out on the "deep, horizontal comradeship" that Benedict Anderson characterized as the bonds of nationality; to stand outside the "instance of virtual racial assembly" and the "moment of simultaneity" that historian Adam Green observed in the wake of the murder of Emmett Till in 1955 was undoubtedly isolating and emotionally enervating.[20] The symbolic meanings of racial identity must be carefully considered in order to create a more accurate and more complete history of the psychological tolls of passing. In stripping away one's ascribed status, passing offers a sharper angle of vision onto the personal meanings of racial identity from the perspective of black communities.

I join scholars who have argued that race is socially constructed and performative, but I keep my eye on what race and racial identity mean to those who are racialized.[21] Rather than seeing racial identity from the racial regime looking down on those who passed as white, I bring into focus what passers saw when they looked out onto their own worlds. From their point of view, race was neither strictly a social construction nor a biological fact. The line between black and white was by no means imaginary; crossing it had profound, life-changing consequences. Race was quite real to those who lived with it, not because of skin color or essentialist notions about biology, but because it was social and experiential, because it involved one's closest relationships and one's most intimate communities.[22] Scholars may view race as a social construction, but this concept does not always correspond to the ways that race operates in everyday life. Echoing the social constructionist argument, W. E. B. Du Bois famously wrote that a black man is "a person who must ride 'Jim Crow' in Georgia."[23] Du Bois's statement raises the question, what would a black man be without Jim Crow in Georgia? Is it possible to remove all of the structures that separated blacks from whites? If such structures were dismantled, what would be done with the recollections, the impressions, and the stories passed down? For these reasons, a black man would still be a black man even without Jim Crow—not because of skin color, or blood, or any other factor inhering in biology, but because of the memories that bind him and social forces that surround him. I argue that it is possible to pass for something without becoming what it is that you pass for. Indeed, it is my contention that the core issue of passing is not becoming what you pass for, but losing what you pass away from.

The chapters that follow examine several historical moments from the late eighteenth century to the present. In each moment, the question of how to live with race was tested and contested. In each period, racially ambiguous people maneuvered around the terrain of a racist society and made choices based on the particular social formation in which they lived. These choices were constrained, anguished, and guided by the structure of the particular racial environment of the historical period. During the 1920s, the racially ambiguous poet and novelist Jean Toomer wondered aloud why he had to choose a racial identity and why he had to be marked. Toomer and Charles Chesnutt called for the birth of a "new race," one that would emerge out of extensive racial mixing. These ideas failed to gain traction in their time.[24] Toomer would resist identification as "the great Negro writer" in similar ways as Barack Obama would demur at being labeled "the black president." Certainly, Toomer faced different limitations in the 1920s than Obama would in the twenty-first century. Throughout this history, there are conflicts between individual aspirations and the realities of the conditions and circumstances. Still, racial ambiguity enabled Toomer to move across boundaries in ways that otherwise he could not as a black writer. Others would make different choices. Langston Hughes often wrote about passing, but he would never dream of doing it himself. Black folks were his muse, his creative inspiration, and his family in deeply personal and emotional ways that his biological mother and father never were nor could be.[25]

Hybridity always existed, but claiming a mixed-race identity only became an option when opportunities to reimagine racial identity arose. These openings have occurred during periods of relative racial openness and pluralism, most notably, after emancipation, during the Reconstruction era and the Harlem Renaissance, and in our present moment in the twenty-first century. During those moments when American society revalued black identity in positive terms, nearly white African Americans could choose to embrace both sides of their putative racial selves. Claiming hybridity seemed to be a plausible substitute for passing. The choices of racially mixed people in these periods—including, most famously, Charles Chesnutt, Jean Toomer, and Barack Obama—reveal moments when racial categories appeared more malleable.

Racial passing in the American context must be acknowledged as a subset of a much larger phenomenon that encompasses multiple disguises and forms of dissemblance. Ralph Ellison characterized disguise as an elemental aspect of American identity: "America is a land of masking jokers.... Benjamin Franklin, the practical scientist, skilled statesman and sophisticated lover, allowed the French to mistake him for Rousseau's Natural Man. Hemingway poses as a non-literary sportsman, Faulkner as a farmer; Abe Lincoln allowed himself to be taken for a simple country lawyer."[26] These are only a handful of examples of a sweeping phenomenon that demonstrate passing's flexibility and adaptability to various historical contexts. The poor passed as the rich, women passed as men, Jews passed as Gentiles, gay men and women passed as straight, and whites sometimes passed as black—and of course, the reverse of each of these dyads was plausible given specific conditions and circumstances. Particularly in societies with relatively open and fluid social orders, the permutations on passing were endless.

In the early to mid-nineteenth century, middle-class Americans worried that young men and women who were steadily migrating out of rural areas and small towns to seek their fortunes in America's booming cities could enter social classes to which they did not belong. American Victorians fretted over women who used makeup to disguise an insincere and immoral character behind a painted face.[27] Loreta Janeta Velazquez, a Cuban-born woman, passed as a Confederate soldier to fight in the Civil War and entered the ranks of numerous women who joined the military or participated in occupations and activities restricted to men. During the era of Chinese exclusion, Chinese immigrants disguised themselves to pass as Mexicans and enter the United States from the United States–Mexico border. In 1907, a U.S. government investigation discovered photographs attached to fraudulent Mexican citizenship papers. When questioned, an immigrant inspector shrugged his shoulders and explained that it was "exceedingly difficult to distinguish these Chinamen from Mexicans."[28] In the early twentieth century, Jewish applicants changed their names to outmaneuver discriminatory admissions policies that limited enrollments at prestigious universities such as Harvard, Princeton, and Yale. Gay men "put their hair up," married women, and worked in professions that would have been unavailable to them had they "let their hair down." Mezz Mezzrow, a "white Negro hipster" born to Russian-Jewish immigrants, passed as black to shore up his musical bona fides.[29] In his 1946 autobiography, *Really the Blues,* Mezzrow explained his decision to pass: "They were my kind of people. And I was going to learn their music and play it for the rest of my days. I was going to be a musician, a Negro musician, hipping the world about the blues the way only Negroes can. I didn't know how the hell I was going to do it, but I was straight on what I had to do."[30]

By no means is the practice of passing exclusively an American phenomenon. Passing has a complex history around the world and especially in nations with similar racial compositions as the United States. For example, in South Africa and Brazil—two countries with very distinct histories, political systems, and patterns of racial relations—national ideologies and cultural practices that value lighter or white skin remain prevalent. In his autobiography, *Long Walk to Freedom,* Nelson Mandela described two laws passed in 1950 that formed the bedrock of the apartheid system: the Population Registration Act that permitted the government to officially classify all South Africans based on race and the Group Areas Act that limited each racial group to living, owning land, and trading only in racially segregated areas.[31] Tragically, members of the same family could be classified differently and separated by chance based on complexion, hair texture, and lip shape. Blacks became coloreds, and coloreds became whites or "play whites" based on an official's whim.[32] Mandela represented a man who was colored but had been mistakenly classified as African. When the man appeared in court, a white magistrate examined him and concluded that he was in fact colored because he had a physique that was stereotypically associated with coloreds. The giveaway was his sharply sloped shoulders.[33] Other coloreds who were light enough to pass refashioned themselves as white South Africans, but this practice became more difficult after 1950 when interracial sex was officially banned. Racially indeterminate men and women were subjected to the infamous and arbitrary pencil test: if a pencil fell out of a person's hair, the person was categorized as white, but if the pencil became entangled or snagged in a curl, the person could only be designated as colored or black. Unlike in the United States where mixed-race people often affiliate with African Americans, some coloreds speak

Afrikaans, worship in the Dutch Reformed Church, adopt the family names of their white ancestors, and support the white leadership of Democratic Alliance in opposition to the African National Congress.[34]

Brazil—a country that has claimed to be a "racial democracy"—has a veritable kaleidoscope of 136 designations to describe skin color, including *alva* (pure white), *alva-rosada* (white with pink highlights), *melada* (honey-colored), *canela* (cinnamon), *preta* (black), and *pouco clara* (not very clear).[35] Although Brazil has the largest population of Africans outside of Africa, the black population lags behind in access to education, employment, housing, and health care. At every level of politics, blacks are almost entirely absent from positions of power. In the media, blacks represent less than 10 percent of the actors and are often cast as domestic workers while their blond-haired, blue-eyed counterparts play the leading roles. The value of whiteness has permeated Brazilian society from its older cultural productions to its more recent vernacular. The 1890 painting, "The Redemption of Ham," features a black grandmother praising God when her mixed-race daughter, who is married to a white man, gives birth to a white baby. Today, a black or mixed-race woman who is pregnant with a white man's baby might be described as "cleaning the plantation." Just as money whitens in Brazil, poverty darkens. Studies have shown that racial identity is deeply imbricated with socioeconomic status; highly educated nonwhite men and women are more likely to marry whites and more likely to classify their children as white than less educated nonwhite parents.[36] In 2004 Brazilian scholars used evidence of a pronounced pattern of racial reclassification on the census from black to brown between 1950 and 1980 and again between 1980 and 1990 to substantiate the "money whitens" thesis.[37]

Perhaps the most celebrated cases of passing have occurred in the United States because of the stark binary between black and white. Within the United States, there has never been an official category like *branquinha* (whitish) in Brazil, "colored" in South Africa, or "Jamaica white" in Jamaica (a term that describes people who appear white enough to pass, yet "everyone" knows that they are mixed race). Although "mulatto" appeared on the U.S. census between 1850 and 1930, it never gained the same traction in American politics and society as the intermediate categories in other nations.[38] The removal of the mulatto category in the 1930s reflected the waning interest in mixed-race populations and national acceptance of bright-line differences between blacks and whites. Although I take account of differences in national racial ideologies, I concentrate on the stubbornness and the resiliency of the white/black racial binary in the United States. The distinctiveness of the bipolar American racial regime—the persistence of the "one-drop rule"; the lack of official categories for multiracial people; the social and economic distance between blacks and whites and the illegality of interracial marriage until the *Loving v. Virginia* case in 1967; and the history of the United States as a white majority/black minority nation until increased immigration led to massive demographic changes in the mid-twentieth century—creates conditions ripe for the singular and spectacular nature of racial passing in the United States.

I have assembled a disparate cast of characters, scenes and settings, and moments of conflict and contradiction to knit together the cultural history of passing. Just like faces in an album of old family photographs, some of the dramatis personae in this book are well known and recognizable. Others resemble a distant uncle who slips to the faded edge of a picture or an estranged aunt who is present early on, but never appears again. Some absences are the result of a move, a clash with a family member, or a death. For the families in this book, passing created absences and left spaces in family photographs that were difficult to explain.

Absence as well as presence can trigger stories. These stories are not social history—their facts cannot be verified—but they are cultural history. They tell us what absence meant to those left behind and the consequences that it had. Passing is difficult to recover in conventional sources given that its purpose was to leave no trace. I have mined passing's historical sources—those threads that escaped erasure—to discover a coherent and enduring narrative of loss. Loss is a complex human sentiment that a historian should not expect to be discussed casually or openly. It can be so transparent and palpable that it leaps off the page. But more likely, the sense of loss is voiced through hesitations, pauses, and other manifestations of the trouble that one finds when looking at an old photograph and trying to recall a family member's name or the location or occasion when the picture was taken. It is the struggle to find the right words or it is the absence of words entirely that conveys the depth of personal loss.

When the sources allowed, I shifted the magnification and the focal point to the lives of particular individuals and families. But frequently, I have recounted the stories of men and women who were barely known, often nameless, sometimes only described through the vague and fuzzy recollections of their relatives. I have tried to create a panoramic view by drawing on testimony of family members to sharpen the resolution at the edges, to bring the distant uncle into view, or to try to explain the estranged aunt's absence.

Recounting the lives of people who sought so assiduously to pass unknown to history inevitably results in a portrait that is at times uneven and blurred. My method rests on restoring as many photographs as possible. It is my conviction that multiple photographs can reveal larger social, cultural, and national dynamics that would be far less visible if viewed through a lens fixed on the idiosyncrasies of a single person, family, or place.

This history of passing is a composite of cultural and political history. I rely heavily on the diverse set of cultural sources that passing produced while keeping my eye on the political and economic conditions that motivated the desire to pass. The curious phenomenon of passing arose precisely out of a confluence of social and political developments. Passing took shape under the slavery regime and later functioned as a response to the laws and changing political environments that defined and regulated racial identities. Passing was by no means a static practice. In each historical period, the conjuncture of political and cultural forces shaped the lived experience of racially ambiguous men and women.

Passing is a continuous and enduring historical phenomenon that opens a wide window onto larger issues about inconstant racial definitions, the changing dynamics of race relations, and the complex and circuitous routes along which African American identity has developed in the United States. The chapters that follow offer a cultural history of racial passing from the late eighteenth century to the moment when it reportedly "passed out" in the 1950s. First, racially ambiguous men and women *passed as free* in the fluid, bustling, and multiracial world of the eighteenth century mid-Atlantic, where opportunities for self-fashioning abounded and where not all blacks were enslaved and not all whites were free. The uneven and uneasy consolidation of a racialized slave society eventually made *passing as white* more commonplace and more fitting with the particular concerns of the antebellum period. The national upheaval and massive ruptures of the Civil War were followed by the fleeting but hopeful moment of Reconstruction that created unparalleled openings for African Americans and offered political, economic, and social logic to the decision *not to pass.* The broken promises of Reconstruction gave way to the tragedy of Jim Crow, but also to massive and unprecedented migrations out of the South and into northern cities. The social and physical mobility of the Jim Crow era, coupled paradoxically with its cramped, segregated living and working arrangements, created the necessary conditions for passing to flourish, but also for this practice to test and to undermine black familial integrity. The unhappy consequences of passing are viewed most starkly in the intimate reaches of black communities. Given the particular and peculiar racial environment of Jim Crow America, it is no wonder that this period witnessed a veritable explosion of literature on passing as a product of the cultural flowering of the Harlem Renaissance.

Optimistic announcements that passing had "passed out" by the end of World War II, a period that coincided with the launch of the civil rights movement, signaled yet another turning point in the history of this phenomenon. In the postwar period, reports of the irrelevance of passing circulated throughout the media. The "passing of passing," social critics observed, was the logical outcome of the collapse of legalized segregation, the sense of racial affinity engendered by civil rights struggles and the aptly named "Second Reconstruction," and promises to deliver economic prosperity—"the good life"—to whites and blacks alike. Such cheerfulness, however, met hard limits: the racial tumult experienced by Betty and Donald Howard captured what historian Arnold Hirsch has described as "the shoals upon which the postwar movement for racial equality would founder."[39] The Howards moved into Chicago's Trumbull Park Homes in 1953 after Chicago Housing Authority officials mistook Betty as a white woman. The arrival of Betty's recognizably black husband, Donald, ignited nearly a decade of racial violence and neighborhood unrest.

Although it is not possible to quantify how many racially ambiguous men and women walked away from plantations and small towns and re-created their racial identities, abundant evidence reveals the contours of a rich and remarkably complex history that encompasses far more than the accounts of the luckless who failed at passing. The portraits of racially ambiguous men and women—often fuzzy and fragmented—explain much more than the unexpected twists and turns of the color line. These intermediary lives reveal the ways that race has been lived on the racial borderlands of American society from the late eighteenth century to the present. This phenomenon has a rich and ever-changing history that warrants an examination over its longue durée.

The chapters that follow reconstruct the world of passing by pairing scholarly discussions of its social, economic, and political context with the personal, emotional, and familial matter that made it human. Passing was not an automatic response to racial proscription. Some African Americans used passing as a crucial channel leading to physical and personal freedom. They declared their rights as American citizens and insisted on their humanity. What they could not fully know until they had successfully passed was that the light of freedom was often overshadowed by the darkness of loss.

1

White Is the Color of Freedom

In the spring of 1859, a Philadelphia newspaper published a humorous account of a slave trader's sudden reversal of fortune. The trader had earned the nickname "Black Matt" because of his dark complexion and reputed skill in breaking recalcitrant slaves. He had recently purchased Sam, a "bright mulatto" who could "scarcely be distinguished from a white man" in that he was "so far removed from pure African," at a reduced price because of his "bad qualities, such as thieving, lying and drunkenness." Despite these flaws, Sam was described as intelligent, literate, and particularly adept at "ape[ing] the airs of a most polished gentleman." Expecting to sell Sam as a body servant at a handsome price, Black Matt dressed him in "fine clothes, calf-skin boots, a silk hat, and kid gloves," and he encouraged Sam to "show himself off" upon his arrival in New Orleans.

While "strut[ting] along with the best of them," Sam overheard a man discussing his interest in purchasing a body servant. Approaching the prospective buyer "with an independent swagger," Sam sold Black Matt to the planter with a glowing review: "[He has] every quality, [he] can shave, dress hair, brush boots, and is besides polished in his manners." But, this body servant came with one troublesome, "ridiculous" fault, Sam confessed to the planter: "He imagines himself a white man." Such a delusion was nothing more than "a funny conceit" to the planter; he boasted of his ability to "cure him of that," given his "considerable experience in training and managing gentleman of color." The planter then "seized the refractory *slave*," and Black Matt's entreaties that he was indeed a white man fell on deaf ears until he was able to produce evidence that identified him as a free citizen of the United States. As for Sam, he swiftly boarded a ship headed for a European port and was never heard of again.[1]

White skin functioned as a cloak in antebellum America. Accompanied by appropriate dress, measured cadences of speech, and proper comportment, racial ambiguity could mask one's slave status and provide an effectual strategy for escape. Many runaway slaves neither imagined nor desired to begin new lives as white; they simply wanted to be free. As literary critics P. Gabrielle Foreman and Cherene Sherrard-Johnson have written, fugitive slaves "passed *through* whiteness"; and once through, they would "*reject* rather than *embrace* the power and superiority whites claimed as their singular possession."[2] Tactical or strategic passing—passing temporarily with a particular purpose in mind—was born at this moment out of a dogged desire for freedom. In later historical periods, this type of passing would allow racially ambiguous men and women to get jobs ("nine-to-five passing"), to travel without encumbrance, and to attend elite colleges. But in the antebellum period, passing was keyed to a larger struggle for freedom. Some scholars have argued that the earliest printed references to passing may have been published in advertisements for runaway slaves in which slave owners warned readers about slaves "of very light color," with "complexion[s] so white," that they might escape "under the pretence of being a white man."[3] At its very origins, then, passing was imbricated with strivings for freedom, but also with slave masters' anxieties about the threat that racial ambiguity posed to the slave regime.

Passing is a flexible strategy that relies heavily on the category of class. The cunning and cleverness of Sam's escape reflect the possibility—even within the constraints of a mature slave regime—of fashioning a new, free self by acting and dressing the part. Sam's disguise (and that of countless others) worked because he presented himself as "a most polished gentleman"; the ruse would likely have failed had he dressed in overalls, been unable to read and write, and displayed coarse manners. Slaves drew on all available resources to construct the appearance of the free person that they resolved to become, and in all but very few incidences, the category of class shaped these disguises. Slaves bought, traded, and stole clothing; they feigned grief, illness, and injury; and they borrowed, reused, and forged passes and certificates of freedom. With one's liberty hanging in the balance, all sorts of disguises were imaginable. As black abolitionist William Still wrote in the preface of his 1871 history of the Underground Railroad, "some, whose fair complexions have rendered them indistinguishable from their Anglo-Saxon brethren . . . with assumed airs of importance, such as they had been accustomed to see their masters show when traveling, have taken the usual modes of conveyance and have even braved the most scrutinizing inspection of slave-holders, slave-catchers and car conductors."[4] Racially ambiguous slaves on the run passed as white to ease the grueling journey to freedom. Their success flouted racial customs and undermined southern confidence in the certainty of racial identity.

Racial ambiguity could be leveraged to secure one's physical liberty but also to articulate broader notions of freedom. Runaway slaves like Ellen Craft, Henry Bibb, and George Latimer relied on racial ambiguity and sophisticated understandings of southern social and gendered norms to escape to freedom; nearly white slaves went to court and pointed to their white skin to convince judges and juries that they had been wrongly enslaved and deserved to be free; abolitionists displayed racially ambiguous slaves to stoke fears about white children falling into slavery; and free black elites passed occasionally to ridicule the wrongheaded assumptions of southern whites. More commonly, those elites, who inhabited an almost impossible position in the antebellum period, used racial ambiguity to remind whites that, but for the accident of color, no meaningful differences separated them. As northern and southern states passed laws to limit the economic and social mobility of free blacks, many black elites rejected passing and instead focused their energies on building independent and politically active communities that dismissed colonization proposals, demanded the right to enjoy public space, and championed social and moral reforms such as antislavery, temperance, and women's rights. Passing in the antebellum period must be viewed in light of the rapidly changing material conditions within free black communities.

The countless men and women who passed successfully demonstrate that there is always some slack even in the most totalizing systems. Passing was an expedient means of securing one's freedom, and in its broadest and most expansive formulation, passing became a crucial means through which African Americans called for the recognition of their own humanity. The desperate acts of enslaved men and women were not freighted with the same internal conflict, tension, or moral angst of other historical periods. Surrounded by loss, enslaved people were motivated by a desire to reunite with their families, not to leave them behind.

Passing illuminates the urgent struggle for freedom and reflects the changing character of the slave regime. Historian Ira Berlin has outlined the transformation from "societies with slaves," where slavery functioned as just one of multiple forms of unfree labor and where the boundaries between slavery and freedom remained pliable, to "slave societies," where slavery operated as the singular and defining system of labor as well as the organizational framework for all social relations in the society.[5] Racialization was part and parcel of this uneven and nonlinear shift: white masters (and sometimes mistresses and children), white indentured servants, and enslaved Africans worked side-by-side in societies with slaves; in slave societies, people of African descent comprised the majority if not the entirety of the unfree laboring class. Although South Carolina judge William Harper's contention in 1831 that "a slave cannot be a white man" would not have made sense in the seventeenth or most of the eighteenth century, it provided an apt description of the evolution and uneasy consolidation of a slave society where labor mapped neatly onto racial categories.[6] But the story of Sam and Black Matt (though surely apocryphal) belies the appearance of a fixed racial system and reflects the sense of disquietude lingering in the air. If being a (white) gentleman meant nothing more than speaking properly and walking with an "independent swagger"—conduct easily "aped" by slaves—

then the racial order was more flexible than white Southerners imagined.

Unprecedented demographic changes further upset traditional social relationships by drawing masses of young men out of rural areas, beyond parental oversight, and into burgeoning cities. As historian Karen Halttunen has written, in an increasingly fluid society, where "no one occupied a fixed social position, the question 'Who am I?' loomed large; and in an urban social world where many of the people who met face-to-face each day were strangers, the question 'Who are you really?' assumed even greater significance."[7] A stranger's arrival had once been a rare and remarkable event, but by the early decades of the nineteenth century, small-town intimacy gave way to "worlds of strangers" where the residents knew nothing about the backgrounds or former lives of their neighbors.[8] Anxieties about racial imperceptibility, and particularly the indeterminate status of free blacks, corresponded with larger concerns about one's proper place in an increasingly mobile and inconstant society. Opportunities for self-fashioning and refashioning abounded in a society where both people and goods circulated widely. Clothing, perhaps the most essential commodity in the process of self-making for the poor and the genteel alike, became increasingly accessible, transportable, and resalable beginning in the mid-eighteenth century.[9] Dressed in "fine clothes, calfskin boots, a silk hat, and kid gloves," Sam assumed the appearance of a refined white gentleman rather than that of an obedient body servant as Black Matt intended. By choosing to rent or to hire slaves out, slave owners authorized slaves' mobility and unwittingly created the necessary conditions for slaves to run away or to pass as free. A reporter's description of Alexandria, Virginia, in 1824 captures the increasingly multiracial character of heavily trafficked public spaces in southern cities: "The street and market-square presented groups of men, women and children, every shade of colour, from the fairest white, down to the deepest black. . . . Some of these were about half-white, some almost white, leaving it difficult to distinguish where the one ends, and the other begins."[10] The social transformations of the late eighteenth and early nineteenth centuries—most visible in the hustle and bustle of streets and market-squares—made possible multiple forms of disguises and dissemblance. Racially ambiguous men and women, both free and enslaved, rushed into the openings created by this fluid, anonymous, and rapidly urbanizing world.

Before "passing as white" became meaningful, racially ambiguous men and women frequently and successfully "passed as free." This form of passing was possible in a world where, as historian W. Jeffrey Bolster explains, racially indeterminate people "faced fewer liabilities because of color than would their black descendants in the New World slave societies that developed later, and in which race became even more cramping."[11] In 1763, a master would have less cause to fear that "a mulatto fellow named Jason" would attempt to pass as white; instead, he might fret that Jason would "endeavor to pass for a Sailor, as he has been for some Time by Water," where, as Bolster explains, "the distinction between enslaved boatmen and quasi-free seaman could easily blur."[12] Similarly, it was assumed that a slave who "took a boat and went to Philadelphia" would soon "endeavour to get Aboard of some Vessel to go to Sea and pass for a free Negro."[13] Maritime life was particularly conducive to passing as free as it offered long stretches of time removed from a master's surveillance, freedom to travel at one's will, and a bustling multiracial environment where few, if any, questions were asked about one's background. Passing as free was also possible by identifying oneself as a tradesman or an artisan or by affiliating with a profession comprising men who were known to be free. By passing as a "Housecarpenter by Trade," "Malato John" assumed both the appearance and the occupation of a free man.[14] To mark the origins of racial passing, it is necessary to locate the shift from "passing as free" to "passing as white" within the context of the massive transformations occurring within the slave system.

Readers perusing the pages of eighteenth-century newspapers would have found it difficult, if not impossible, to overlook advertisements for runaway slaves, such as the following:

> RUN AWAY, on Tuesday the 9th from Turtle-Bay, a Mulatto Wench named Lens, 17 Years old, can speak good Dutch and English, and sings a good Song; is a handsome Wench, and may pass for a free person, as she is very well featured all but her nose, and lips, which are thick and flat, has long black curld hair and a mould on her face: Had on when she went away a homespun Josey and Pettycoat, but no shoes nor stockings. Whoever takes up and secures said wench on the Island of New-York, so that she may be had again, shall have Forty Shillings Reward. All Persons are forbid to harbour or entertain said Wench at their peril. Likewise, all Masters of Vessels are forbid to carry her off.[15]

Papers contained exhaustive descriptions of slaves' complexions, personalities, facial features, clothing, language skills, and even musical talents. Deft manipulation of these attributes could obscure one's slave status and allow a slave to present him- or herself as a free person. Runaway slave advertisements offered two competing narratives: they provided slave owners' best attempts at explaining and papering over the fissures in the slave regime, and they announced the success of slaves in besting the system and securing their freedom.[16]

During the eighteenth century, racial identity was fluid, and race was disaggregated from slave status. These two categories would not become fully intertwined until the early nineteenth century.[17] Describing the racial dynamics in the eighteenth-century mid-Atlantic colonies, historian David Waldstreicher explains, "to be white was not necessarily to be free; to be black was not necessarily to be a slave; and to be a mulatto or racially mixed was not necessarily to be either of these." Considering the terms used to identify slaves and servants—" 'tawny,' 'swarthy,' 'dark,' 'brown,' or even 'black' " (a color often used to describe Irish immigrants)—the eighteenth-century mid-Atlantic had yet to reach the conclusion that blackness signaled slavery and whiteness signaled freedom.[18] Passing as free became a viable strategy in the context of a highly mobile, flexible, and multiracial workforce whose labor was interchangeable and where variable and seasonal labor demands did not require large clusters of slaves on plantations.

Written passes, issued by masters with the intention of curbing the mobility of slaves, could easily be borrowed, forged, or duplicated by slaves who could read and write or by white or free black confidants.[19] To a master's mind, a literate slave was inherently a dangerous slave. Fugitive slave Henry Bibb recognized the importance of "striving to learn [himself] to write" and copied the passes that he was given as a house servant when his master sent him on errands: "Whenever I got hold of an old letter that had been thrown away, or a piece of white paper, I would save it to write on. I have often gone off in the woods and spent the greater part of the day alone, trying to learn to write myself a pass."[20] The ability to read and write had significant economic consequences and often lowered a slave's value in the market. Slaves, mindful of the social capital and power that literacy conferred, worked tirelessly to acquire it.[21] A slave named Harrison learned to read and write, as he had a "strong aversion to both the 'wholesome regulations' of the peculiar institution . . . [and] saw that the only remedy he could avail himself of was to learn to write his own passes."[22] A master wrote in a runaway advertisement that his thirty-five-year-old slave could "read and write both English and Dutch," making it "likely [that he] will forge a pass."[23] As historian Jill Lepore observed, "To write was to defy bondage. . . . In a world in which literacy marked a kind of dividing line between 'savagery' and 'civilization,' writing and, more, *authorship* became crucial to blacks' insistence on their own humanity."[24]

Masters cautioned even the most astute and "the most careful" slave catchers of the likelihood of being duped by a fugitive slave who would "write any Pass . . . he thinks necessary." They also feared that slaves might collude with others willing to write passes for them. One master alerted slave catchers, "it is imagined he has got a pass, being very intimate with a Negro fellow, who can write."[25] In October 1764, Moses Grimes was taken to a Pennsylvania jail on the suspicion that he was a runaway slave. His master explained that Grimes was likely to "pass for a free man, and get somebody to forge a pass for him." Similar to many eighteenth-century runaways, Grimes assumed the guise of a free man without looking white: he was described as "very yellow," able to "pass for a Mulattoe," and with the right pass, he could pretend to be free and blend effortlessly into the racially heterogeneous city of Philadelphia.[26] C. H. Gay in Laurel, North Carolina, published an advertisement offering a $100 reward for the return of his slave, Edgar, who "can read and write well"; the master had "no doubt he has provided himself with papers of some kind," perhaps by purchasing "the papers of some free negro."[27]

Some masters underestimated the talents of their slaves. A master assumed that his slave, characterized as "very flippant" and "a plausible smooth Tongue Fellow," had not designed his own escape but instead had been lured away by a white man who wrote him a pass that enabled him to travel to Norwalk, Connecticut, and "pass there for a free Negro."[28] The wonderful irony that James Alexander, a colonial statesman from New York who famously juxtaposed liberty ("How amiable is one!") and slavery ("How odious and abominable the other!"), had a slave who escaped from his attic by writing a pass with his own hand represented, as Lepore explains, "an act of forgery that defined, better than anything Alexander could put to paper, the liberty of freely writing."[29]

When masters hired their slaves out, they often furnished them with written passes to prevent their arrest while en route to their next job. Slaves were also given permits to visit family members on neighboring plantations on Sundays and during holidays. But in easing a slave's travel, the passes could easily be reframed to assist a slave's flight. In 1775, a master wrote that his slave, Jenney, had fled with her husband after she had been given a "note to look for a Master," but he now feared that it was "likely she may make a traveling pass of it."[30] Another slave used a pass and "pretended that he belonged to a Butcher in New York, and was going in to the country to fetch cattle for his master."[31] Masters regretted that old and outdated passes failed to expire and could easily be borrowed, sold, or otherwise recycled. Henry and Joseph Robinson warned that Benjamin Moore, a black servant previously indentured to Job

Throckmorton, carried old contracts and "shows them for a pass, pretending to be a free Negro."[32]

Runaways who played the role of free men with confidence found that their actions raised few eyebrows. Making quite a performance of it, Isaac Williams and his traveling companions "went so far as to light cigars, tilt their hats jauntily to one side, and stroll through the streets when they entered Washington." By "look[ing] at everyone directly, not cowering," Williams and his friends walked directly past several officials, but "not one asked to see their papers."[33]

Hoodwinked masters bristled at being cleverly outmaneuvered by their slaves. Many used runaway advertisements to save face. One master described an escaped slave as "an artful, cunning, plausible villain, [who] will make use of every specious and fairy tale to induce belief of his being a freeman." But in the next breath, he insulted him, denigrating his behavior as "excessively complaisant, obsequious, and insinuating."[34] His slave may have spoken "good English, smoothly and plausibly," but his speech was marked by "a cringe and a smile," and he was "ready at inventing specious pretences to conceal villainous Actions or design." An advertisement published in the *Pennsylvania Gazette* on April 29, 1762, reported that a slave named Charles had absconded with a "Variety of Clothes," including "two or three Coats of Suits . . . and several other Waistcoats, Breeches, and Pairs of Stockings; a blue Great Coat, and a Fiddle." Irked by this loss of property, Charles's master was most undone by the way that Charles misused his name, exploited his kindness, and betrayed his trust:

> When he became my servant I intended to have him shipped to the West Indies and sold him there, and kept him in prison till

> I should get an Opportunity, but on his earnest request solemn Promises of his Good Behavior, and seeming Penitence I took him into my Family upon trial, where for a Time he behaved well and was very serviceable to me. Deceived by his seeming Reformation, I placed some Confidence in him, which he has villainously abused; having embezzled Money sent him to pay for Goods, borrowed money and taken up goods in my Name unknown to me, and also put on his own Account, pretending to be a Freeman.[35]

Humiliated by their slaves and forced to accept the limits of their mastery, slave owners made earnest yet often futile efforts to prevent the production and misuse of slave passes. An excerpt from a letter from Petersburg, Virginia, dated August 19, 1785, expressed one community's incredulity about a suspicious character who came into town and began "selling out" slave passes:

> Some days ago it was discovered that a person unknown in this town was selling out Certificates of Freedom and Passes to the Slaves, and forging such people's names as were most likely to answer the purpose. By the activity and vigilance of some gentlemen in town, this dangerous villain was apprehended last night, about ten o'clock, in company with some slaves, and just as he had finished a pass for one of them. He was carried before a Magistrate, who committed him to prison for further trial. He at first called himself Joe Thompson, but says his name is Thompson Davis.[36]

That "a person unknown in this town" could consort with slaves, forge names, and create counterfeit freedom certificates and slave passes was unthinkable. The slipperiness of this man's identity—

first identified as Joe Thompson but later as Thompson Davis—parallels the elusiveness of the identities of the slaves for whom he falsified passes.

Although passing as free was largely a phenomenon of the eighteenth century, it remained a viable strategy in any setting where not all black people were enslaved. The turmoil and dislocation brought about by the Civil War created new and unanticipated opportunities to pass as free. An advertisement promising a "$200 Reward," published in a Philadelphia newspaper sometime between 1860 and 1862, described a negro man "of black complexion" named Henry who was living in Lexington, Kentucky. According to his master, Henry had "left home some time last fall in the employ of the 15th regiment of Ohio Volunteers, went with them to their camp on the Nashville Railroad, and remained there until the 17th day of December last, at which time he was ordered to return home by the commanding officer." His master, having not heard from him since, noted in the advertisement that "he is said to pass himself for a free man, and may have secured employment in some camp near Louisville."[37] It can only be speculated as to how many men and women, once removed from the confines of plantation life and amid the chaos of the impending war, took advantage of the opportunity to blend in among scores of others who hoped to secure their freedom by running to the Union lines. In a society where not all blacks were enslaved, passing as free remained plausible and increasingly probable during moments of massive disruption and dislocation.

By the 1820s, the fluid and cosmopolitan Atlantic world began to give way to a new racial regime. As it hardened, this regime neatly aligned one's status with one's race. Correspondingly, the phenomenon of passing as free gave way to the phenomenon of passing as white and reflected rearrangements within the slave system as well as larger changes in American society, namely: the massive importation of African slaves; a voracious internal slave trade that carried slaves from resource-depleted farming lands to points south; the increased production of staple crops such as rice, indigo, and cotton that required closer attention and tending; and higher-pitched hysterics about maintaining the boundaries of whiteness. The rush of the plantation regime overwhelmed the more flexible and varied forms of labor that existed previously and formalized the equations of slave equals black and white equals free. White-indentured servitude declined as servants completed their indentures and became tenants and small landholders. As historian Ira Berlin explains, "*African* slavery was no longer just one of many forms of subordination—a common enough circumstance in a world ruled by hierarchies—but the foundation on which the social order rested."[38]

As the system of racialized slavery matured, nineteenth-century Americans underwent a moral panic about the parameters of whiteness. Perhaps the greatest concern was that if black could be mistaken for white, then white could just as easily be mistaken for black. Abolitionists, seeking to bolster antislavery sentiment among Northern audiences, made fears about racial misrecognition more urgent by distributing images of "white slaves" and by arguing that if Southern slave power continued to expand and encroach on freedom and liberty, whites—and most catastrophically, white children—could easily be stolen into slavery. Reverend Henry Ward Beecher, known for "dazzling imagery and oversize emotional gestures" and for presiding over mock "slave auctions" where he exhorted crowds to donate money to emancipate enslaved women, drew on images of little slave girls "of sweet face, large eyes, light hair, and fair as a lily" to appeal to Northern audiences that "as long as children who looked so white were enslaved, no white child was safe."[39] Writing in his 1860 narrative about his escape from slavery, William Craft reminded readers, "It is almost impossible for a white child, after having been kidnapped and sold into or reduced to slavery, in a part of the country where it is not known (as often is the case), ever to recover its freedom." Craft also used white slavery as a device to trouble Northerners about "such inhuman transactions" of "worthless white people to sell their own free children into slavery."[40] Unnerved by the near-white complexion of fugitive slave Henry Bibb, abolitionists in Cincinnati asked, "Could it be possible that a man so near white as myself could be a slave? Could it be possible that men would make slaves of their own children?"[41] An article in a Philadelphia newspaper announced an event at a church where three slave children would be exhibited: "two pretty girls of about eight years of age, who would 'readily pass for whites,' as the chattel advertisements say, and a boy of the same age and equally white."[42] The original plan, found objectionable by the church hosting the event, was to display the three nearly white slaves alongside "some of the peculiar instruments of the peculiar institution." In this instance, the intention may have been to make obvious the interconnectedness of two of the most appalling but elemental facets of the slave regime: the sexual economy of slavery and the brutality of the violence that held the system together. Historian Mary Niall Mitchell argues that in these light-skinned, "passable" slaves, Northerners saw "living proof of the ruling passions of the South," and could "read in [their] white skin a history of 'miscegenation,' generations of it, resulting from the sexual interaction of white masters with their female slaves."[43] Dogged by accusations of advocating "amalgamation," abolitionists could now reveal the South's history of race mixing, its "dreadful amalgamating abominations," and make the antislavery argument that such would "experience, in all probability, a ten fold diminution" with emancipation.[44]

The nineteenth-century courtroom provided another stage on which to scrutinize racial difference and the likelihood of white slavery. Legal scholar Ariela Gross has discussed numerous "trials of racial determination" in which light-skinned slaves sued their masters by claiming that they were white and had been unjustly and illegally enslaved. Most Southerners, Gross argues, believed that a "racial essence" existed in the blood. They ran into trouble, though, when they tried to come to an agreement as to how it would be disclosed. In many cases, by being known to "do the things a white man or woman would do," slaves increased their chances of gaining the sympathy of judges and winning their cases. Testimony from white neighbors and friends that the plaintiff "visited among white folks as an equal," "was kind of a favorite at school," "exhibited genteel actions and movements," "had no clumsiness about him," and "dined with whites just the same as any gentleman would have done" offered evidence of a racial competency that juries considered more reliable and ultimately more conclusive than skin color. Gendered norms also played a crucial role in reinforcing one's claim to whiteness: a white man was expected to actively participate in civic affairs by voting, mustering in the militia, and serving on juries; a white woman was presumed to hold "moral power and weight" and to be "neat in her person, simple in her array, and with no ornament upon her not even a ring on her fingers."[45] Determining an individual's racial identity—which, in the nineteenth century, often meant deciding whether one would be freed or enslaved—was tricky business. Neither judges nor juries entered into this exercise lightly.

The wide range of evidence taken into account in nineteenth-century trials of racial determination reveals that at times, passing had very little to do with skin color. This is not to suggest that passing as white is not contingent on a racially ambiguous or white appearance, but rather that a racially ambiguous or white appearance is contingent on a brew of actions, behaviors, and mannerisms. Looking white is, in many ways, contingent on *doing* white. Racially ambiguous slaves drew on highly sophisticated understandings of racial, gender, and social norms to enact whiteness; by doing so, they successfully passed to freedom.

Risky Property

By her husband's account, Ellen Craft was a reluctant, but sensational, runaway. It was he, William Craft, who conceived their elaborate plot and encouraged Ellen's acquiescence: "It occurred to me that, as my wife was nearly white, I might get her to disguise herself as an invalid gentleman, and assume to be my master, while I could attend as his slave, and that in this manner we might effect our escape."[46]

It was necessary for Ellen to pass as a man, the Crafts reasoned, because it was unconventional for a white woman to travel alone with a male slave; such a coupling would attract the kind of attention that a pair of fugitive slaves wished to avoid. Literary critic Marjorie Garber argues that even by William's telling of the story and despite her initial misgivings, "It was Ellen Craft who invented the persona of the young invalid gentleman that was to prove so effective."[47] Concerned that "the smoothness of her face might betray her" and that her illiteracy would render her incapable of registering her name in hotel visitors' books, Ellen improvised the accoutrements needed to shore up her white male identity, hitting on a clever solution: "'I think I have it! I think I can make a poultice and bind up my right hand in a sling, and with propriety ask the officers to register my name for me.'" She then created another poultice that would be "worn under the chin, up the cheeks, and to tie over the head. This nearly hid the expression of the countenance, as well as the beardless chin."[48] By beginning their "desperate leap for liberty" at Christmas, a time of the year when masters allowed slaves to visit friends and family members on neighboring plantations, the Crafts believed that their request for visiting passes was more likely to be granted and that their absence would be less conspicuous. With spectacles, boots, a short haircut, men's trousers, and a top hat, the physical metamorphosis was complete. The slave Ellen Craft had become the free white man, Mr. William Johnson. Hesitating at first, an emboldened Ellen now played the role to the hilt. En route to Philadelphia, young southern women swooned in the presence of this "most respectable looking gentleman."[49]

For her performance to be convincing, or even plausible, it was essential that the disguise extend beyond Ellen's physical appearance. Becoming a white man required far more than white skin and the concealment of a beardless face. It was Ellen's ability to "get on . . . in the company of gentleman" that would ultimately determine the success of the Crafts' undertaking. Such a feat required a nuanced understanding of southern social and gender norms, thus revealing the crucial linkages that passing forged between race and class. Ellen successfully passed as white by presenting herself as a well-dressed, courteous, and honorable gentleman; the Crafts' plan would not have worked had Ellen appeared as an

Figure 1.1. Ellen Craft, disguised as a Southern gentleman during her escape from slavery. *Courtesy of Louisiana State University Press, Baton Rouge, Louisiana.*

uncouth, unrefined man of low social standing. To become a white southern gentleman, Ellen's inability to read and write would have to be explained; her absence from "general conversation, of which most Yankee travelers are passionately fond," would need to be excused.[50] The poultice, wrapped under her chin, indicated illness and provided a useful prop to discourage verbal exchange. And, when it failed to fend off eager conversationalists, including a friend of Ellen's master who inauspiciously sat beside Ellen on the train, she feigned deafness. Another poultice, binding Ellen's right hand in a sling, masked her inability to write and offered an explanation for her reliance on desk clerks to sign her name in hotel registers. When the clerk refused to sign for her at a hotel in Charleston, a man whom Ellen had met on the ship "stepped in, somewhat the worse for brandy," shook Ellen's hand and "pretended to know all about him." As luck would have it, this man's assertion that he knew Ellen's "kin like a book" persuaded the hotel clerk to reassess Ellen's impairment and reverse his earlier decision.[51] Read as an injury and a source of sympathy, Ellen's bandaged hand no longer undermined her white male identity; instead, her presumed literacy functioned, as literary critic Lindon Barrett writes, as an "indispensable correlate to [her] racially ambiguous skin."[52]

William's careful enactment of the role of the faithful, if not obsequious, slave bolstered the credibility of Ellen's southern white male persona. "You have a very attentive boy, sir; but you had better watch him like a hawk when you get on to the North," one passenger warned Ellen. A slave dealer surmised that not only was William "a keen nigger," but he could see "from the cut of his eye that he is certain to run away."[53] Although Ellen's certitude in William's fidelity sounded naïve to some passengers, it reprised familiar southern refrains about the loyalty of slaves and the humane aspects of slavery. Over the course of the Crafts' travels, several passengers weighed in on Ellen's treatment of William, making it a frequent yet contentious conversation topic. A Southern military officer chastised Ellen for being "very likely to spoil [her] boy by saying 'thank you' to him," and an "uncouth planter" announced that she was "'*spiling*' that ere nigger of yourn, by letting him wear such a devilish fine hat." When the planter's friend cautioned him against "speak[ing] so to a gentleman," the irony of the planter's retort could not have been lost on the Crafts: "Why not? It always makes me itch all over, from head to toe, to get hold of every d——d nigger I see dressed like a white man."[54] Still, these passengers did not intend to cast aspersions on Ellen's whiteness nor were they disputing her masculinity or her honor (in her role as Mr. William Johnson). Instead, they hoped to dissuade Ellen from treating her slave so mildly. They saw William, at best, as an easy target for abolitionists, and, at worst, as a likely runaway.

An anxious moment arose when Ellen and William were detained and interrogated about their travel plans. "It was rather sharp shooting this morning," one passenger explained when the Crafts were finally released, only after the official took pity on Ellen/Mr. Johnson, who appeared to be a frail gentleman clearly in need of medical attention. "It was not out of any disrespect to you, sir; but they make it a rule to be very strict at Charleston. . . . If they were not very careful, any d—d abolitionist might take off a lot of valuable niggers."[55]

Ellen and William Craft were not alone; other fugitive slaves replicated many of the elements of their legendary plot. Henry Bibb, who was also racially ambiguous, made a "regular business" of running away, an art he honed "to perfection" after many attempts and over several years. He finally "broke the bans of slavery, and landed [himself] safely in Canada, where [he] was regarded as a man, and not as a thing." Born a slave in May 1815 in Shelby County, Kentucky, to a mother who was "so fortunate or unfortunate, as to have . . . slaveholding blood flowing in her veins," but "not enough to prevent her children though fathered by slaveholders, from being bought and sold in the slave markets of the South," Bibb endured the physical and psychological horrors of slavery. He was driven to work under the lash and beaten savagely by masters and overseers. Most painfully, he was powerless to protect his wife and his young daughter from repeated acts of violence and sexual abuse.[56]

Bibb planned his first escape for the fall or winter of 1837, and he prepared by saving money (about two dollars and fifty cents) and purchasing a suit that he "had never been seen or known to wear before," to avoid being detected.[57] Traveling aboard a southern steamboat bound for Cincinnati, "surrounded by the vilest enemies of God and man, liable to be seized and bound hand and foot, by any white man, and taken back into captivity," Bibb kept himself "back from the light among the deck passengers, where it would be difficult to distinguish [him] from a white man." According to Bibb, this was "one of the instances of my adventures that my affinity with the Anglo-Saxon race, and even slaveholders, worked well for my escape." He was "so near the color of a slaveholder," he was not discovered among the white passengers. As soon as the ship neared Cincinnati, Bibb was able to "pass off unnoticed" as the passengers became absorbed with their arrival in the city.[58] When Bibb arrived at the New Orleans slave market after being captured by a slave trader and dressed in the trader's old suit, he was immediately mistaken as white. A potential buyer retracted his offer to purchase Bibb, fearing that he was "a little too near white," could read and write, and was likely to run away.[59]

Over the course of multiple escape attempts, Bibb both reproduced and inverted the class dimensions of Ellen Craft's performance as a southern gentleman. In one instance, he passed as an inebriate, drawing on popular assumptions that "Indians were generally drunkards"; that it was not unusual for a drunken white man to be "found straggling among them"; and that in an intoxicated state, a white man "would be more likely to find friends from sympathy than an upright man." Bibb "walked up to the door of one of their houses, and fell up against it . . . opened [the door] and staggered in, falling about, and making a great noise." Disturbed by the commotion, an old woman finally awoke and covered Bibb with a blanket.[60] During other escapes, Bibb passed as free by possessing intimate, "inside" knowledge about various places. Bibb convinced some white travelers that he was a resident of Ohio by being "well acquainted with its location, its principal cities, inhabitants, &c." And, as he gained confidence in his newly found white identity, Bibb "stayed in the best hotels, ate at the best tables, slept in the best beds . . . and acted with as much independence as if [he] was worth a million dollars." At times, he went so far as to "talk about buying land, stock and village property." Chatty and conversant on the right topics, Bibb was "treated just like other travelers." As Bibb explained, "No man ever asked me whether I was bond or free, black or white, rich or poor; but I always presented a bold front and showed the best side out, which was all the pass I had."[61]

Yet another ingenious ploy allowed Bibb to travel on a steamboat from Jefferson City to St. Louis, Missouri. To board the boat, Bibb knew that he would have to provide proof of his status; he would need to show free papers to prove that he was free or he would be required to provide his master's name if he was a slave. Cleverly passing himself off as a body servant of one of the passengers boarding the boat, Bibb purchased a large trunk, struggled with it as if it were full of clothing, and followed the passengers onto the boat.[62] In this instance, Bibb successfully passed as black. This practice of "darkening up" has been described as a way "not only to escape but also to see without being seen."[63] When he was not pretending to carry a heavy trunk at the heels of white passengers, Bibb's nearly white appearance created confusion. Mistaken as a white man, he was invited to dine at the captain's table. Once the captain realized that Bibb was not white, he would not allow him to eat until everyone else had been served. When Bibb took umbrage at this insult, the captain replied casually, "No one has misued you, for you ought to have known better than to have come to the table where there were white people." When Bibb insisted that he had been invited to the table, the captain replied, "Yes, but I did not know that you was a colored man, when I asked you; and then it was better to insult one man than all the passengers on board of the boat . . . you have imposed upon me in a way which is unbecoming a gentleman."[64] The captain may have felt offended and embarrassed, but perhaps he could have taken some solace in knowing that he was hardly alone in mistakenly welcoming black guests to the dinner table.

The historical record is replete with stories of slaves "so near white that a microscope would be required to discern [their] colored origin" who passed their way to freedom. William Still wrote, "Not that quite a number of passengers, fair enough to pass for white, with just a slight tinge of colored blood in their view, even sons and daughters of some of the F.F.V. (First Families of Virginia), had not on various occasions come over the U.G.R.R. (Underground Railroad)."[65] In one such case, George Latimer ran away from Norfolk, Virginia, in October 1842 with his pregnant wife, Rebecca. This couple reversed the roles played by the Crafts: George, who had been advertised by his master as a fugitive slave with a "bright yellow" complexion, passed as a white slave master, while Rebecca, a dark mulatto, played the role of his slave.[66]

Charlotte Giles and Harriet Eglin "contrived each to get a suit of mourning, with heavy black veils, and thus dressed, apparently absorbed with grief," as they began their journey to Philadelphia. In this case, gender helped Giles and Eglin. Heavy black veils and a mourning suit would only serve women. Horror followed by an equal measure of relief when one of their masters boarded the train, asked for their names, but mercifully did not recognize the women dressed in mourning clothes.[67]

Not "the faintest shade of colored blood was hardly discernible" in John Wesley Gibson, so he resolved to be free by first "hold[ing] up his head and put[ting] on airs." He arrived safely in Baltimore and found passing as white quite easy; indeed, it "proved a success beyond his expectation," and "he could but wonder how it was that he had never before hit upon such an expedient to rid himself of his unhappy lot."[68]

Nineteen-year-old Wiley Maddison escaped from Petersburg on the train by passing as a white man. With a "promising appearance," Maddison "found no difficulty whatever on the road."[69] Daniel and David Bruce of Prince William County, Virginia, passed as white and worked as mail carriers. A white identity offered both men "access to education and other advantages, routinely denied free black youth," and convinced them of the expediency of "mov[ing] in and out of the white world, but also guaranteed them a privileged position in the free black community."[70] Jeremiah Colburn, who was described as a "bright mulatto, of prepossessing appearance, [who] reads and writes, and is quite intelligent . . . and was fair enough to pass for white," traveled from Charleston to Philadelphia without detection "under the garb of a white gentleman." Cornelius Scott of Stafford County, Virginia, "had been very much bleached by the Patriarchal Institution, and he was shrewd enough to take advantage of this circumstance," even if it meant leaving his mother and half brother behind in order to travel as a white man.[71] Scott's story prefigures the devastating family separations that passing often required.

"Entirely too white for practical purposes," Lewis Lee could not "content himself under the yoke" and grew tired of working for less money than he knew he deserved. He believed that "it was now time to 'strike out on his own hook'"; since "he was about as white as anybody else, and that he had as good a right to pass for white as the white folks, . . . he decided to do so with a high head and a fearless front." He decided to "boldly approach a hotel and call for accommodations, as any other southern gentleman," and refused to "skulk in the woods, in thickets and swamps, under cover of the darkness." Despite receiving "first-rate" treatment in Washington and Baltimore, Lee had little education and "coming among strangers, he was conscious that the shreds of slavery were still to be seen upon him." With "no intention of disowning his origin" and "once he could feel safe in assuming his true status," Lee, like many other racially ambiguous runaway slaves, actively avoided entering the white world upon securing his freedom.[72]

Passing as free was possible in a society where not all African Americans were enslaved. Passing as white was possible in a society where whiteness was not based solely (or arguably, even primarily) on appearance, but also on dress, comportment, and social knowledge. But after the passing was over, after freedom had been won and ex-slaves reunited with their families, something was still amiss. An article published in a Philadelphia newspaper in the early 1850s commented, "The question of what shall be done with the free negroes is becoming as important as what shall be done with the slaves."[73] The freedom that these daring men and women had so doggedly pursued was incomplete and imperfect.

Racially ambiguous people—both enslaved and free—moved to urban centers with the intention of blending into racially heterogeneous cities and taking shelter in free black communities. The new arrivals comprised "a peculiar society of their own."[74] In northern cities such as Boston, Philadelphia, New York, and Cleveland, the population of free blacks had increased dramatically in size but also in financial worth by the 1850s. Free black communities grew as a result of gradual emancipations that followed the American Revolution, the flight of fugitive slaves, and early migrations of elite blacks who saw their social and economic prospects diminish.[75] Most free blacks still had one foot squarely in the slave system owing to relationships with enslaved family members. A smaller number had been born to free parents or worked as mechanics or artisans and lived beyond slavery's reach. Some had purchased their own freedom, the freedom of their spouses, and their children or were freed by white masters (who often doubled as fathers and occasionally provided for their children's education). But regardless of their particular path to freedom, free blacks created a veritable moral panic in the North and the South as their very presence unsteadied the slave system and the larger social order. In a speech in Philadelphia on July 4, 1830, abolitionist Peter Williams bemoaned the hostility directed at free blacks: "Ah! . . . the sight of *free* men of colour is so unwelcome, that we know not what they may think themselves justifiable in doing, to get rid of them."[76]

Free blacks rushed into already swelling urban areas at a moment when the physical arrangement of antebellum cities brought wide swaths of people into close contact, despite the efforts of the newly forming middle class "to insulate themselves from the 'dangerous classes,' who threatened not only their persons and property but their status as well, by jeering and insulting them in public."[77] Confrontations between black and white city dwellers, like the one below, could be expected given the hurly-burly of antebellum city streets:

> Sally Moore (white) and Cora Pearson (yellow) were arraigned yesterday morning on the charge of committing a breach of the peace. Miss Moore appeared on the street . . . dressed in a

> fawn-colored silk. Her hair was neatly arranged. . . . She was rather tall, walked with ladylike dignity. . . . Now it so happened that Cora, whose face was rather darker than a quadroon, appeared on the same pavement, and walking in the same direction. She was short in stature. . . . The dress in which she was habited was of dilapidated silk. Cora dashed ahead, and her long train was trod upon accidentally by Sally; and now a scene ensued which would have been doubly interesting had it not been accompanied with remarks too profane and immoral for repetition. . . . The yellow female sprang at the other with all the ferocity of an untamed tigress. A short rough-and-tumble struggle ensued, which ended in Cora going sprawling on the pave, divested of the largest proportions of her dress. . . . Sally had her face scratched. Four finger marks down her rosy cheeks gave evidence of the feline powers of her antagonist on the evening before. The case concluded by binding the parties over to be of good behavior and to keep the peace.[78]

Before the altercation, the reporter described Cora "following in [Sally's] wake, as though apeing the other." A quadroon's inelegant attempt to imitate the "ladylike dignity" of a white woman was so absurd that it created a "general laugh among the spectators who find time to lounge in front of large hotels." But Sally's feminine modesty was hardly unblemished by the fracas; her face may have been scratched by the "feline powers of her antagonist," but it was Sally who had sent Cora "sprawling on the pave."

Railway cars represented another turbulent and contested site. In Philadelphia, for example, blacks were only allowed to ride in a small section of the smoking car, making for a miserable experience, which was captured by an article in a Philadelphia newspaper:

"Bundled with his wife into that foul apartment, in hearing of brutal jests liable to insult, he must feel if he have feelings, the hopelessness of his degradation."[79] In 1862, James Barrett, a passenger on a railway car, was charged with assault and battery against another passenger, George W. Goines, who was described as "a colored man of respectable appearance . . . [whose] hair is straight and his complexion is a shade lighter than is usually seen in the colored race." The first leg of Goines's trip was unremarkable and "no objection was made to his riding." On his return, he went unnoticed until the conductor approached him to collect his fare and insisted that Goines travel in the front platform, a cramped and uncomfortable space designated for black passengers. When Goines refused, a scuffle ensued, and with the help of Barrett, the conductor roughly cast Goines off the train. Goines complained of a severe bruise on his arm and testified that he had been kicked, though he was not sure by whom. The jury ruled in favor of the conductor who maintained that proper procedures had been followed and "no more force than was necessary had been used against Goines."[80]

Allowed little physical space on city streets and admitted to only the most offensive railway cars, this "peculiar society" was afforded even less discursive space given that it was assumed that blacks were only fit to be slaves. Debates about who should be considered a lady and who should be considered a gentleman were rarely decided in favor of blacks. The presumption that virtue and honor inhered only in whiteness vexed black elites who complained that despite their mastery of the subtleties of upper-middle-class culture, they could still be violently ejected from railway cars or ridiculed for "putting on airs."[81] Charlotte Forten, a teacher and reformer from a prestigious free black family in Philadelphia, spoke French fluently, played the piano, enjoyed classical music, and appreciated the poetry of Tennyson and Wordsworth. Forten was so ensconced in upper-class culture that the vast social and cultural distance separating her from the black masses became strikingly evident when she moved to South Carolina to educate newly freed men and women in the early days of emancipation. Forten described the ex-slaves as "kind and polite," but she barely understood the way they spoke, she was entirely unfamiliar with their religious practices, and she questioned why it was necessary for their preachers to "scream." Before moving to South Carolina, Forten attended an integrated school in Salem, Massachusetts (her father hoped to shield her from the prejudice of Philadelphia's segregated schools), but she still encountered bigotry and intolerance, even in a reputedly liberal environment. On Wednesday, September 12, 1856, Forten wrote in her journal:

> I wonder that every colored person is not a misanthrope. Surely we have everything to make us hate mankind. I have met girls in the schoolroom—they have been thoroughly kind and cordial to me—perhaps the next day met them in the street—they feared to recognize me; these I can but regard now with scorn and contempt, once I liked them, believing them incapable of such measures. Others give the most distant recognition possible.[82]

Forten conceded that such slights were "but trifles, certainly to the great, public wrongs which we as a people are obliged to endure," but she still felt their sting: "to those who experience them, these apparent trifles are most wearing and discouraging; even to the child's mind they reveal volumes of deceit and heartlessness, and early teach a lesson of suspicion and distrust." A few years later, Forten described being insulted by a man while dining aboard a train: "A *gentleman* took umbrage at sitting at the same table with one whose skin chanced to be 'not colored like his own,' and rose and left the table. Poor man! He feared contamination."[83]

These kinds of snubs and rebuffs were emblematic of the wide range of indignities endured by free blacks. In January 1858, G. E. Stephens wrote to Jacob Cook that he "dare not smoke" a cigar or walk with a cane in the street as both were against the law in Charleston. On crowded streets, blacks were expected to walk in the middle and "give way" to white pedestrians, and especially to white women. Stephens was troubled by warnings that "if I had run against one of them [a white woman], they would have had me flogged."[84] Perhaps the most humiliating measure was a law that compelled free men and women to register before country clerks every three years and to carry numbered badges with them at all times.[85] An article published in a Philadelphia newspaper described a "handsome married woman, almost white," who carried a badge with the inscription, "Charleston. 1860. Servant. 1243"; her husband carried a similar one that identified him as "Porter." The couple had been fined the astronomical amount of $40 for being a day late in "taking out" these badges.[86] "Virtually, they were made to be slaves," one reporter wrote, commenting on the flimsiness and negation of black freedom in the mid-nineteenth century. Laws coupled with local customs deprived blacks of the most mundane signifiers of freedom and the most basic expressions of independence and autonomy.

The involvement of black soldiers in the Civil War augured new possibilities for recognition. Writing to his uncle, James P. Thomas, on August 19, 1864, John Rapier Jr. described the deference paid to black soldiers at the Freedmen's Hospital in Washington, D.C.: "But I must tell you coloured men in the U.S. Uniform are much respected here, and in visiting the Union's Department if the drefs [dress] is that of an Officer, you receive the Military Salute from the guard as promptly as if your blood was a Howard or Plantagenet instead of Pompey or Cuffee's." Melvin Patrick Ely's work on the settlement of free blacks on Israel Hill in Prince Edward County, Virginia, demonstrates that there were places where whites did not simply tolerate free blacks, but where they worked side by side, occasionally married, and raised families together.[87] But Rapier's letter to his uncle contains a striking admission of the lack of hospitality that blacks could expect to receive upon arrival in Washington, D.C., regardless of their dress or military rank. Rapier warned his uncle: "In all of Washington there is not [a] number one place for a Col'd Gentleman to stop." It would be necessary, Rapier explained, that his uncle provide "due and timely notice" of his travel plans so that Rapier could properly "fix [him] up."[88]

The delight of passing as white, of "fooling white folks," is plain to see, particularly in light of the everyday humiliations that free blacks suffered, on the streets, on railway cars, and in dining rooms. Robert Purvis, the nearly white abolitionist born in Charleston, reveled in poking fun at countless whites that misrecognized him.[89] In 1834, on a ship bound for England, Purvis dined, danced, and discussed horses with Southerners who earlier had refused to sail with a black man. Invited to give a toast on the last night, Purvis received a standing ovation from one of the most rabid, proslavery Southerners on board. But this man's enthusiasm for Purvis quickly cooled when Purvis informed the captain of his racial background, and the news spread like wildfire around the ship. At a poultry exhibition, a man approached Mr. Purvis's booth and admired the "rare beauty" of his exhibit but flippantly remarked, "And these belong to that black nigger down in Byberry." Purvis responded impassively, "Why friend, you put it in rather strong lan-

Figure 1.2. Robert Purvis, African American abolitionist who occasionally passed as white to disprove beliefs in white racial superiority.
Courtesy of the Moorland-Spingarn Research Center, Howard University.

guage, but you can judge for yourself—I am that man."[90] When the Bensalem Horse Traders threatened to expel Purvis from a competition, his friend Miller McKim responded, angrily: "Still, we are told, that his color made him objectionable; which allegation we deny since it is with difficulty, such is the fairness of his complexion, that any one, unacquainted with him, could, without being informed of the fact, tell that he is a colored man at all." This sentiment was at the heart of Purvis's critique of race relations: if it was impossible to identify Purvis as black, then race must be an arbitrary and biologically meaningless category. If education, class, comportment, and taste rendered Purvis even more indistinguishable from whites, there was no reason why he should not have access to any social or economic circle according to his own lights.[91]

Occasionally, attempts at passing failed. In 1863, John Rapier wrote his father to inform him that the University of Michigan was "thrown into convulsions" when an "American of African descent dared to present himself as a candidate for admission to the Medical class." When it was discovered that the student, Mr. Tucker, was a "Col'd gentleman from the West Indies," the administration initially allowed him to matriculate, but wavered when his attendance at a lecture became the "signal for commotion among the Copperhead Students, and many unprincipled Republicans." Mr. Tucker was soon asked to leave the University because, as Rapier explained, "Col'd Men are not admitted here." The letter implies that Rapier was also passing. He wrote, "Tucker's Col'd friends are in arms against me because the faculty retained me in my seat after his expulsion. They say I pretend to be white when I am nothing but a 'nigger.'" Rapier was passing, and he found himself in an increasingly insecure position after the luckless Mr. Tucker was unceremoniously outed. Perhaps Rapier was simply more adept at the passing game. There is no evidence in his correspondence to indicate that his roommate, "a good fellow from Wisconsin," knew that he was sharing a room with a "Col'd gentleman."[92]

"A Nigger's Honour"

"Became white" is neatly handwritten beneath St. John Appo's name on the Cook family's genealogical chart. St. John Appo's birth and death dates are not recorded, but according to the 1880 census, he was born "abt 1848 or 1849." His mother, Betty Brady, listed as "colored," was born in 1822. He was the second oldest of five children. Another family tree provides a few more data points: Appo is listed parenthetically as "(w.?)" and it is noted that he married a white woman, Alice Hartford, with whom he had three children. No further information is provided; neither the date of his marriage nor his children's names or any descendants are noted. The thinning out of information about St. John Appo in his family's records creates a striking, if not eerie, similarity between Appo and his two brothers who died untimely deaths, without progeny: Garnet Appo, who died at 18, and William Appo, who was killed in the Battle of Bull Run. Other branches of the Cook family have more robust genealogies: Appo's cousins became well-known ministers, educators, and abolitionists. Several family members enjoyed privileged positions and high social standing in Philadelphia's elite black community.

Census data offers a more detailed account of St. John Appo's life and his wanderings across the color line. In 1880, he is listed as a mulatto merchant tailor living in Hartford, Connecticut. In 1890 and 1900, he is a black journalist in Brooklyn, New York. But by 1920, Appo is a white newspaper publisher, still living in Brooklyn.

Why, when St. John Appo's family members were actively engaged in building an economically viable and socially vibrant black community, did Appo choose to walk away and leave it behind? Family records offer sparse documentation of his life. The census is often an unreliable source, but in this case, it confirmed his family's speculations that he "became white" and it revealed more about his life "on the other side" than his family could have known. A census taker might read one person's race one way one year and another census taker might have an entirely different opinion of the same person a decade later. Within one person's lifetime, one could be black, mulatto, and white. Still, one can only conjecture as to what Appo expected to gain professionally and personally by becoming white at that particular moment.[93]

The descendants of Thomas Jefferson and Sally Hemings offer a more familiar example: Beverley and Harriet Hemings both married whites of "good circumstances" and "good standing" and passed in Maryland; Eston Hemings, known for his musical talents, spent some time in Chillicothe, Ohio, before changing his name to Eston H. Jefferson and moving to Wisconsin with his "colored" wife in 1852, where both identified as white; Madison Hemings nestled himself in the black community of Chillicothe and enjoyed a modest life as a skilled carpenter.[94] By 1873, all of the Hemings siblings with the exception of Madison were living as white. The differences in the lives lived by members of the same family demonstrate the range of choices available to racially ambiguous people in the mid-nineteenth century.

But simply identifying the range of choices available to racially ambiguous people avoids more elusive questions about the kinds of benefits that passing offered and what passing meant to those who practiced it during this period. The efficacy of passing as a means of rescuing one's self from slavery is unmistakable, but little hint appears in the historical record about the reasons why some chose to pass after their freedom had been won. And the lion's share of evidence points to light-skinned African Americans who made the decision to identify as black and who worked tirelessly to build and sustain burgeoning free black communities. To reconstitute the fainter and less perceptible meanings that passing held, meanings that often elude the historical record, it is helpful to turn to an episode from a mid-nineteenth-century novel.

If the census records are correct, St. John Appo fared better as a white man than Clarence Garie, one of the characters in Frank J. Webb's 1858 novel, *The Garies and Their Friends.* Clarence's life falls apart when a figure from his past (and the son of the man who murdered his father) arrives on the eve of his wedding and reveals Clarence's identity. Clarence had been coaxed into passing by white benefactors who feared that he would be sold as a slave after the death of his father, a white slave owner who had married a mulatto slave. When Clarence is exposed, he becomes "very wretched and lonely"; he not only is "completely excluded from the society in which he had so long been accustomed to move" but also experiences dramatic changes in his appearance, becoming "bent and emaciated to a frightful extent."[95] Mr. Bates, the father of Clarence's fiancée, frames passing as a fundamentally dishonorable act: "There are laws to punish thieves and counterfeits—but such as you may go unchastised except by the abhorrence of all honourable men. Had you been unaware of your origin, and had the revelation . . . been as new to you as to me, you would have deserved sympathy; but you have been acting a lie, claiming a position in society to which you knew you had no right, and deserve execration and contempt." Mr. Bates demands that Clarence return the letters that his daughter has written to him, but Clarence pleads for one more day with his beloved's correspondence:

> "Tomorrow I will send them," said Clarence. "I will read them all over once again," thought he.
>
> "I cannot believe you," said Mr. Bates.
>
> "I promise you upon my honour I will send them tomorrow!"
>
> *"A nigger's honour!"* rejoined Mr. Bates, with a contemptuous sneer.
>
> "Yes, sir—a nigger's honour" repeated Clarence, the colour mounting to his pale cheeks. "A few drop of negro blood in a man's veins do not entirely deprive him of noble sentiments.

> 'Tis true my past concealment does not argue in my favour. I concealed that which was no fault of my own, but what the injustice of society has made a crime."[96]

Earlier in the novel, Clarence's father, Mr. Garie, enjoys a good laugh at the expense of Mr. Priestly, a white man who "prides himself on being able to detect evidence of the least drop of African blood in any one," yet he is fooled into treating the nearly white Mr. Winston "with the most distinguished consideration," even requesting that he accompany his daughter to the grand ball. "A Fifth-avenue belle escorted to church and to balls by a coloured gentleman!" Mr. Garie exclaimed, bursting into wild laughter. But Mr. Garie harbored hope that the revelation of Mr. Winston's racial background would convince Mr. Priestly that "a man can be a gentleman even though he has African blood in his veins."[97] Mr. Garie's hope was ultimately false: Mr. Priestly's racial views would not be reversed, and the shame and humiliation of being bested by a black man would have only made matters worse.

That a black man could possess honor and dignity was unimaginable almost everywhere in mid-nineteenth-century America, and certainly in the South where, as scholars have written extensively, an honor culture thrived and predicated a white man's honor on a black man's dishonor.[98] It is not surprising that one would choose to pass as white at a time when "prejudice against blacks extend[ed] to every class"; when blacks suffered the daily affronts of being restricted to far-flung galleries in theaters, concert halls, and churches; when blacks could expect to cause "immediate rebellion" among white workers when they were employed as apprentices or journeymen, which limited them to "dull, manual labors" where at best one might aspire to be "a hotel-waiter, a vendor of peanuts and cakes, or a mere beast of burden." But the exchange between Clarence and Mr. Bates broaches much broader reasons for passing. During the antebellum years, passing as white served primarily to deliver slaves from bondage, but it also provided a vehicle to reclaim one's honor and dignity by upending the assumption that "the existence of a 'gentleman' with African blood in his veins, is a moral and physical impossibility."[99]

On the eve of the Civil War, Richard Walpole Cogdell moved his mulatto family from Charleston to Philadelphia. Similar to Mr. Garie, Cogdell worried about the fate of his children in a slave state after his death, and he hoped that Philadelphia would offer a less oppressive environment for his black mistress, Sarah Martha Sanders, and their children. In the aftermath of the Civil War, Cogdell lost his estate due to mismanagement, and he died deeply in debt in 1866. Despite his financial ruin, many of his descendants prospered and became members of Philadelphia's black elite while others decided to pass as white.[100] The family produced successful tailors, carpenters, hairdressers, and wigmakers. In 1880, the Chew branch of the family would bring legal suit to abolish racially segregated schools in Philadelphia. Richard Sanders Chew, a beneficiary of these efforts, studied engineering at the University of Pennsylvania. According to family lore, a professor advised Chew to leave Philadelphia and pass as white, convincing him that such a route would ease what might have otherwise been a frustrating path to success. Chew followed his professor's advice: he moved to the west coast, married a white woman, and enjoyed a distinguished career as an engineer. He often visited his family in Philadelphia, but these relationships ended abruptly with his death.[101] The Cogdell-Sanders-Chew extended family provides another example of a mixed-race family that included relatives who made different choices about their racial identities.

The massive dislocation and disruption brought forth by the Civil War as well as the anxious uncertainty about the war's aftermath reshaped the meaning of passing and led African Americans to ask new questions about where they wanted to live and who they wanted to be. In the midst of the war, William Parham carefully assessed his life chances in America and, with great frustration and disappointment, decided to opt out. In a letter dated September 7, 1862, he wrote to the wealthy barber Jacob White:

> You have of course, already seen by the papers that we are at present, to all appearances, in imminent danger of an attack from the Confederates. . . . there are rumors enough, but nothing reliable. Last night it was rumored that the 'rebs' had made their appearance within 5 miles of this city; and when I retired to rest, I knew not whether I should wake up a subject to Jeff Davis or Abe Lincoln: however, the rumor proved unfounded, and—I therefore find myself still under the government of the colonizer. After much deliberation, I have almost concluded to go to Jamaica. . . . I shall unless my mind should undergo a very sudden and radical change, make an effort to get out of this slavery-cursed and Negro-hating country as soon as I can make it expedient so to do. My dear friend, you do not [k]now how much I yearn to be a man, and having found that I can only be so by leaving the country, I am willing to accept the conditions.[102]

The impossibility of being a man in a "slavery-cursed" and "Negro-hating" country made America an intolerable place to live. For racially ambiguous people, passing represented one strategy of escape, but for all African Americans, the end of the Civil War signaled the emergence of new possibilities: some took part in the first waves of a great migration that brought thousands of blacks out of rural areas and into northern and southern towns, whereas others carefully vetted plans to leave the country altogether and settle in Jamaica, Liberia, or Canada.[103] But, the war's end, emancipation, and the beginning of the experiment of Reconstruction confirmed that the world had turned upside down. Perhaps blacks could find a more complete freedom in this country. Just one year later, Parham wrote another letter to Cook that captures the brisk pace of change and explains why Parham reassessed his plans:

> I have for several reasons given up the notion of migrating to Jamaica for the present. . . . The present aspect of things in this country,—the injustice and outrage to which we are still subject, notwithstanding—gives evidence of the coming of a better and a brighter day. . . . When this war is over, the next struggle will be against prejudice, which is to be conquered by intellect and we shall need all the talent that we have among us or can possibly command, then will be your time to be found in the thickest of the fight; where the battle rages fiercest and the danger is most imminent.[104]

The optimism of Parham's letter captures the hopeful tenor of the early years of Reconstruction and anticipates the unprecedented opportunities that would emerge after the Civil War. Reconstruction was the moment black elites had been waiting for: as Parham suggests, black elites would assume leadership positions by contributing "all the talent" they had or could command; it was their time to be "found in the thickest of the fight." This historical moment was nothing short of revolutionary, as was the possibility that the honor, "noble sentiments," dignity, and humanity possessed by black men and women might finally be fully acknowledged. And, under these new conditions, the meaning of passing would take on another valence as it adapted to the conditions of a new social regime. Parham closed his letter to Cook by writing, "the present is not always. Better days will come."[105] He had good reason to believe this to be true.

2

Waiting on a White Man's Chance

Walking along the road in Fayetteville, North Carolina, on the afternoon of July 31, 1875, the African American novelist Charles Chesnutt was "taken for 'white'" at least three times. Chesnutt identified as black, but he had fair skin and sandy hair. His racial composition—seven-eighths white—legally classified him as white in several southern states. At the pond, one man said that "'he'd be damned' if there was any nigger blood" in Chesnutt; another man saw Chesnutt buying trunks at Colonel Coleman's, a general store, and assumed that he was a white student on his way to school. An older man, startled by Chesnutt's appearance, yelled out to a friend, "Look here Tom, here's a black fellow as white as you air." Recording the day's events in his journal that evening, Chesnutt wrote, "At Coleman's I passed. I believe I'll leave here and pass anyhow, for I am as white as any of them."[1]

Figure 2.1. Charles Waddell Chesnutt, African American author, activist, and lawyer. His novels and short stories examined racial identity in the postemancipation South.

Courtesy of the Moorland-Spingarn Research Center, Howard University.

Chesnutt would change his mind. He would not leave North Carolina and pass as white, but he would spend his career writing about the illogic of the color line and the absurdity of racial categorizations.[2] Hemmed in by the racial codes of small town life in postemancipation North Carolina, Chesnutt gave serious thought to walking away from his dull hometown where he was known as a black fellow with an almost indiscernible fraction of "nigger blood." Facing a problem that he described as similar to that of Mahomet's Coffin, Chesnutt lamented his in-between, racially ambiguous status: "I am neither fish, flesh, nor fowl—neither 'nigger,' 'poor white,' 'buckrah.' Too 'stuck-up' for the colored folks, and of course, not recognized by the whites."[3]

Chesnutt was part of an increasingly visible, well-educated, and economically ascendant class of light-skinned black elites who hoped to widen the distance between the slave past and their rising social, economic, and political stations. Well poised to take advantage of new openings for advancement during the years immediately following emancipation, these blacks perceived themselves as vastly different from the black masses, particularly in terms of class, cultivation, and color. Their intermediate racial standing posed new problems in the aftermath of the Civil War—both for numerous mixed-race people and for the whites who struggled to locate them within fixed racial categories. At this radical historical juncture, these blacks had a choice: they could trade on their light skin and pass as white or they could continue to live as black. If they chose to remain black, they hoped to play a role in reconstructing a nation where blackness would no longer limit their claims for full personhood and equal citizenship. This brief period presented an auspicious time, a chance to be a part of a black rebirth, and to cast one's lot with one's people. No one knew just where this moment might go.

The national upheaval of the Civil War, followed by the favorable but fleeting moment of Reconstruction, marked an important turning point in the history of racial ideology. This period was America's first experiment in creating a "postracial" society. The destruction of slavery and Lincoln's announcement of "the birth of a new freedom" signaled a thoroughgoing transformation of the racial order. These heady times—when the prospect of being both black and a citizen existed—were nothing short of revolutionary, but this period was also fleeting and marred by violence. Extensive political enfranchisement of black men and vocal and vigorous political participation of black women combined to create a determined belief in the power of a collective franchise and to make the early days of Reconstruction in America profoundly different from other postemancipation societies.[4] In the moments of massive rupture, dislocation, and racial upheaval that followed the Civil War, racially ambiguous men and women found new avenues to renegotiate their lives and to embrace a black racial identity. The bright promises of Reconstruction affirm that the American racial order was neither fixed nor timeless, but rather fluid and unpredictable. For a brief moment, this period offered compelling reasons to choose not to pass as white.

In the antebellum era, racial indeterminacy was the precondition to pass as white, to escape slavery, and to live as a free man or woman. During Reconstruction, racial indeterminacy was a platform to make compelling claims for black humanity and equality. The lives of light-skinned blacks, including novelist Charles Chesnutt and Reconstruction-era political figures Blanche and Josephine Bruce, P. B. S. and Nina Pinchback, and Robert Harlan demonstrate that passing was not an automatic response to racial proscription; instead, it was a practice that corresponded to and depended upon particular historical contexts and circumstances. In the postemancipation moment, many racially ambiguous men and women decided against passing and instead waited in anticipation of the new possibilities for social, economic, and political freedom that the Reconstruction era promised to bring. A window of possibility opened during Reconstruction—a hopeful yet unstable moment when light-skinned black elites aimed to carve out space for themselves within a tripartite racial world—before the consolidation of legalized segregation under the Jim Crow regime.

Reconstructing the lives of racially ambiguous men and women who chose not to pass does not suggest that the practice of passing ended altogether during Reconstruction. In the chaos that attended the Civil War and followed in its wake, it is impossible to know how many white-looking freedmen and freedwomen walked away from the plantations and towns where they were known, assumed a white identity, and never looked back. The outline of the missing person—a relative who made the decision to pass as white and quickly disappeared from the historical record—is visible even during a period when it would seem that, for some, to be black was to be "somebody" whereas to be white was to be "nobody." That passing continued throughout the Reconstruction era is not surprising. Instead, it is the play in the system, the increased political and social flexibility that intersected with a new moment of opportunity for blacks, that the Reconstruction era reveals. Stepping along and around the color line, racially ambiguous men and women made powerful claims for a more robust definition of freedom that included equal treatment, equal rights, and the full recognition of their humanity.

In a world suddenly made anew, one question loomed large for African Americans of all complexions: "Who am I going to be?" A wide range of new strategies and possibilities came to light for both black elites and the black masses: Charles Chesnutt and others weighed living as black against taking advantage of their light skin and passing as white; rural blacks took part in the "first Great Migration" and began new lives amid the anonymity of burgeoning northern and southern towns and cities; and other blacks, questioning whether they would ever realize civil rights in a country rife with racial antagonism, made plans to emigrate to Liberia and pinned their hopes on new lives as Africans rather than as Americans. The cast of characters in this chapter carefully vetted these strategies, leaned away from the prospect of emigration, and sought political, economic, and personal success in America. Some, like Chesnutt, were self-made, and believed that in this moment of national reconstruction, their futures and their fortunes might not be dictated by racial restrictions. The dawn of freedom strengthened institutions and expanded networks within the black community. Concentrated matrices of associations supported members of the black elite and forged linkages through friendships, marriages, and political alliances. Situated within dense familial and institutional networks—including promising new opportunities within Republican Party politics—these blacks chose not to pass. Their lives tell stories not simply of ambitious and independent men and women on the make. Instead, these racially ambiguous men and women operated within the constraints imposed by their notions of kinship, community, leadership, and respectability.

The beginning of Reconstruction signaled a dramatic opening of opportunity for all blacks, not just elites. Freedmen and freedwomen greeted this profound transformation with optimism and expectancy, anticipating the unprecedented changes that would reshape their labor practices, their social relations, and their very personhood. As newly autonomous individuals, many blacks changed their names as a crucial first step toward remaking themselves. Names such as Deliverance Belin, Hope Mitchell, and Chance Great reflected the newness and the possibility of the moment.[5] As African Americans selected new names for themselves, they also rejected names that were not of their own choosing. Blacks recoiled at the provisional term "contraband" that was often used by Union army officials to denote the value of slaves who fled to Union army lines, without contesting their status as property. Frederick Douglass complained that contraband is "a name that will apply better to a pistol, than to a person."[6] As blacks secured their freedom and as emancipation became permanent, the term "contraband" no longer made sense as a legal designation. As the temporary term "contraband" gave way to the more permanent titles of "freedmen" and "freedwomen," blacks continued to wrestle with how to define and express the meaning of their newly acquired status.

Where to begin? "Everything among us indicates a change in our condition, and [we must] prepare to act in a different sphere from that in which we have heretofore acted," wrote a black man in California. Even before the signing of the Emancipation Proclamation, he could envision the opening of new possibilities and the coming of a new day: "Old things are passing away, and eventually old prejudices must follow. The revolution has begun, and time alone must decide where it is to end."[7] To many, it seemed that a sea change had taken place during the first few years that followed the end of the Civil War. In May 1867, a politician speaking at a convention captured the profound transformations of this moment, comparing the louder calls for black suffrage and the realization of a biracial democracy to the incremental development of a child: "As the growth of a child is scarcely perceptible to the family who see it day by day, although clearly apparent to a periodical visitor, so you may not so plainly perceive the progress of republicanism here . . . the idea of negro suffrage was abhorrent to the ruling classes; now they talk of electing colored gentlemen to office." Old masters had given up the hope of a compensated emancipation and now "read with composure a decision of our Supreme Court, rightly declaring that slavery never had any legal existence." That former slaveholders read about the Thirteenth Amendment "with composure" was an overstatement, but the politician captured the spirit of the day and concluded his speech on an upbeat note: "Galileo was right—the world moves."[8]

The optimism of this moment temporarily tabled otherwise animated conversations about emigration. After twelve hundred emigrants sailed to Liberia with the American Colonization Society between 1866 and 1867, a white colonizationist wrote, "You could not get one of them to think of going to Liberia now."[9] In this moment, freedmen and freedwomen turned away from Africa and imagined a future as Americans. In a letter to Senator Blanche Bruce, a constituent from Yazoo County, Mississippi, wrote: "I also hope you will use your influence against the Petition now before congress 'asking appropriations to assist colored persons to emigrate to Liberia.' We are not Africans now, but colored Americans, and are entitle[d] to American citizenship by every just consideration."[10] Whether he was personally opposed to the Liberian settlement plan or swayed by his constituents, Bruce rejected colonization and in an article published in the *Cincinnati Commercial* on February 19, 1878, he argued, "The Negro of America is not African, but American,—in his physical qualities and aptitudes, in his mental development and biases, in his religious beliefs and hopes, and in his political conception and convictions, he is an American. He is not a parasite, but a branch, drawing its life from the great American vine, taking on the type of American civilization and adapting himself to the genius of her institutions as readily and unreservedly as his Caucasian brother." The experience of a speaker at a black convention in 1876 further demonstrated the shift away from Liberia and a new faith in the promises of life in America. After receiving "positive signs of disapproval" by raising the issue of emigration, the speaker declared, "Damn Africa . . . if Smith wants to go let him; we'll stay in America."[11]

The end of slavery also raised new questions about property relations and how elements of the informal antebellum economy would be transformed after slavery. During slavery, blacks in some areas of the South, the Georgia low country in particular, owned property with the consent of whites. In the aftermath of slavery, blacks expected their property claims to be recognized.[12] Questions were raised about whether slaves could logically or legally own property or whether slaves' belongings were simply an extension of their masters' households. Other debates surrounded the issue of how land should be allocated and how time should be spent. Laboring under the task system with relatively easy access to land, low-country slaves worked to finish their tasks quickly to spend time planting personal crops. This informal economy led to conflicts over the boundaries between "the master's time" and "the slaves' time."[13] Emancipation continued older debates and raised new concerns about property ownership, land allocation, and time management. For newly freed men and women, it also signaled greater autonomy and independence from whites. Control over their daily routines and "get[ting] their own time" carried more weight for some blacks than settling the land that General Sherman was rumored to have set aside on the coast.[14] As one freedman, Peter Winn, explained, "I am not willing to be a slave again because now I can stop & rest & go about & walk some, then, when I was a slave I could not till I got through with my task. No sir, be a slave I am not willing to be that anymore."[15]

Black suffrage became a widely discussed and pressing topic, and soon it would take center stage in American political debates, forcing President Lincoln to address the issue in a letter to Governor Michael Hahn of Louisiana in March 1864. In a delicately written note, Lincoln gestured toward a limited extension of the franchise: "I barely suggest for your private consideration, whether some of the colored people not be let in—as for instance, the very intelligent, and especially those who have fought gallantly in our ranks. . . . But this is only a suggestion, not to the public, but to you alone."[16] Advocates of black male suffrage repeatedly pointed to blacks' military service and sacrifice to argue that the vote was their due. General Rufus Saxton, head of the Freedmen's Bureau, facilitated black political organizing in South Carolina and made this connection most explicit: "If the nation asks you to help in time of war, you certainly have a right to call for the help of the nation for your rights in time of peace. . . . I want the colored men in this department to petition the President of the United States and Congress for the right to exercise the elective franchise—the right to vote for those who are to rule over them."[17] Members of the black elite shared Lincoln's hesitation about offering the franchise to the black masses and worried that they were not yet ready for such responsibility. Most worrisome was that their lack of preparedness might jeopardize or delay the extension of rights to their betters. P. B. S. Pinchback, elected to the Senate from the state of Louisiana, anticipated a limited extension of the franchise and urged blacks to be ready for this moment: "I am of the opinion that most of the states will in their legislatures make Such laws as they think Best for their own interest, among those laws I think will be one conferring the right to vote upon the more intelligent of our People . . . I say to you let us conduct ourselves in a manner to obtain the respect of all men and merit this great privilege."[18] The right to vote had never been a universal guarantee; rather it was a privilege enjoyed by white men, property holders, and others who held high status. Suffrage was fundamental to full citizenship and equal treatment. Pinchback and other black elites knew that if they were to have a stake in the future of American democracy, they could not risk losing it.

With such profound transformations in the offing, many wondered if color would carry the same weight as it had in the past or if a form of equality, no longer based on color, was realizable. Robert G. Fitzgerald, a black teacher, wrote in his diary, "I heard a white man say, today is the black man's day; tomorrow will be the white man's. I thought, poor man, those days of distinction between colors is about over, in this (now) free country."[19] When Martin Delany tried to speak of color in South Carolina, he was abruptly interrupted with the retort, "We don't want to hear that; we are all one color now."[20] Some blacks may have predicted the blurring or erasure of the color line, but most remained acutely aware of the stark color and class differences that divided the black population. Historian Thomas Holt's work on Reconstruction in South Carolina has shown that intense infighting occurred between mulattoes and blacks who were divided by their goals and by their ideas about who should lead the race.[21] Wealthy and well-educated blacks saw a chasm of social distance between themselves and their darker and unenlightened brothers, and hoped to maintain it. To them, a "strange error" had occurred. They believed that they were closer in intellect and comportment to white men but despite these enormous differences, it was the former slaves to whom their fates were inextricably linked.[22]

But even in this season of hope, dark clouds were lurking. The lives of many black elites unfolded against the backdrop of a highly unstable and increasingly volatile social and political world. Questions remained unsettled about how customary forms of discrimination that mimicked the slave system and prevented African Americans from exercising their rights of citizenship freely would be eliminated after emancipation. Beginning in 1865, black codes struck directly at the economic and personal freedoms of the black bourgeoisie. These laws threatened the very survival of this class by mandating that all blacks carry special licenses in order to work in any profession outside of agriculture. A constituent in Aberdeen, Mississippi, wrote to Blanche Bruce to describe the visceral reaction that these laws prompted and predicted the potentially ruinous results of such restrictive policies: "The Colored people are more disturbed now in this section than I have ever seen them and if they are not better protected in their Constitutional rights: there will be an *'Exodus'* that will destroy the labor of this Country."[23]

Access to plentiful and high-paying patronage jobs gave some blacks compelling reasons to stay in the South, but beginning in 1875 with the Democrats' political resurgence, patronage positions became less secure. Many black employees wrote to Blanche Bruce in a panic, asking for his help in finding other forms of employment. "I have been compelled to sleep in the woods and cotton pens night after night in order to save my life, and even now they are loud and deep in their threats as ever," Albert D. Thompson wrote in December 1875, adding that "there are some persons in this county, who the democrats determine must leave, and I am one." Thompson, who "dare[d] not appear on the streets after dark without being fired upon," hoped to secure a position in a government department as a messenger, "or in fact anything to keep soul and body together."[24] Once a lucrative and steady source of employment, patronage jobs became potentially dangerous, if not life-threatening, liabilities for blacks. Sensing the changing circumstances of the Republican administration in Mississippi, one man humbly asked Bruce if he could "find a suitable place for me in [the] event the worst comes; one in which I can make a respectable living for myself and family. I don't want to leave this State, and didn't intend to if I can possibly help it but you know at this time, a republican engaging in any kind of business here is almost certain failure."[25] Some had been met by violent white mobs who ordered them to leave town, and many requested that Bruce work "as expeditiously as possible" to find new positions where they might "live away from this . . . Hell on Earth."[26]

In addition to the difficulty that blacks faced as they tried to hold on to government positions, the violent campaigns of the Ku Klux Klan, the White Camelias, and the White Leagues kept blacks away from the ballot box. Race riots engulfed the South and in cities such as Vicksburg and Colfax, blacks were massacred while waiting in vain for relief from the federal government.[27] Disturbing dispatches from Vicksburg circulated in an attempt to arouse the dormant sympathies of Northern readers: "There is a reign of terror and bloodshed at present in Mississippi that you up North, accustomed as you are to peace and good order and security of life, could hardly realize unless you were here to see for yourself the actual state of the case. . . . the bad men of the South went gunning for negroes as a Northern hunter went gunning for squirrels."[28] A critical and recurrent question—"Are we to have soldiers?"—was asked but left frighteningly unanswered in much of the correspondence between black constituents and their representatives.[29] In an 1875 article published in the *New Orleans Times,* a white lawyer described the precarious nature of the public offices held by Republicans and commented that no "radical could hold an office twenty-four hours in Louisiana but for Grant's bayonets."[30] Responding to the circumstances that blacks faced in Louisiana, Pinchback offered the gloomy assessment that the "condition of colored people is but little, if any, better than it was before the war." Buoyed by the argument that "the colored people of the county furnish an aggregate of political and commercial force that, in contact with and under the quickening influences of a Christian civilization . . . needed but the summer of liberty to spring into life and fruitfulness," Pinchback still believed that the federal government would live up to the Constitution and protect blacks' newly won rights. As Pinchback explained, "To let it alone, would be the most fatal blunder that the Nation could make. To let this question alone, would be to turn the lamb over to the Wolf." The stakes had never been higher: every political right and every legal entitlement that had been conferred to African Americans would be lost.[31]

The tragic denouement of this story is well known—the collapse of Reconstruction, the clobbering of the Republican Party, widespread violence and intimidation, and the consolidation of the Jim Crow regime—but it must be underscored that as late as the 1880s, when Reconstruction may have appeared old to contemporary eyes, there were still grounds for blacks living through this period to be sanguine. To be sure, there were solemn fears and frightful speculations, including one expressed by Blanche Bruce's brother, H. C. Bruce, in 1876, that "slavery is to be reestablished."[32] But when the Democrats came to power in 1875 and 1876 in every southern state except South Carolina, Florida, and Louisiana, it did not necessarily mean that the curtain had fallen, never to be raised again. Indeed, in April 1879, a constituent in West Point, Mississippi, wrote to Bruce and optimistically predicted Republican success in the next election: "Let me Say to you that if we can have a fair Show in 1880 this State will go Republican Beyond a doubt."[33] The election results of 1875 did not spell the end of Reconstruction, nor did they foreshadow an inexorable march toward Jim Crow. For those living at this time, other likelihoods still existed, as did signs that things might have been different.

"A Grave Social Question Has Arisen"

One of the most stunning changes to the American political landscape during Reconstruction was the election of black men to state and federal office throughout the South. In South Carolina alone, between the years of 1867 and 1876, more than half of the 487 men elected to public office were black.[34] Although histories of Reconstruction take note of the tenures of black elected officials, few accounts have paid attention to the ways that the entrance of black men into politics created opportunities for new forms of interracial encounters. The bugbear of "social equality" became even more frightening when mixed-race politicians and their wives could boast of similar if not even more impressive social and educational credentials than those of their white counterparts.

Coupled with the usual paranoia about black men in the public sphere getting too close to white women were new concerns about how the social landscape in Washington would be rearranged and just what place these wealthy, well-educated, and nearly white wives would occupy. Calls for black male suffrage and interracial political collaboration made the boundaries between public and private worlds even more porous. Historian Jane Dailey has explored the equation of black political power with sexual power as black men joined the interracial Readjuster Party in Virginia.[35] But the light-skinned wives of black politicians posed a different kind of problem that was less about sexual power and the potential to physically encroach on white women, and more about a worrisome blurring of racial and class boundaries.[36] With the arrival of these women in Washington, the social sphere grew dramatically larger, rendering the line between social and political worlds increasingly faint, if not altogether invisible.

Bruce was born a slave in 1841. He later studied at Oberlin, became a wealthy planter, and entered politics in Mississippi in 1868, just two years before Hiram Revels, also from Mississippi, became the first black man to enter Congress.[37] Bruce and Revels are best characterized as conservative accommodationists, though Revels consistently expressed more conciliatory, if not obsequious, positions. Revels supported lenient measures that would restore the right to vote to ex-Confederates, and he joined the Democratic Party after a violent and ultimately successful campaign to return to power in Mississippi in 1875. Most egregiously, Revels testified before the Boutwell Committee that he knew nothing of the ferocious savagery, fraud, and intimidation that attended the 1875 elections.[38] Revels's identification with southern Democrats, as one historian has argued, "reflected in the quality of leadership which

Figure 2.2. Blanche Kelso Bruce, Republican senator from Mississippi, 1875–1881. Bruce was the first African American senator to serve a full term. *Courtesy of the Moorland-Spingarn Research Center, Howard University.*

he offered his constituency: too little, and never too much."[39] Blanche Bruce, nicknamed the "silent Senator" because he never entered into debates on the Senate floor, was hardly outspoken on black civil rights.[40] In fact, an article published in the *Washington Bee* commented that Bruce was "a really whitened African . . . not so much that his features are more negro-like nor that his hair curls more tightly. It is rather in his mental attitude, which is reflected in his deferential manner."[41] A letter from one of Bruce's constituents in Vicksburg criticized him for "not strongly enough represent[ing] the grievances we have and now suffer."[42]

Few newspapers took note on March 4, 1875, when Blanche Bruce became the second black man to be seated in the U.S. Senate. Despite the threat that Bruce might have posed as a black man slated to serve a full term, it was Bruce's wife, Josephine, who nettled Washington society. It is likely that Hiram Revels's wife did not accompany her husband to Washington in 1870, given that there are no discussions of her arrival in Washington; the accounts of Revels's arrival describe him boarding with his friend George Downing, a wealthy black caterer. Reports of the Bruces' relocation are replete with descriptions of their stately home and its elaborate furnishings; there are no comparable accounts for the Revels. Perhaps Mrs. Revels, overlooked in articles about the wives of prominent black leaders, decided to stay at home with her five daughters during her husband's short one-year term. The absence of Mrs. Revels—when viewed in light of the panic caused by Mrs. Bruce—underscores the gendered dimension of the entrance of black politicians in Washington. When present, some wives, Josephine Bruce in particular, received as much, if not more, scrutiny as their husbands. By staying at home, Mrs. Revels did not raise the troubling questions about the racial contours of Washington's social world that Josephine Bruce would ignite four years later. Although Revels may have created other anxieties as the first black man to be seated in Congress, he was a less controversial figure. Fewer social codes were breached by the arrival of this modest, religious, and politically conservative man who chose to stay close to the segregated world of black elites during his brief sojourn in Washington.[43]

Despite the theatrics of the occasion of Bruce's seating in the Senate—the failure of James Alcorn, the senior senator from Mississippi, to follow custom and escort Bruce to the Vice President's desk where Bruce would be sworn in; the painful, awkward pause followed by the benevolent gesture of Roscoe Conkling, the senator from New York, to notice Alcorn's insult, rise quickly from his chair, and accompany Bruce down the aisle—reporters spent little time covering this story. Instead, the press turned its attention to Bruce's elegant, well-educated, and light-skinned wife, Josephine. One reporter described her as "quite beautiful" and noted that "it requires much more than usual attention to notice that she has any African blood in her veins." To the reporter's surprise, Josephine appeared to be "an ordinary brunette," but the telltale signs of black ancestry were still discernible. "Close scrutiny," the reporter explained, "will reveal her peculiar lips and hair."[44] As Josephine prepared to move to Washington, her husband wrote to her to describe the commotion she had already created: "A great deal of curiosity is manifested here, for what reason I know not, to know where you will stop. . . . It is very amusing. Washington is all ablaze to see you."[45] Despite Blanche Bruce's history-making political success, reporters fixated on a much more urgent question: What was Washington society going to do with this woman? Given her beauty, her sociability, and her status as the wife of a senator, Mrs. Bruce should have expected to be welcomed into Washington society. But it was not clear whether the white senators' wives would cross the color line and extend their hospitality or return Josephine Bruce's invitations.[46]

The article, "Ought We to Visit Her?," predicted some of the conflicts that Josephine's arrival might cause, explaining: "There is some social agitation here with regard to the manner to which Mrs. Bruce will be received by Washington. She is a lady of fine personal appearance, and is perhaps, better educated than most of the women who intend to snub her if she presumes to enter society."[47] As another reporter commented, "Ever since the colored Senator from Mississippi brought his bride to the capital, Washington society has directed a curious gaze upon Mrs. Bruce and wondered what part she would take in the social life here. There was no inconsiderable fear that a grave social question had arisen, which would not only create much unpleasantness but might bring out the 'color line' in an awkward relief. The social rank of a United States Senator is not to be disregarded, hence the position occupied by Mrs. Bruce was felt to be a delicate one that called for consummate tact."[48]

Northern Republicans rebuked the Democrats who snubbed the Bruces for being too provincial to recognize the couple's intelligence and sophistication. An editorial titled "Snobbery," published in a Wisconsin weekly in 1879, described at length the trouble that the Bruces created for Southerners. Remarkably, the author expected southern Democrats to cast off "the old race prejudice" and to accept Blanche and Josephine Bruce into their social world. The author's frustration did not stem from a misplaced innocence or naiveté, but instead evinced "a reasonable expectation" of "the new

Figure 2.3. Josephine Beall Willson Bruce, wife of Senator Blanche Bruce and daughter of Dr. Joseph Willson, a prominent dentist, and Elizabeth Harnett Willson, a singer and musician.
Courtesy of the Moorland-Spingarn Research Center, Howard University.

order of things" after emancipation, a steadfast belief that a new day in race relations had dawned in the South. The time had come for slaveholders to "ignore their prejudices of caste," and treat the wife of a U.S. senator with the respect that a woman who occupied such a station deserved, especially because she was "an educated, refined and highly accomplished lady." But to the author's outrage, the Democrats had "studiously ignored her existence," and given in to "the old race prejudice."[49] Other articles commented on the infrequent visits received by Mrs. Bruce from the wives of Democratic senators. According to one report, although some of the wives of the cabinet members and the justices of the Supreme Court had visited Mrs. Bruce, "no person of Democratic connections who comes from the south of Mason & Dixon's line" had called on Mrs. Bruce while she was at home.[50] One of the most egregious examples of such "snobbery" was that of the wife of Senator Thurman, who, along with her daughter, had called on Mrs. Bruce but later "[made] an earnest denial," so as to reverse the damage done to her husband's popularity and presidential aspirations and to "[set] himself right with his Southern masters." Disgusted, the author declared, "No more humiliating exhibition was ever made in Republican America."[51]

Other reports offered more cheerful pronouncements, indicating that acceptance of the Bruces reflected the changing times. An article from the *InterOcean* pointed to the fact that when the Bruces traveled from Cleveland to New York and stopped at the exclusive white hotel, the Hoffman House, they met with no protest from Democrats. But the article's statement that "a wonderful change has come over the Democratic press" might have been overly optimistic. The author's evidence of such a change in editorial direction among Democratic newspapers rested upon the explanation that a few years before, the Bruces' nuptials would have been "heralded as a 'Nigger Wedding,'" but these days "the marriage of the colored Senator from Mississippi is gracefully mentioned as a 'Wedding in High Life.'"[52]

Josephine Bruce—comfortably perched at the top of colored society yet only grudgingly accepted by white Washingtonians—exemplified the new problems that racially ambiguous people posed in a social world remade in the aftermath of the Civil War. Her appearance raised questions about whether older social customs could be maintained or whether behaviors would have to be reshaped to accommodate this unprecedented moment. Josephine Bruce's family enjoyed an affluent lifestyle in Philadelphia where they were ensconced in a largely independent world of black elites. Josephine's father, Joseph Willson, published a book in 1841, *Sketches of the Higher Classes of Colored Society in Philadelphia,* in which he called for the recognition of class divisions within the black community and worried about the public's inclination to "regard the people of color as one consolidated mass, all huddled together, without any particular or general distinctions, social or otherwise."[53] Willson, who began his career as a printer and who would later become a successful dentist, took an active role in the Philadelphia Young Men's Anti-Slavery Society, as well as in literary societies, debating groups, and social clubs hosted by Philadelphia's black elite.[54] Willson was part of a cohort that included Robert Purvis and James Forten (the wealthy sailmaker and also the father of Charlotte Forten). His definition of the "higher classes," however, was not limited to those with white ancestry. Ex-slaves including John Hart, a modest porter who became a vestryman at the historic St. Thomas's African Episcopal

Church and the secretary to five benevolent societies, and the darker-skinned Reverend William Douglass were both recognized by Willson as among the upper echelons of colored society.[55]

There is no evidence to suggest that Willson, born to a wealthy merchant of Scots Irish descent and a free woman of color, considered passing even though he was occasionally classified as white by census takers.[56] Unlike his brother John (who was also categorized as white by the census), who chose to live in a mostly white neighborhood of Spring Garden, Joseph and his wife moved from Spring Garden to Shippen Street, which was located in the predominantly black district of Moyamensing. This area of Philadelphia was just a short walk to the church and to many of the black community institutions to which the Willsons belonged. It was also near the less desirable and more impoverished sections of the South Street corridor, which had been the target of racial violence in the 1830s and 1840s.[57] Perhaps Joseph Willson decided to move his family to this neighborhood to signal his identification as a black man. In the 1840s, he married Elizabeth Harnett, a woman with a similar background who was the daughter of a free woman of color and a Scottish immigrant. Joseph and Elizabeth would later move to Cleveland in the early 1850s with the hopes of climbing even higher on the social ladder in a newer city with a more fluid social register as well as integrated schools, a strong abolitionist tradition, and growing black and liberal white populations. The family worshipped among mostly white congregants at St. Paul's Protestant Episcopal Church but continued to socialize with the colored aristocracy of Cleveland and joined the Social Circle in 1869. It is not surprising, then, that Josephine, the daughter of this old-line family with a keen sense of itself and its history, who was enmeshed in rich social networks, would have little reason to walk away from this intimate community and pass as white.

Despite the fanfare surrounding Josephine and Blanche Bruce's wedding on June 24, 1878, it was an uncharacteristically private event hosted by Josephine's parents at their home on Perry Street in Cleveland. When Blanche Bruce looked out from the altar at the wedding guests, he did not see a single relative of his own. He may not have seen one familiar face. The invitation list was carefully vetted to omit Blanche Bruce's family; reminders of the slave past were decidedly unwelcome on this happy occasion. Already intrigued by the couple (and especially by Josephine), reporters jockeyed to provide coverage of a wedding ceremony deliberately concealed by heavy draperies. Reporters who were able to catch a glimpse of the bride and groom described Bruce as "a splendid specimen of his race, standing nearly six feet in his stockings with a finely formed head and pleasing countenance," and added that Josephine's choice of a plum-colored silk gown trimmed with velvet accentuated "her very handsome features." Most newspaper accounts remained fixated on Josephine's appearance and took note of the couple's dissimilarity: "The contrast between them as regards to color was very marked, she being a pale brunette with light colored hair and would readily be taken for a white woman."[58]

The decision to omit Blanche Bruce's family from the guest list captures the uneasy relationship between the "better sort" of blacks and those from slave origins. A letter from Bruce's brother confirms that no invitations were extended to the Bruce family and that the family would learn of the marriage only through newspaper accounts. Six months after the wedding, on December 16, 1878, Calvin Bruce wrote, "Dear Bro I write to say we are all well I see in quite a number of Newspapers that you have Marred is it so or not if so my wife says you must send her your [wife's] photograph."[59] Unlike Josephine, who was deeply connected to her family and to black society, Blanche Bruce had lost touch with his family long before his wedding in 1878. With the help of his white father, Bruce left the Virginia plantation where he was born in 1841, settled in Missouri, and became a printer's apprentice. After attending Oberlin and working as a steamboat porter on the Mississippi River, Bruce became a wealthy planter and held a number of public offices including registrar of voting, tax assessor, and sheriff. By striking out on his own, away from his darker-skinned family members, and by choosing to marry a racially ambiguous and well-connected woman, Bruce created new opportunities for personal and political advancement.

Although Josephine Bruce remained close to her well-known family and ascended to even greater heights in the world of the black elite, her brother chose a very different path. In 1872, Leonidas Willson passed the Ohio state bar; later, he went into partnership with a white lawyer and married a white woman. When his first marriage ended in divorce, Leonidas remarried a nearly white schoolteacher named Anna Foote. It is likely that Josephine's light-skinned brother passed as white. If Leonidas had been known as a black man, it would have been highly unusual for him to partner with a white man and to enjoy such a high level of professional success. It is also striking that Leonidas fell out of correspondence with his family after the dissolution of his second marriage, to a light-skinned black woman.[60] Leonidas offers only the shadowy outlines of a missing person: once he left his family behind, married a white woman and, later, a light-skinned woman who could easily pass, and pursued a career in the almost exclusively white legal field, it becomes increasingly difficult to locate him or to trace the remainder of his life.

If Leonidas chose to pass as white in the 1870s, his decision provides a useful counterpoint to the choices of many light-skinned blacks in the same historical moment. His story reveals the forked road that many racially ambiguous men and women faced. Similar to the histories of antebellum families, Leonidas's story also demonstrates that within one family, two entirely different trajectories were possible. In contrast to Josephine Bruce, Blanche Bruce and Leonidas Willson both left their families behind, prefiguring two strategies for advancement that would become more routine just a few decades later. Both men rehearsed a painful, yet ultimately effective, plan of action: for Bruce, it was breaking away from his family to enter a new world of possibility that opened during Reconstruction; for Leonidas, it was leaving behind the dense familial and institutional networks that sustained his sister and buttressed the elite black communities in Philadelphia and Cleveland to take advantage of a different kind of opportunity—and one that would become even more fraught with the coming of Jim Crow.

In Search of a White Man's Chance

The Bruces' story, and especially Josephine's decision not to pass as white, recalls a similar notion held by P. B. S. Pinchback, a racially ambiguous politician, who won a contested election in 1873 and served as the governor of Louisiana for only thirty-five days. Pinchback, the son of a wealthy white planter and a mixed-race slave, was born free in 1837 because his father, enamored with his mother, manumitted her two years before Pinchback's birth. Upon his father's death, Pinchback and his nine siblings were hurried to Cincinnati out of a concern that they might be reenslaved by their father's white heirs, who already had swindled them out of their rightful inheritance. At the age of twelve, Pinchback struck out on his own and worked as a cabin boy before becoming a steward on a steamboat, the highest position that a black man could attain. He ran the Confederate blockade during the Civil War and later settled in New Orleans, where he joined the First Louisiana Volunteer infantry. When Benjamin Butler, a Union general whose administration occupied New Orleans, issued order No. 62, which called upon free men of color in Louisiana to take up arms in defense of the Union, Pinchback opened an office to recruit black soldiers.

Given Pinchback's stormy personality, it is no surprise that he had several conflicts while in the army, attributable to the unjust treatment that his men received at the hands of white officials and to his own frustration when he was denied a captain's commission. Still, Pinchback could have enjoyed a comfortable life and a profitable career; instead, he chose to get involved in politics. In 1867, he ventured into the political world and organized the Fourth Ward Republican Club, and in 1870, he published the *New Orleans Louisianian.* Pinchback served as the head of the police force in New Orleans before he was nominated in 1872 to be governor of Louisiana. The impeachment of Governor Warmouth carried him into office until January 1873, when he was elected to the Senate for a six-year term. The election was bitterly contested; it would take Pinchback two years to bring his case before the Senate, and he met with resistance that was both personal and political. As a reporter for the *New York Commercial Advertiser* explained, "McCreery, Senator from Kentucky, declares, privately, in that pastoral phraseology proverbially peculiar to blue grass Democrats, that he 'will give that nigger some sleepless nights before he gets his seat.'"[61]

Like Joseph Willson and many other black elites, Pinchback felt a deep sense of ambivalence toward the black masses. On one hand, he perceived the vast social and cultural distance that separated their lot from his, but on the other hand, he realized that he needed the support of black constituents to win his seat. In a letter to Blanche Bruce, Pinchback described his discomfort when around rural folk, far away from his cosmopolitan home of New Orleans: "I am in the country; and by all the Gods I must confess it is all I can bear to remain here. The Fleas, Mosquitos, Nigs, Carpetbaggers and scalawags are determined to 'make it warm' for me; but by the help of the Lord I am managing to hold my own."[62]

Even with the support of black voters, Pinchback would spend most of his political career struggling to be seated in the Senate; ultimately, he would hold this position for only thirty-five days. In the 1887 chronicle of black leaders, *Men of Mark,* William Simmons argued that a conspiracy kept Pinchback out of office. Pinchback's tireless efforts on behalf of black civil rights have been "especially noted," Simmons wrote, because even though Pinchback was "so fair that he could readily pass for a white man, he is known to stand up for his race."[63]

Yet it was not only Pinchback's dogged support for black suffrage and black civil rights that breached southern social customs. His perceived arrogance and his overambitious wife were also mentioned as vexing Republicans and Democrats alike. Although one reporter commented that Nina Pinchback had been received favorably—"being both beautiful and accomplished, she was not only treated with civility but was made quite a lioness"—her social motivations still raised eyebrows within Washington society. A reporter for the *Philadelphia Times* predicted the Pinchbacks to be social climbers and wrote that Pinchback is "a smart and ambitious mulatto, with a wife of the same origin who came with him to Washington naturally enough bent upon social distinction." The problem was a social one. For once Pinchback was accepted into the Senate, Mrs. Pinchback, like Josephine Bruce, would have to be accepted into Washington society. The social question rankled both Republicans and Democrats, the author explained, as it was "an open secret that certain Republican statesmen voted against [Pinchback's] admission as a matter of race prejudice when the Democrats voted against it as a matter of political principle." Indeed, the author noted that if Pinchback had been a white man, "or even a negro with an unpretentious wife," he likely would have won his seat.[64]

Reported to "glide around the [Senate] Chamber like a bronze Mephistopheles, smiling sardonically and buzzing his supporters," Pinchback irritated those who bristled at his swagger but admired his good looks. "His features are regular, just perceptibly African, his eyes intensely black and brilliant," one reporter wrote, adding, "His most repellent point is a sardonic smile which, hovering continuously over his lips, gives him an evil look, undeniably handsome as the man is." In a rare showing of sympathy, however, the reporter speculated on what might be the cause of Pinchback's "evil look": "It seems as though the scorn which must rage within him, at sight of the dirty ignorant men from the South who affect to look down upon him on account of his color, finds play imperceptibly about his lips."[65] Indeed, such a rendering of Pinchback was unusual; most accounts echoed an article that maligned Pinchback for an arrogance that was described as if it were an inherent racial trait: "The over-stimulated vanity of a vain race developed abnormally in Pinch, doubtless prompts him to attribute his notoriety to merit and strength in himself." It

Figure 2.4. Pinckney Benton Stewart Pinchback, the first person of African American descent to become governor of a U.S. state. He would only serve 35 days.

Courtesy of the Moorland-Spingarn Research Center, Howard University.

was this case of extreme vanity that led Pinchback to believe himself. To be a power" who could sway the next senatorial race in his favor.[66]

Pinchback was well aware of the limits that he faced as a black man trying to wrest control of his seat in the Senate. Charges of "impertinence" and an "over-stimulated vanity" would hardly help his case. In a letter to the editor of the *New York Herald,* Pinchback pleaded for "a white man's chance" after he had been personally attacked on the Senate floor. "A white man's chance," according to Pinchback, was a courtesy extended to blacks by white Southerners who "exhibited a manly fairness in their contests." In the event of a fight between a white man and "his legally disabled and embarrassed colored opponent," the white man would "invite the contest by offering to relieve the colored man of his disabilities."[67] Now that blacks were free, Pinchback hoped to claim as a right what had previously been considered a favor. Without a white man's chance, Pinchback worried that the personal prejudices of the other senators would prevent him from being seated: "It is asserted that one of the reasons is that several Senators . . . think me a very bad man, if this be true I fear my case is hopeless. . . . I am bad because I have dared on several important occasions to have an independent opinion, I am bad because I have dared at all times to advocate and insist on exact and equal justice to all mankind. I am bad because having colored blood in my veins I have dared to aspire to the United States Senate." Pinchback refused to truckle to white politicians. He argued back with candor: "If I cannot enter the Senate except with bated breath and on bended knees I prefer not to enter it at all."[68]

Without the courtesy of a "white man's chance," Pinchback would struggle to find an audience willing to listen to his appeals.

After years of tirelessly arguing his case, Pinchback became particularly discouraged by the double standard that prevented whites from taking the plight of blacks seriously: "Were I a white man, speaking for the rights of white men, I should have no difficulty, every race of people in this country except the colored people are accorded the same rights and privileges, there are no discrimination made in regard to entertaining them in the public places, or on steamboats, cars, or other conveyances when they pay the same fare and conduct themselves properly."[69] Attacked as "personally a corrupt and dishonorable man," Pinchback fired back, "I shall do this with the plainness of speech demanded and justified by the rights involved, and yet with the moderation inspired by the full appreciation on my part that such is the public sentiment of the country that language emanating from a white man which would be considered appropriate and manly, when uttered by me one of the proscribed race—would be deemed impertinent and turbulent."[70] Anxious about the reception that one of his speeches would receive at the Capitol, Pinchback confided in Blanche Bruce that he "was fearful that it was a little too bold for a colored man." Had it been "the utterance of a white man," it would have been doubtlessly well received, if not resoundingly applauded, but from a black man, it would be "generally considered impudent and impertinent."[71]

Read by white politicians as too outspoken and presumptuous, even "turbulent," Pinchback, similar to Blanche and Josephine Bruce, raised uncomfortable and unanswerable questions about how the social environment might be reshaped by black political success. Pinchback worried that the senators who opposed his seating were too blinded by their own prejudices to recognize the legitimacy of his claims: "It is possible there may be Senators sufficiently narrow-minded to be governed by their *personal* prejudices on this question, supposing that I might desire to take advantage of my official position to force myself unasked upon their social life. Such a supposition would not only proceed upon an unjust estimate of the purposes of my race, but would be in opposition to my own personal respect and manliness which would prompt me as sacredly to respect the social sanctity of others, as it would to protect the integrity of my own."[72] Galled by charges that blacks desired more intimate social contact with whites and overstepped the boundaries that maintained social inequality, Pinchback countered that blacks and whites "meet, mingle and separate daily," in multiple ways and in numerous arenas, but that these interactions, while they created "a community of interests and of wants," and made both blacks and whites "the bearer in some sort of his brothers' burdens," in no way compromised the "sanctities of the family circle," or created a sense of intimacy or social equality. African Americans were not seeking social equality, Pinchback argued; indeed, "no such claim is ever felt or preferred." Pinchback's arguments were for political and economic equality; he did not wish to use any legislation "to force unasked their companionship upon the white race." Such demands for "so much dreaded" social equality were neither asked for nor desired. Instead, Pinchback argued that African Americans desired to protect and preserve their own privacy, to have the time to develop and grow into a responsible citizenry, not to invade the social sphere of white men and women.[73]

Pinchback wanted a white man's chance, but he did not want to be a white man. He wanted blacks, and particularly "the better sort," "to be acknowledged for what [they] had achieved instead of what [they were] in a society where to be of discernible African ancestry was to be forever excluded from the inner circles of power and prestige." He wanted to be afforded respect and common courtesy. He hoped to be relieved of his "disabilities" and treated with a "manly fairness." It was fair for white politicians to dislike him because he was arrogant, but it was not fair for white politicians to believe that he was arrogant because he was black. He wanted to remain separate—to have the chance to "protect our own privacy" and to acknowledge that "our own social wants, in our own circle need development and perfecting"—but not to be excluded or insulted. He and many other black elites wanted to possess all the rights and privileges that white men possessed, but they did not want to be white men. Though eventually he would be proved wrong, Pinchback believed for a moment, during this unprecedented historical juncture, that winning a "white man's chance" just might be possible.

The Coming of *Plessy*

As the lone dissenter in the landmark *Plessy v. Ferguson* (1896) case, Supreme Court Justice John Marshall Harlan argued for the same white man's chance that Pinchback desired. Harlan's half-brother Robert had claimed a white man's chance for most of his life. Robert Harlan lived a highly unusual life for a slave in Kentucky. Born in 1816 to a white father and a mother who was described as three-fourths white, Robert Harlan was raised in James Harlan's household. Some scholars have argued that the special treatment afforded to Robert Harlan was because he was James Harlan's son, making him the half-brother of John Marshall Harlan.[74] James Harlan attempted to send Robert to school with his other sons, but when it was discovered that Robert was black, he was sent home. At the time, Kentucky schools would neither admit black students nor make any arrangements for their education. One can only muse as to whether James Harlan believed that Robert could pass as white and be admitted to the school or if he assumed that by sending Robert along with his other sons, his own reputation and high social standing in the community would ease the path to Robert's admittance. The older Harlan sons provided Robert with an education, and later, Robert was granted uncommon opportunities to travel, to operate two businesses, and perhaps most surprisingly, to present himself as a free man of color with James Harlan's consent through the 1840s.[75] It was also anomalous for a slave to use the surname of his master; that Robert Harlan did so further suggests that James and Robert shared a close relationship that may have been publicly acknowledged (or at least rumored).[76] Recognizing Robert's exceptionality, James Harlan emancipated him on September 18, 1848. According to the memoirs of his daughter-in-law, Harlan offered "gifted" slaves the opportunity to purchase their own freedom by providing them with a financial sum equal to being hired out for half a year.[77] After Robert became a free man, he remained in contact with James and John Marshall Harlan. Some scholars have written that the decision in *Parker v. Commonwealth* in 1847—that it was illegal for slaveholders to allow slaves to hire themselves out—may have played a role in Harlan's decision to formalize Robert's emancipation. James Harlan's paternalism provided a platform for Robert to move to California at a moment when racial conditions were worsening in the South. Robert made a $45,000 fortune during the gold rush and returned in 1850 to Cincinnati where he bought two grand homes in a high-end neighborhood and opened real estate and photography businesses.[78]

How Harlan presented himself during the gold rush is open to conjecture. He may have passed as white as he amassed his riches, or perhaps his racial identity became less relevant in California in the late 1840s, amid the confluence of people of many different and unknown backgrounds who were all eager to get rich quick. Photographs of Harlan show that his white skin, straight hair, and ruddy complexion made his racial identity discernible only to those who already knew of his background. Perhaps upon Harlan's arrival in California, he said nothing about his racial identity and, instead, let the people around him draw their own conclusions.

After living in England for ten years, Robert Harlan decided to bring his family back to Cincinnati in 1868.[79] There were many reasons for his departure from Cincinnati in 1858. One of the most infamous rulings in the nineteenth century, the 1857 *Dred Scott* case, put the bleak prospects for both enslaved and free blacks in plain view. The Supreme Court's decision—that blacks were not citizens and could not claim to be free when they traveled to and settled in free states—and Chief Justice Roger Taney's acerbic pronouncement that blacks "had for more than a century before been regarded as beings of an inferior race, and altogether unfit to associate with the white race, either in social or political relations, and so far inferior that they had no rights which the white man was bound to respect" not only foreshadowed increasingly strict limitations on blacks' geographic mobility but also seemed to foreclose the possibility that African Americans could ever become citizens of the United States. Worst of all for people like Robert Harlan, the *Dred Scott* decision concentrated all blacks together, regardless of the distinctions of class and color. As the national outlook grew increasingly gloomy for blacks, changes at the local level foreshadowed an even more dispiriting future. Had Harlan stayed in Cincinnati, he would have been disfranchised in 1857 when the Ohio state legislature, controlled by a Democratic majority, repealed three statutes favorable to blacks and enacted a law that denied the right to vote to those with "a visible admixture of Negro blood." The well-educated, urbane, and nearly white Harlan must have smarted at the provisions of this law.

During the 1870s, Harlan plunged into Republican politics in Ohio. In 1871, he garnered widespread support as a candidate for the state legislature, and during that summer, he met President Grant and became one of his key campaigners. Elected in 1872 to the Republican State Central Committee, Harlan was only the second black man to serve in this position. In 1872, he attended the national Republican convention in Philadelphia as an alternate delegate-at-large, and in the presidential election of the same year, Harlan canvassed tirelessly in support of Grant. He received the first federal patronage job given to a black man in Ohio and served as special inspector of the U.S. Post Office in Cincinnati until he was removed from office in January or February 1875. Robert Harlan acquired a great deal of power and prestige through his positions within the Republican Party. In fact, when John Marshall Harlan's appointment to the Supreme Court was under consideration, Robert Harlan made it seem as though he might be able to "put in a good word" for him.[80] The political world had been indisputably turned upside down—the very image of the formerly enslaved brother having the ear of the president and advancing the career of the more favorably situated sibling revealed the dramatic racial transformations of this period.

Harlan was one-eighth black, but there is no evidence that he made any efforts to pass, although he likely was mistaken as white.

Given the political ascendancy of some blacks in the Republican Party, passing as white was not a particularly expedient strategy for advancement at this historical moment. Indeed, Robert Harlan's political success and usefulness lay in his ability to be a representative and an agent for his race. In 1872, at the Republican National Convention, Harlan announced his racial identity to reporters to avoid any confusion. Described as a "tall man, almost white, with a heavy moustache," Harlan came to the convention with his pockets filled with printed speeches and bundles of pamphlets in support of John Sherman, a Republican candidate for Senate from Ohio. During an interview, Harlan told reporters that he attended the convention to promote the candidacy of Sherman, but he was intent that the reporter "not make a mistake about his identity: 'I look as if I am on the other side, but I am entirely on the dark side.'" The reporter clarified Harlan's statement by putting it even more bluntly: "Mr. Harlan meant that he is a colored man. He is originally from Kentucky, and has twice been returned to the Ohio Legislature from Hamilton county, and for years has been visiting New Orleans with race horses. He claims to be a blood relation of Justice Harlan, of the United States Supreme Court."[81] Harlan's correspondence openly discussed his African American identity. He presented himself to white politicians as a spokesperson for black interests and white politicians commonly noted Harlan's racial status in their discussions of him. In a letter dated December 6, 1881, in support of Harlan's efforts to become the special U.S. customs inspector at Cincinnati, President Grant wrote: "His long service as a Republican, his capacity for usefulness and the fact that he is a representative man of his race give him strong claims which I hope you can find it practical to recognize—his many friends of whom I am one, would be gratified if this can be done."[82]

Other letters in Harlan's recommendation file directly address his racial identity and underscored the significance of a black man holding a high position in public office.

It is plausible that John Marshall Harlan's relationship with Robert Harlan shaped the Supreme Court Justice's enlightened views on race and particularly his dissent in the landmark 1896 *Plessy v. Ferguson* case.[83] John Marshall Harlan's path to the Republican Party had taken a long and winding course: he had been affiliated with the Whigs, the Know-Nothings, and the Constitutional Union Party, which passionately opposed secession. He became a Republican around 1871, just a few years before President Rutherford Hayes appointed him to the Supreme Court. A number of factors may have influenced Harlan's conversion. He relocated from Frankfort, Kentucky, an anti-black and pro-Democratic bastion, to Louisville, a Republican stronghold. He believed that the "general tendencies and purposes of the Democratic Party were mischievous," and he aligned with the Republicans who he believed would be more successful in securing the results of the Union's victory in the Civil War. He recoiled at the Democratic-sponsored campaigns of terror and violence that swept through Kentucky between 1868 and 1871.[84] In defense of his political about-face, Harlan wrote that it was better to be "right rather than consistent."[85] He delivered an extemporaneous dissent against the Court's majority opinion that the Civil Rights Act of 1875, which prohibited discrimination against blacks in inns, in theaters, and on public carriers, was unconstitutional. Countering Democratic challenges that the act gave blacks greater privileges and legal rights than whites, Harlan argued, "the clear and manifest purpose of the Act, as seen upon its face, was to secure equal, not superior, privileges to the colored race."[86] Yet, Harlan's mixed record on civil rights should not be overlooked. He was comfortable with the extension and protection of certain civil rights to blacks, but he did not speak out against discrimination in matters of social rights. In 1882, in *Pace v. Alabama,* Harlan voted with a unanimous Court to approve a law that punished an interracial couple that had committed adultery more severely than a same-race couple who committed the same crime, and in an 1889 decision, Harlan ruled in favor of an all-white school board sued by black parents for closing the black high school.[87] Earlier in 1871, he had argued that it was "right and proper" to keep "whites and blacks separate" in public schools.[88]

By offering a lonely dissent to *Plessy,* Harlan argued for the equality of all citizens before the law and wrote, "Our Constitution is color-blind and neither knows nor tolerates classes among citizens." To Harlan's mind, the Reconstruction amendments were crafted to eradicate the principle sanctioned by *Dred Scott* that blacks possessed no rights as citizens. Instead, as Albion Tourgée, a carpetbagger, a novelist, and one of Plessy's attorneys, explained, the Court had "virtually nullified the fourteenth amendment . . . and emasculated the thirteenth."[89] Lambasting the majority opinion that legal distinctions based on race did not produce feelings of inequality, Harlan wrote, "The arbitrary separation of citizens on the basis of race . . . is a badge of servitude wholly inconsistent with the civil freedom and the equality before the law established by the Constitution."[90] Harlan rejected the view that a distinction required by law did not create a legal discrimination. "Everyone knows," he explained, "that the statute in question had its origin in the purpose, not so much to exclude white persons from railroad cars occupied by blacks, as to exclude colored people from coaches occupied by or assigned to white persons."[91] Mandating equality of accommodations was but a "thin disguise," and the pernicious result of this ruling, Harlan worried, would be to "permit the seeds of race hate to be planted under the sanction of law."[92]

It is likely that John Marshall Harlan observed the rhetorical and phenotypical (both men were seven-eighths white) similarities between Homer Plessy and Robert Harlan. Perhaps in Homer Plessy, John Marshall Harlan saw something that others might not have seen. He may have seen someone who he believed deserved certain civil rights, and he may have believed that the extension of a limited set of privileges need not raise the bugbear of social equality. The *Plessy* decision effaced the possibility of a white man's chance and sounded the death knell of Reconstruction. When Homer Plessy lost, so did a much larger class of black elites. The final blow of *Plessy,* its "untroubled endorsement of racial separation," signaled the dawn of a much bleaker day. The beginning of Jim Crow brought the larger narrative of race relations from the apogee of optimism to its tragic finale.[93]

Neither Fish nor Fowl

The journal entries of Charles Chesnutt, recorded between the years of 1874 and 1882, move away from the cosmopolitan world of black elites in Washington, D.C., and cast light on the stifled character of black life in postemancipation North Carolina. Chesnutt was a self-made man, but to be black and self-made in late nineteenth-century American society was not to live out the conventional Horatio Alger narrative, but rather to encounter limitations and restrictions at every turn.[94] Chesnutt yearned for self-advancement, but his efforts would not bear fruit: the small town of Fayetteville lacked the cosmopolitan musical culture that he longed for, he was unable to take German classes because the instructor had been warned by the mayor that he would lose all of his students if he chose to work with Chesnutt, and he experienced the humiliation of being asked to withdraw from a local political race by "supporters" who were discomfited by the prospect of a black man holding public office. Scoffing at talk that Chesnutt is "a perfect gentleman in every respect" and "every bit as good as a white man," a poor white clerk made plain the social, political, and economic ceilings that Chesnutt could not break through: Chesnutt is "a nigger," and despite all of his efforts, self-discipline, and nearly white appearance, "nothing in the world can make him anything else but a nigger."[95]

Chesnutt decided against passing as white, even when he had the opportunity on the road to Coleman's general store. He could have chosen to play the role of a student returning from school, as one traveler presumed him to be. The road itself represents a paradigmatic site of passing. As a space unattached to any particular community where nameless strangers meet, the road provides a necessary condition for passing—it creates the physical distance from a place where one's identity is known and the means of entering a new place where one's identity can be re-created. Once dislocated from Fayetteville and removed from the racial and familial knowledge of the town's residents, Chesnutt's appearance became hazy and indeterminate, allowing the other travelers to formulate an alternate and plausible story—that Chesnutt, carrying trunks, was no longer a "black fellow," but instead a white student heading home from school.

A vast social and cultural distance separated Chesnutt from rural black folk in North Carolina and further blurred his racial identity. While teaching in remote areas of Charlotte in the 1870s, Chesnutt found little companionship among his students or their families. Chesnutt saw himself as a profoundly different type of person than his country hosts: his speech was articulate and refined, he longed for intellectual engagement and read Byron and Cowper while others performed backbreaking and tedious farm work, and he adhered to strict standards for bodily decorum and bathing. Chesnutt copied the pages of *A Handbook for Home Improvement* by hand in a fastidious effort to master the proper customs of bodily care. But when Chesnutt violated Christian principles by cleaning his shoes on Sunday, an old country woman questioned his manners. Chesnutt "couldn't fault the country people," the woman remarked quizzically, because Chesnutt was "from town" yet still did not know better than to clean his shoes on Sunday. Chesnutt's excuses for this violation fell on deaf ears; he wrote that the old woman "did not exonerate me . . . but she hoped the Lord would forgive me."[96]

Chesnutt also saw the value of education through a starkly different lens. When the "deplorably ignorant" parents of Chesnutt's students complained about the high cost of education, Chesnutt felt little sympathy for them. The parents grumbled, "You want us to pay you thirty or forty dollars a month for sitting in the shade, and that is as much as we can make in 2 or 3 months. . . . We all of [us] work on other people's, white people's, land, and sometimes get cheated out of all we make."[97] Chesnutt asked the parents to consider that by sending their children to school, they will "qualify them to look out for themselves, to own property, to figure and think about what they are doing, so that they may do better." Frustrated with what he perceived as the parents' simple and shortsighted response, Chesnutt wrote in his journal, "'We can't do it,' was all I could get out of them."[98] Exasperated by their devout yet misguided religious practices, their credulous beliefs, and their disregard for education, Chesnutt felt the cultural distance between him and the country folk growing wider and wider. Writing in his journal, Chesnutt bemoaned, "Well! Uneducated people are the most bigoted, superstitious, hardest-headed people in the world! These folks downstairs believe in ghosts, luck, horse shoes, cloud-signs, witches, and all other kinds of nonsense, and all the argument in the world couldn't get it out of them. These people don't know words enough for a fellow to carry on a conversation with them." Universal education, Chesnutt concluded, was "much-to-be-wished-for," but regrettably, a "little-to-be-hoped-for blessing."[99]

Chesnutt lived and worked in closer proximity to poor blacks than the Bruces or the Pinchbacks, but he shared similar feelings of ambivalence—and sometimes outright disgust—toward the folk. An earlier sense of sympathy, charity, and identification gave way as Chesnutt began to feel acutely that these were not his people. Chesnutt found himself in a bind: he was eager to leave the tedium and cultural isolation of life in small town North Carolina as well as the "home folks" who failed to recognize his talents, yet he felt an obligation to continue the "good work" of teaching. Growing tired of the South, Chesnutt wrote in his journal that he "pine[d] for civilization and companionship," but he hesitated to leave because he knew that his work was necessary to improve the conditions in the town. Still, he wondered if he could better serve the race in another occupation, and he feared exposing his children to the "social and intellectual proscription to which [he had] been a victim."[100]

But when Chesnutt decided to move to Washington, D.C., feeling "buoyed up with the high hopes of success and bright visions of the privileges and rights enjoyed by colored men in the blessed land to which [his] steps were turned," he was sorely disappointed with what he discovered upon his arrival. To Chesnutt's surprise, the class structure in Washington was far less flexible than he imagined, and he regretted that he was unprepared to keep up with the city's fashionable set. Chesnutt hoped that moving to the metropolis would both benefit him and open new opportunities for his children. Relying on the simple virtue of "work, work, work," Chesnutt was convinced that he could "live down this prejudice" and "see if it's possible for talent, wealth, genius to acquire social standing and distinction."[101] But, to Chesnutt's disappointment, the society was not pliant; one had to be born into Washington society as it was largely closed to newcomers. He wanted to escape the provincialism of Fayetteville, yet he lacked the bona fides to enter into the elitist world of Washington. The bright promises of the city lay beyond Chesnutt's grasp, and he struggled to make sense of why the city was not the right place for him: "The unfavorable ideas which I conceived were more against city life in general, than against life in Washington alone. There is too much noise, too little fresh air. The water from the hydrants is good, but I prefer to draw mine from a well."

But there was something else that drove Chesnutt out of Washington; it is not simply that he failed to keep up with the fast pace of the city or that he preferred the quaintness and the simplicity of country life. As he left Washington, Chesnutt lamented, "There are so many people, and so many men of wealth and distinction that a man must be very rich or very distinguished to attract any notice. Colored people have a great many 'privileges' which they do not possess further South, but it requires money to enjoy them to any considerable extent. The colored people of Wash. are very extravagant and spend all their earnings, great and small, in a vain attempt to keep up 'style' and a high-toned society."[102] In Washington, Chesnutt recognized that he would lose the stature that he enjoyed in Fayetteville because his academic credentials would not carry the same weight in a city where wealth, more so than education, determined one's status.

But perhaps Chesnutt's most unexpected realization was that he longed for the closeness and the kinship that he felt with the country folk in Fayetteville. Despite the occasionally tense and often conflicted nature of these relationships, the rural folk felt more like Chesnutt's people than the "many men of wealth and distinction" that he met in Washington.

In 1887, Chesnutt moved his family from Fayetteville to Cleveland, where he found a more mobile class structure and more lucrative employment opportunities as a stenographer and later as a lawyer. He took part in Cleveland's vibrant community life, socializing with both whites and blacks and becoming a member of the prestigious Rowfant Club. Years later in 1933, Chesnutt was asked by a white member of the Rowfant Club, "Why don't you 'pass'? You could, and you'd have so much better time." Chesnutt responded, "Ah, but I married a woman darker than myself, and I will never go where she is not welcome, too."[103] The member commented that he did not believe that Chesnutt "ever had any desire to deny his Race. I have heard him accused of trying to do so by people who did not know him—who I thought were maybe jealous of him—but he never said anything leaned that way to any of our mutual friends."[104] Married to a recognizably black woman, raising children in a relatively open and integrated social world, enjoying a notable and prolific writing career, and taking part in the cultural offerings of the city, Chesnutt finally seemed at home in Cleveland.

New People

It is useful to return to literature and to Chesnutt, who relied on literature to make sense of the dilemmas created by indeterminate racial identities. He explored these themes in *The House Behind the*

Cedars, published in 1900. Unlike Chesnutt, John Warwick, the novel's light-skinned protagonist, leaves his small North Carolina town, passes as white, and settles in a city in South Carolina, where he becomes a successful lawyer. He convinces his sister, Rena, to pass as well and plans for her to marry George Tyron, a wealthy white man. Before John introduces Rena to George, he makes the following confession: "I think you ought to know, George, that my sister and I are not of an old family, or a rich family, or a distinguished family; that she can bring you nothing but herself; that we have no connections of which you could boast, and no relatives to whom we should be glad to introduce you. You must take us for ourselves alone—we are new people."[105]

At first, the term "new people" seems a misnomer. People like John and Rena were hardly "new." As a result of the massive migrations during the nineteenth century, thousands of people with "no connections" brought nothing but themselves as they began new lives in northern and southern towns and cities. But Chesnutt's formulation gets at the demise of the black elite and the emergence of new political, economic, and familial contexts. When the disintegration of black political power spelled the end of numerous patronage jobs awarded to blacks during Reconstruction, working as white became an effective strategy for blacks to earn their bread by taking part in emerging urban economies that offered a wide range of white-collar and white-only work in salesrooms, offices, and department stores. By conveniently lacking relatives in South Carolina, John and Rena need not have worried about recognizably black family members who might turn up at just the wrong moment.

This disclosure to George, however, situates John and Rena within the context of a family (though not an old, rich, or distinguished one) and allows Chesnutt to prefigure the psychic tolls that passing would exact on familial relationships. "And what about our mother?" Rena asked when John proposed a new life for her in the white world. John and Rena arrive at an awkward and agonizing decision: "It would be necessary to leave her behind, they both perceived clearly enough, unless they were prepared to surrender the advantage of their whiteness and drop back to the lower rank. The mother bore the mark of the Ethiopian—not pronouncedly, but distinctly; neither would Mis' Molly, in all probability, care to leave home and friends and the graves of her loved ones. . . . She would not fit into Warwick's scheme for a new life."[106] Rena and John are reminiscent of Clarence and Emily Garie, the orphaned brother and sister in *The Garies and Their Friends,* published almost fifty years before *The House Behind the Cedars.* Both novels end tragically, with particularly devastating consequences for the characters—John, Rena, and Clarence—who each decide to pass. Emily Garie is the only exception: she marries a black man and remains untroubled by her decision to walk "with the oppressed," rather than "on the side of the oppressor," as her brother has fatefully chosen.[107]

On October 27, 1877, John Lynch, a black congressman from Natchez, Mississippi, wrote a disturbing letter to Blanche Bruce: "In Ohio the Republican Convention . . . strongly endorsed the Southern policy and the result is a humiliating Republican defeat. I confess that the outlook is anything else but favorable . . . the Senate in all probability will be Democratic. . . . It now begins to look as though the South will be united and the North divided in 1880 which of course will result in a Democratic victory. We may as well therefore prepare for the worst."[108] Just a few weeks earlier,

Lynch had teased Bruce when a newspaper, the *InterOcean,* alluded to him as a "United [States] Senator from Mississippi [who] is actually afraid to come home."[109] He was. To return to Mississippi was not only to leave behind the sumptuous lifestyle in Washington but also to suffer the loss of a social circle that he and Josephine had so carefully cultivated. Widespread racial violence, political instability, and targeted attacks on black Republicans who had held onto positions of power meant that by going back to Bolivar County, Bruce might be taking his life into his hands.

In the early days of Reconstruction, Bruce's constituents, along with many other African Americans, believed that they were witnessing the dawn of the first "postracial" society. A racially revolutionized society seemed possible given the broad extension of the franchise, the protections of the federal government, and the shifts in ideology about the meaning of race in the aftermath of the Civil War. But by the late 1870s and early 1880s, as the bright promises of Reconstruction dimmed, such a world became increasingly difficult to imagine. When Congress reconvened in 1879, there were no black representatives, and by 1889, according to Henry Grady, the owner of the largest newspaper in the South, the *Atlanta Constitution,* "The Negro as a political force [had] dropped out of serious consideration."[110] In 1902, Colonel A. K. McClure, writing for the *Washington Post,* commented, "The negro race is entirely unrepresented in either branch of the present Congress, and I cannot recall a negro Senator, Representative, or State officer in any one of the Northern States. For the full period of a generation, with a single brief exception, the negro was represented in one or both branches of our national legislature, but he is now retired and apparently without hope of reasserting himself as a factor in national legislation."[111] As early as the 1880s, there were far fewer blacks in public office, a Democratic resurgence was under way throughout the South, the Supreme Court declared the watered-down Civil Rights Act of 1875 unconstitutional, and Northerners had shifted their attention away from the plight of blacks in the South and onto increasing racial and ethnic tensions in their own cities. In a speech, Pinchback asked plaintively, "Can it be possible it means that this great nation—one of, if not the greatest and most powerful on earth—this new world power can not, or will not, respect its own constitution, nor enforce its laws when the rights and privileges to have one of them [has been] repealed?"[112] Race relations continued to decline throughout the 1880s, and in September 1889, the editor of *The Progressive Educator* would write to Chesnutt, "I am sorry that I cannot say that the relations between the races in this state are improving. There has been so much bitterness in N.C. since emancipation barring the years immediately succeeding Reconstruction. . . . We feel keenly the hardship of our present situation and are determined under God to find relief. We can no more stand the oppression of the Southland than a magazine can stand the application of a torch."[113]

As the hopefulness of Reconstruction faded into the grim reality of Jim Crow, those who could pass used this practice to deftly maneuver an increasingly restrictive and despairing racial climate. In part, these transformations reflected the changing circumstances and loss of status for black elites. Summarizing Blanche Bruce's accomplishments, an observer wrote, "His career demonstrated the opportunism of the politicians of Reconstruction. Had he lived into the twentieth century, he would probably have been less influential."[114] Hopes of maintaining the social and cultural distance between black elites and the black masses were dashed as restrictive racial codes overlooked distinctions based on class or color.

The overturning of the Civil Rights Act in 1875 and later the *Plessy* decision in 1896 effaced the possibility of a "white man's chance" and sounded the death knell of Reconstruction. The lives of the children of Blanche and Josephine Bruce set the new racial constrictions of the Jim Crow era in stark relief. Roscoe Conkling Bruce Jr. would have to comply with segregated housing policies at Harvard in 1923 even though his father, Roscoe Conkling Bruce Sr., had spent his college years in integrated dorms a generation earlier; and Clara Bruce Jr. (the Bruces' granddaughter) would drop out of Radcliffe after a few unremarkable semesters and marry Barrington Guy. The two would eventually pass as white and Indian, respectively, in order to advance Guy's fledgling acting career.[115]

When the "more intelligent members of the race" found it increasingly difficult to distinguish themselves from the black masses, when their constituents were disenfranchised and could no longer support them electorally, when their family names carried less weight, and when older institutional support systems diminished, passing became an increasingly expedient strategy for self-advancement. The tripartite world that Joseph Willson described in 1841 and painstakingly maintained behind the closed draperies at his daughter's wedding in 1878 had buckled. This collapse signaled the beginning of a new era in race relations, which in turn opened and closed opportunities for blacks who looked white.

Perhaps, then, Rena and John in Chesnutt's *The House Behind the Cedars* are best described as "new people." They are two individuals, seemingly unencumbered by familial relationships, who, like many Americans at the turn of the century struck out on their own to create better lives for themselves. Chesnutt's use of "new people" provides an ironic twist on the term: unlike those who have come before them, they are uprooted, dislodged, and trying to make their way alone, without the sustenance of family ties or the support of institutional networks. As the Reconstruction era closed and the sobering future of Jim Crow came into view, African American identity—so recently reshaped and redefined by emancipation and the tumult of the first years of freedom—would be refashioned once again by a new social and racial regime. As a season of hope gave way to decades of rigid and cramping racial segregation, the practice of passing would also change to respond to new political circumstances, economic contexts, and social conditions.

3

Lost Kin

In the December 1926 issue of *Opportunity,* Radcliffe-trained anthropologist Caroline Bond Day published a semiautobiographical story about Sarah, a "Negro woman of mixed blood," who enjoyed countless courtesies while wearing a pink hat. The hat was plain and made of straw, but it metamorphosed into a "magic-carpet" and an "enchanted cloak," remaking Sarah's drab life into one of possibility and adventure. A gentleman offered her a seat on the train, a young man helped her off of a railway car and retrieved her lost gloves, and a salesgirl addressed her as "Mrs.," a respectful title reserved for white women only. "Lo! The world was reversed," Sarah observed once she allowed the hat to conceal her curly brown hair, accentuate her ruddy complexion, and cast a pink hue over her face. For a few fleeting moments, Sarah glimpsed the pleasures of life beyond the limits of her Jim Crow world—a cold drink at a soda fountain, a pair of shoes purchased in the town's best shop, a comfortable seat in a movie theater, a stroll through an art gallery, a clean ladies' room—all on account of a pink straw hat. But Sarah's world would take a sudden turn when she broke her ankle. Bedridden in her black neighborhood, Sarah relied on the care of her black family when no white physician would treat her. As her ankle slowly healed, so too did her fractured identity. The pink hat had lost its usefulness. As Sarah concluded, with her good health, her loving family, and all the pleasures that her neighborhood had to offer, "Who'd want a hat?"[1]

With the bright promises of Reconstruction dashed and the consolidation of the Jim Crow regime complete by 1900, light-skinned blacks had plenty of reasons to pass. Jim Crow's assaults on African American life came in myriad forms: daily frustrations, humiliations, and indignities; political disenfranchisement; economic discrimination; widespread racial violence in threat and in fact; and the pseudoscience of eugenics that announced the biological and physiological inferiority of African Americans. Legalized segregation drew the color line more starkly in both the North and the South, excluding blacks from restaurants, hotels, Pullman cars, and other public accommodations. The rise of a new spokesman, Booker T. Washington, and the pronouncements made in his 1895 Atlanta Compromise address accelerated and sanctioned racial inequality in all forms of political, social, and economic life. Historian C. Vann Woodward wrote of Washington, "In proposing the virtual retirement of the mass of Negroes from the political life of the South and in stressing the humble and menial role that the race was to play, he would seem unwittingly to have smoothed the path to proscription."[2]

More than half a million black men became voters in the South after the ratification of the Fifteenth Amendment on March 30, 1870, which extended the right to vote to all American citizens regardless of race, color, or previous condition of servitude. But disenfranchisement by way of white primaries, poll taxes, literacy tests, and "grandfather," "good character," and "understanding" clauses systematically removed blacks from the political sphere.[3] When Mississippi was readmitted to the Union in 1870, ex-slaves comprised half of the state's voting population. Between 1870 and 1880, Mississippi voters elected two black U.S. senators as well as several black state officials. But in 1890, Mississippi held a convention to rewrite its state constitution to be consistent with the imperative expressed by the convention's president: "We came here to exclude the Negro."[4] The new state constitution included a number of restrictions, including a steep poll tax that had to be paid two years in advance of an election and that was far too expensive for the poorest segment of Mississippi's population. A literacy test required blacks to read and interpret technical and opaque sections of the state constitution to the satisfaction of a white clerk. These policies, known as the Mississippi Plan, made voting a nearly impossible feat for Mississippi's black citizens. Other southern states implemented similar policies of restriction. Ninety percent of African Americans were registered to vote during Reconstruction. By 1892, black voting registration had diminished to less than six percent. By 1940, only one percent of blacks in Mississippi were registered voters.[5]

During Reconstruction, an estimated 2,000 African Americans held political office. The U.S. Congress seated sixteen African Americans, approximately 600 blacks were elected to state legislatures, and hundreds more served in local offices throughout the

South. George Henry White, a congressman from North Carolina elected in 1897, was voted out of office in 1901. White was the last black congressman to serve, and his ouster signaled the symbolic end of black political power, even though some blacks continued to work in local offices. Many lost their positions when President Woodrow Wilson dismissed blacks from the federal bureaucracy in 1913. Congress remained lily white until 1929 when Oscar de Priest was elected to represent Chicago.[6]

Alleged upswings in "Negro crime," including a particular paranoia about black men's desire for white women and a bemoaning of the passing of the "old Negro" (African Americans born into slavery whom southern whites perceived as harmless and acquiescent to the racial power structure), were used to justify frightening increases in racial violence. Race riots swept through Wilmington in 1898, Atlanta in 1906, and Tulsa in 1921; the second Klan rose in 1915, "white cap" riders and lynch mobs went on "nigger hunts," and between the years of 1890 and 1917, two to three black Southerners were murdered each week.[7]

A compelling motive to pass as white is expressed most grotesquely at the climax of James Weldon Johnson's 1912 novel, *The Autobiography of an Ex-Colored Man.* It is the sight of a lynched black body—"the scorched post, a smoldering fire, blackened bones, charred fragments sifting down through coils of chains, and the smell of burnt flesh . . . in [his] nostrils" that "fixed" the Ex-Colored Man "to the spot where [he] stood, powerless to take [his] eyes from what [he] did not want to see."[8] The omnipresent threat of violence, the likelihood of injury, and the chance of death cast a pall of terror over the everyday lives of African Americans. James Weldon Johnson was nearly lynched by a white mob when he shared a park bench with a light-skinned companion who was mistaken as white.[9] In the novel, the Ex-Colored Man, "escaping the agonizing dilemma of black manhood," later feared that he had "chosen the lesser part" and "sold [his] birthright for a mess of pottage." But the gruesome scene, the spectacle of lynching as a form of white entertainment for a cheering mob, and his realization of the "cheapness of black life" prompted him to pass: "All the while, I understood that it was not discouragement, or fear, or search for a larger field of action and opportunity, that was driving me out of the Negro race. I knew that it was shame, unbearable shame. Shame at being identified with a people that could with impunity be treated worse than animals. For certainly the law would restrain and punish the malicious burning alive of animals."[10]

The eugenics movement reached a fever pitch in the 1920s. The science of heredity traveled from Europe around 1900 and found fertile ground in American nativist circles, where conversations about "race suicide" troubled those who believed in white racial superiority. Eugenicists lamented the failure of the "grand old New England stock" to reproduce and argued that the human species would progress only if those with the best genes reproduced.[11] They focused their efforts at "race improvement" on immigration restriction, lent their voices to calls for "100% Americanism," and applauded the passage of the Johnson-Reed Act in 1924, a bitter restrictionist attack that prohibited Japanese immigration and established a quota system designed to reduce the flood of southern European immigrants to a mere trickle.[12]

Closing the border was at the heart of this crusade, but eugenicists also worried about the consequences of racial intermixture. In Virginia, the state legislature passed the Act to Preserve Racial Integrity in 1924 out of a fear that, as one eugenicist explained, "Many thousands of white negroes . . . were quietly and persistently passing over the line."[13] This act enshrined the "one-drop rule" into law by defining a white person as one with "no trace of other blood." Never before had racial identity been defined by such a strict standard. The law also forbade interracial marriage between whites and anyone with even the slightest amount of racial mixture.

Walter A. Plecker, a physician and the state registrar of Virginia, worked closely with other eugenicists and members of white-supremacist Anglo-Saxon clubs to pass the law. Plecker was meticulous, zealous, and fanatical. He treated the work of enforcing the law classifying all Virginians based on color as if it were a religious calling. The achievement of white racial purity in Virginia was a "great struggle,"[14] Plecker wrote, especially because nineteen northern states and the nearby District of Columbia allowed intermarriage.[15] Plecker was especially concerned that mixed-race Virginians were becoming legally white by passing as Indian first. A subsection of the Virginia law, known as the Pocahontas Exception, allowed those with one-sixteenth Indian ancestry to be classified as white and enabled Virginia's oldest families to claim descent from Pocahontas and John Rolfe without tainting their white racial identity.[16] Relying on records that dated back to 1853, Plecker worked tirelessly to disprove the claims of those whom he believed had black ancestry and were trying to pass as Indian or as white. Plecker wrote to the director of the U.S. Census to "state as positively and emphatically as possible" that there were clusters of Virginians in several counties that "should under no circumstances be given classification as Indians in census records."[17] This was a ploy, Plecker surmised, to use identification as Indian as a gateway to passing as white.

Day in and day out, from 1924 until his resignation at the age of 85 in 1946, Plecker wrote hundreds of harassing letters to Virginians in a vain attempt to enforce the law. Aileen Hartless was hounded for "false statements" made by her parents, whom Plecker believed were free blacks before the Civil War and who "look[ed] almost white . . . and are trying to pass as white." When she submitted her birth certificate to obtain a marriage license, she was reminded by Plecker that "giving false registration as to race" was punishable with one year in the penitentiary. Plecker warned Hartless that her case might make it to court "if you continue to try to be what you are not."[18] Miss Blanche Cunningham received a letter reminding her that interracial marriage was illegal in the state of Virginia and instructing her to "immediately break off entirely with this young mulatto man" that she presumed was white and intended to marry.[19] Circuit court clerks in counties across the state were told to delay marriage licenses until the couple's ancestry could be proven to Plecker's satisfaction.

Plecker sounded the alarms at the Riverview Cemetery by alerting the superintendent and secretary that black bodies had been laid to rest in an ostensibly all-white burial ground. "We are under the impression that the Riverview Cemetery is reserved for white internments [*sic*]," Plecker wrote, but William H. Moon, who was from a mulatto family that was "striving in every way possible to gain white recognition," had been buried in Riverview on March 17, 1940. Plecker did not insist that the superintendent disinter Mr. Moon, but he certainly suggested it: "We are giving you this information to take such steps as you deem necessary. You probably know whether the State law permits use of a white cemetery by colored people."[20] When the secretary asked what could be done to rectify this situation, Plecker let him draw his own conclusions. This issue would not be so urgent in the "Pauper Section," Plecker wrote, but to a grieving white family, "it might prove embarrassing to meet with negroes visiting with one of their graves on an adjoining lot."[21]

Doctors and midwives received missives cautioning them that it was illegal to classify any child as white without clear evidence that neither parent had a drop of black blood.[22] Plecker badgered midwife Mary Gildon: "This is to notify you that it is a penitentiary offense to willfully state that a child is white when it is colored. You have made yourself liable to very serious trouble. What have you got to say about it?"[23] Another midwife, Mrs. Robert Cheatham, was browbeaten by Plecker after she assisted in the delivery and racial classification of a baby in 1924: "This is to give you a warning that this is a mulatto child and you cannot pass it off as white . . . See that this child is not allowed to mix with white children. It cannot go to white schools and can never marry a white person in Virginia. It is an awful thing."[24]

It was all "an awful thing" to Plecker. Midwives misclassifying black babies as white, the specter of integrated public schools and cemeteries, and the possibility of interracial sex and marriage were all appalling, dreadful, and unspeakable. Perhaps Plecker's efforts were so determined and so dogged because he knew that he was fighting a losing battle. No matter how many letters he wrote, he could not control the actions of all Virginians. To make matters worse, he was surrounded by states with more lenient racial laws. On occasion, Plecker sent letters outside of Virginia to sway public opinion against intermarriage. Plecker chastised the editor of the popular New York publication *Survey Graphic* for "deliberately and apparently approvingly" featuring interracial marriages on the pages of the magazine.[25]

Plecker was struck by a car and died at the age of 86 in 1947, one year after his retirement. By that time, eugenics had been discredited by the horrors of the Holocaust. Hitler had studied American eugenics. The Nuremberg laws were based on the same concepts about racial purity that Plecker had swallowed whole. But the Holocaust seared chilling images into the world's mind of atrocities that could result when racial laws were taken to the extreme. Twenty years after Plecker's death, the landmark Supreme Court decision *Loving v. Virginia* (1967) repudiated the Racial Integrity Act and declared all race-based restrictions on marriage unconstitutional. Although the era of eugenics reached its low ebb with the *Loving* decision in 1967, during the 1920s it was at its high watermark. So was the motivation to pass.

With the memoirs of Anna Julia Cooper and W. E. B. Du Bois in mind, historian Thomas Holt observed that early in these lives "there comes some traumatic confrontation with the Other that *fixes* the meaning of one's self before one even has the opportunity to *live* and *make* a self more nearly of one's own choosing." In the Jim Crow era, "traumatic confrontations" were bound to happen. And, as Holt notes, these confrontations need not be "dramatic street encounters." More likely, these were "quiet stories of one's parents" or "silences about a painful past."[26]

Passing, sometimes compelled by the kinds of traumatic confrontations that were recounted in African American autobiographies, provided an unusual yet effective means of authoring one's own life. The practice allowed those who could pass a means of clandestinely navigating the Jim Crow order. Passing offered much, but it could not mend splintered relationships with one's family; it could not ease a deep-rooted sense of alienation and longing for one's people. Passing was unfit for the task, borrowing from Du

Bois, of merging two selves "into a better and truer self." This curious phenomenon granted economic privileges and social courtesies, even transformational opportunities for self-fashioning, but often at a terrible cost.

During the Jim Crow era, the personal stakes of passing could not have been higher. Unlike the antebellum period where desperate leaps for freedom offered moral cover for an otherwise questionable act, and unlike the Reconstruction era when many African Americans chose not to pass, passing in Jim Crow America was predicated on the racial separation that defined the times. As racial barriers grew higher, so too did the incentive to pass and the finality of the loss one endured.

The lines from a Negro spiritual, "chilly waters, crossing over," frame a 1926 article published in *Opportunity* and express "the tragedy and pathos of that yearning for freedom persisting in the soul of the Negro during the period of bondage." The elasticity and the doubled (in fact, tripled) meanings of "crossing over" allow the article's author to fit three major forms of movement—emancipation, migration, and passing—beneath one rubric.[27] The sweeping demographic changes of migration produced new opportunities for "crossing over," as demonstrated by Alexander Manly's flight from Wilmington to Philadelphia during the race riot of 1898 and his subsequent decision to pass as white to work as a painter and join a union. He struggled to find work at first; when employers found out that he was black, they insisted that they could not hire him because of union restrictions.[28] "So I tried being white," Manly explained; "that is, I did not reveal the fact that I had coloured blood, and I immediately got work in some of the best shops in Philadelphia. I joined the union and had no trouble at all." Manly soon tired of living "the life of a sneak," and he took a job as a janitor so he could live openly with his recognizably black wife and children.[29]

The social and physical mobility of the Jim Crow era began with what Carter G. Woodson called the early migrations of the "Talented Tenth" in the 1870s and 1890s and culminated in the first waves of the Great Migration that saw the exodus of hundreds of thousands of blacks from the South between 1890 and 1930. According to the census of 1900, eighty-three percent of African Americans lived on farms or in rural areas and ninety percent of African Americans lived in the South.[30] Over the course of the twentieth century, these southern peasants would become members of the first African American working class and the backbone of the northern proletariat.[31] By 1970, the unofficial end of the Great Migration, only forty percent of blacks lived in the South. More blacks lived in the city of Chicago than in the state of Mississippi.[32] Migration allowed racially ambiguous people to travel and try on different identities once they were no longer associated with or known in a particular place.

The transformative processes of urbanization and migration and the anonymity offered in cities made these "worlds of strangers" particularly safe spaces to re-create one's racial identity. The term *passing* itself suggests a type of instability, a "moving through," or the lack of a stable home or place. Capturing the possibilities that migration and the cityscape presented in re-creating one's identity, one family member wrote of another, "He realized he looked like any white boy, so he started his journey North."[33] Legal scholar Cheryl Harris described her grandmother's journey from Mississippi to Chicago in the 1930s that preceded her decision to pass. Once in Chicago and no longer instantly recognizable as "'Lula's daughter,'" Harris's grandmother could easily enter the white world. When she looked for work in Chicago's all-white retail district, "no one ever asked if she was Black; the question was unthinkable." Unwritten codes of racial decorum at the high-class establishment where she worked prevented such inquiries.[34]

For some, leaving home for college created new possibilities for one's racial identity to be either mistaken or altogether reconstituted. In the late 1890s, Anita Hemmings, "a beautiful dark young woman . . . eagerly sought by the men from Yale, Harvard and other universities," arrived at Vassar College. Her boastful and insistent claims about the purity of her patrician background, "about her relatives—their style of living, the splendor of her home, &c.," rang false to a blue-blooded roommate, who instructed her father to investigate the matter. Suspicions that "her ancestors might have had colored blood mixed with the New England 'blue blood' of which she was fond of talking" were soon revealed to be true: the Hemmingses were a respectable black family of moderate means, but they were certainly not to the manor born, as Anita had insinuated.[35] Hemmings's racial identity was revealed a few days before commencement. In a secret session, the faculty decided to allow her to receive a diploma with her class. Perhaps Vassar did not want to betray its reputation as a liberal institution. Anita Hemmings would become the first black woman—at least as far as the university knew—to graduate from Vassar.

For others, graduating from college or graduate school created opportunities to refashion one's life. Theophilus John Minton Syphax, the son of an elite black family in Philadelphia, legally changed his name and decided to pass after graduating from Columbia Law School in 1902. As his friends explained, "He went away and never, so far as anyone could recall, came back." Syphax found himself in an awkward, impossible position when his parents offered their Washington, D.C., home for the wedding reception of longtime family friends Roscoe Conkling Bruce Sr. and Clara Burrill. As a courtesy, the African American couple removed Syphax from the guest list. Bruce wrote to Burrill on March 10, 1903, "Yes, let's omit Sie from the list of ushers; he *would* be embarrassed."[36] But, after marrying a white woman and spending almost forty-five years as a prominent Wall Street lawyer, Syphax (now known as McKee) traversed the color line once again in 1948 when he realized that he stood to inherit an $800,000 fortune left by his black grandfather.[37]

Some reports note that McKee maintained that neither he nor his grandfather was black. He stated that he would "not deny nor affirm" whether he was a Negro when he was asked directly. He held his ground by stating that he belonged to the "best clubs" and had "influential people—lawyers, judges" as his closest friends. Even his wife did not know of McKee's background until he decided to claim his grandfather's fortune. McKee would not live to inherit the trust fund. He died from complications following a serious kidney operation shortly after he made the claim to his inheritance.

The choices made by Syphax/McKee offer a striking example of the contingencies and vagaries of racial identity and the opportunism it sometimes produced. Heading off to college provided a break from one's past and a chance to reimagine one's future. A sudden financial windfall could be a powerful incentive to return to the race.

Like Theophilus McKee, Elsie Roxborough was born to a storied African American family. She also chose to pass as white after her college graduation in 1937. Her story also ends in death, but unlike McKee, she took her own life.

During the Depression, the Roxborough family lived a life that few Americans could imagine. The family had maids and chauffeurs. Elsie rode horses and drove her father's cars—a Pierce Arrow, a Packard, and a Cadillac.[38] The family vacationed with other black elites at Idlewild, a lakefront resort in western Michigan nicknamed the "Black Eden."[39] As one family friend explained, "We knew things were bad, but not for our crowd. We knew people sold apples on street corners but we wore white lapin jackets in Sunday School."[40]

When Elsie Roxborough arrived in Ann Arbor and moved into Mosher Jordan Hall in September 1933, she became the first black woman to live in a dormitory at the University of Michigan. Her father, Charles Roxborough, a renowned Detroit lawyer and the first black state senator elected in Michigan, had passed the Roxborough Bill in 1931 that prevented discrimination in university housing. At Michigan, Elsie wrote for the student newspaper, the *Michigan Daily,* majored in journalism, and became active in theater. Elsie was at best a mediocre student, and the plays that she directed were panned by critics and audiences alike, but as her friends and family explained, a dogged determination and raw ambition made Elsie both restless and relentless.[41]

Elsie was tall and slender, glamorous and vivacious, with beauty and charm that few men, black or white, could resist. She dated the heavyweight boxing champion Joe Louis, who was managed by her uncle, John Roxborough. Their relationship would not last. Family members speculated that John ended the affair. Louis, nicknamed the "Brown Bomber," was beloved by the black community, and he was one of the first African Americans to become a national hero. But he was born to sharecroppers in rural Alabama, and he lacked the culture and sophistication of a high-society woman like Elsie Roxborough. Louis may not have been worldly, but Elsie was certainly not a conventional woman of her time. Known as a "hell-raiser," Elsie once smashed Louis's car when she felt that he was not paying enough attention to her.[42] Langston Hughes was undeniably a better match, but their relationship also failed. Hughes described Elsie as "a lovely-looking girl, ivory white of skin with dark eyes and raven hair like a Levantine," but he was rumored to be gay, and Elsie was, as her friends explained, too in love with her work to be serious about any man.[43] Ernest Lehman, the future screenwriter, admired her. Her classmate, the future playwright Arthur Miller, called her "a beauty . . . the classiest girl in Ann Arbor."[44]

Langston Hughes wrote that Elsie would "tell him her dreams, and wonder whether or not it would be better for her to pass as white to achieve them."[45] After graduating from college in 1937, Elsie moved to California and passed as white to work as a model and a screenwriter. When her fortunes ran dry out west, Elsie moved east. In New York City, she dyed her brown hair a "titian red" and dropped the famous Roxborough name to become the unattached Mona Manet. As her brother-in-law explained, Elsie had "the most exciting life of any black girl of her time"; she was at the top of the Motor City's vibrant social world, but still, she chose to move to New York and "go on the other side." Elsie's departure from Detroit's black community did not go unnoticed by the black press. The *Michigan Chronicle* echoed Elsie's brother-in-

Figure 3.1. Elsie Roxborough during the period when she changed her name to Mona Manet to pass as white in New York City.
Courtesy of the Burton Historical Collection, Detroit Public Library, Detroit, Michigan.

law and reported, "Detroit did not supply the exuberant Elsie with the creative outlet that she needed."[46] The *Baltimore Afro-American* published the article, "Elsie Roxborough Reported Living Incognito in Gotham," and noted that "much to her family's undisguised disgust," Elsie was trying out a life in New York as a "Nordic."[47] Elsie would come back to Detroit for visits to "see the folks." Her sister Virgie, who could also pass, was the only family member to visit her in New York.[48] Langston Hughes was in Spain when Elsie wrote him to tell him that she "intended to cease being colored." For several years, Elsie wrote letters to Hughes and sent him gifts at Christmas, without a return address on the package. In time, Elsie's letters and gifts stopped altogether, and Hughes never heard from her again.

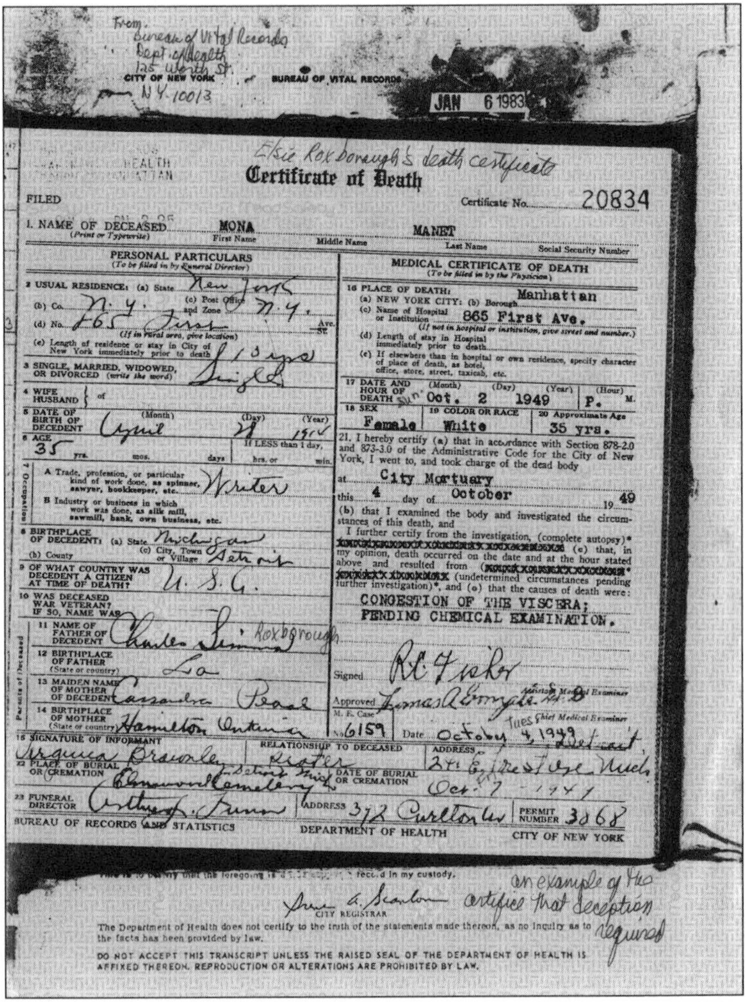

From:
Bureau of Vital Records
Dept. of Health
125 Worth St.
N.Y. 10013

CITY OF NEW YORK — BUREAU OF VITAL RECORDS

JAN 6 1983

Elsie Roxborough's death certificate

Certificate of Death

FILED

Certificate No. 20834

1. NAME OF DECEASED (Print or Typewrite) MONA (First Name) (Middle Name) MANET (Last Name) (Social Security Number)

PERSONAL PARTICULARS (To be filled in by Funeral Director)

2 USUAL RESIDENCE: (a) State New York (b) Co. N.Y. (c) Post Office and Zone N.Y. (d) No. 865 First Ave. (If in rural area, give location) (e) Length of residence or stay in City of New York immediately prior to death 1 1/3 yrs

3 SINGLE, MARRIED, WIDOWED, OR DIVORCED (write the word) Single

4 WIFE / HUSBAND of

5 DATE OF BIRTH OF DECEDENT (Month) April (Day) 28 (Year) 1914

6 AGE 35 yrs. mos. days. If LESS than 1 day, hrs. or min.

7 Occupation: A Trade, profession, or particular kind of work done, as spinner, sawyer, bookkeeper, etc. Writer. B Industry or business in which work was done, as silk mill, sawmill, bank, own business, etc.

8 BIRTHPLACE OF DECEDENT: (a) State Michigan (b) County (c) City, Town or Village Detroit

9 OF WHAT COUNTRY WAS DECEDENT A CITIZEN AT TIME OF DEATH? U.S.A.

10 WAS DECEASED WAR VETERAN? IF SO, NAME WAR

Parents of Deceased: 11 NAME OF FATHER OF DECEDENT Charles Simmons Roxborough. 12 BIRTHPLACE OF FATHER (State or country) La. 13 MAIDEN NAME OF MOTHER OF DECEDENT Cassandra Pearl. 14 BIRTHPLACE OF MOTHER (State or country) Hamilton Ontario

MEDICAL CERTIFICATE OF DEATH (To be filled in by the Physician)

16 PLACE OF DEATH: (a) NEW YORK CITY: (b) Borough Manhattan (c) Name of Hospital or Institution 865 First Ave. (If not in hospital or institution, give street and number.) (d) Length of stay in Hospital immediately prior to death (e) If elsewhere than in hospital or own residence, specify character of place of death, as hotel, office, store, street, taxicab, etc.

17 DATE AND HOUR OF DEATH Sun. (Month) Oct. (Day) 2 (Year) 1949 (Hour) P. M.

18 SEX Female 19 COLOR OR RACE White 20 Approximate Age 35 yrs.

21. I hereby certify (a) that in accordance with Section 878-2.0 and 873-3.0 of the Administrative Code for the City of New York, I went to, and took charge of the dead body at City Mortuary this 4 day of October 1949 (b) that I examined the body and investigated the circumstances of this death, and I further certify from the investigation, (complete autopsy)* [XXXXXXXXXXXXXXXXXXXXXXXXX] (c) that, in my opinion, death occurred on the date and at the hour stated above and resulted from [XXXXXXXXXXXXXXXXXXXXX]* [XXXXXXXXXXXXXX] (undetermined circumstances pending further investigation)*, and (e) that the causes of death were:

CONGESTION OF THE VISCERA; PENDING CHEMICAL EXAMINATION.

Signed R C Fisher, Assistant Medical Examiner
Approved Thomas A Gonzales M.D., Chief Medical Examiner
M. E. Case No. 6159 Date October 4, 1949 Tues

15 SIGNATURE OF INFORMANT Virginia Braxonley — RELATIONSHIP TO DECEASED Sister — ADDRESS 241 E. Forest Ave. Detroit Mich.

22 PLACE OF BURIAL OR CREMATION Elmwood Cemetery, Detroit Mich. — DATE OF BURIAL OR CREMATION Oct. 7 1949

23 FUNERAL DIRECTOR Arthur J. Turner — ADDRESS 372 Carlton Av. — PERMIT NUMBER 3868

BUREAU OF RECORDS AND STATISTICS — DEPARTMENT OF HEALTH — CITY OF NEW YORK

This is to certify that the foregoing is a true copy of a record in my custody.

CITY REGISTRAR

The Department of Health does not certify to the truth of the statements made thereon, as no inquiry as to the facts has been provided by law.

DO NOT ACCEPT THIS TRANSCRIPT UNLESS THE RAISED SEAL OF THE DEPARTMENT OF HEALTH IS AFFIXED THEREON. REPRODUCTION OR ALTERATIONS ARE PROHIBITED BY LAW.

an example of the artifice that deception required

Figure 3.2. Elsie Roxborough/Mona Manet's death certificate. Note that she is listed as white.

Courtesy of the Burton Historical Collection, Detroit Public Library, Detroit, Michigan.

When Elsie's white roommate returned from a weekend trip, she found Elsie in her bed. It appeared that Elsie had committed suicide. As her brother explained years later, "maybe Elsie swallowed life whole and had trouble digesting it."[49] Her sister, Virgie, and her aunt, Cutie, could both pass as white, so they traveled to New York with the wrenching assignment of claiming the body. The arrival of these two ostensibly white women allowed Elsie to remain white, even in death. In Elsie's apartment, Virgie and Cutie found a pair of stockings waiting to be washed in the bathroom sink. Elsie must have wanted to live, they reasoned, but perhaps she had too much to drink and had accidentally overdosed on sleeping pills. Elsie had written to her uncle and her father for financial help. They refused her, and three days later, she was dead. Virgie would never speak to her father again.

After Elsie's death, Virgie received numerous letters of condolence from Elsie's bereaved white friends in New York. One friend expressed the anguish she felt because she could not pay her last respects or contribute flowers to the funeral.[50]A grief-stricken Ernest Lehman wrote, "Mona Manet had many friends in NYC . . . apparently we have failed her, the whole world has failed her, all of us, her friends, her family, the world are to blame. We allowed sweet Mona to be lost. Why did this terrible thing have to be? Why?"[51]

Years later, Elsie's cousin explained that Elsie was just one of the Roxboroughs' tragedies.[52] Elsie's mother died when Elsie was five years old. Known as the "divorcing Roxboroughs," Elsie's father and stepmother's marriage unraveled at a time when divorce was uncommon.[53] Family members and friends described the Roxboroughs as "aloof, private, and withdrawn"; they were not affectionate or demonstrative and they rarely kissed or hugged.[54] Some family members turned to alcohol as they struggled to negotiate the pressures of sitting at the very top of Detroit's black social and professional worlds. Virgie's husband had an uncle who was a lawyer but whom he never met because he was "on the other side." His uncle would see Virgie's father, who also was a lawyer, at court hearings and he would ask about him, even though he could never see him. He invited Virgie to lunch, but Virgie never went. This was as close as he could get to his nephew.[55]

After Virgie's death, a relative sent her condolences to Virgie's husband. "I don't think her life was an easy one," she wrote. "So many secrets to keep to herself as well as hurts and disappointments, the lack of closeness in her own family, meaning . . . the Roxboroughs, has poisoned many possible relationships . . . I never felt there was enough interest . . . to get close to many of my relatives." As she read the letters that Virgie received after Elsie's death, she said solemnly, "I truly wish I had known her—so much creativity and spirit in that woman." Reflecting on the loss of family members who had passed as white and the absence of family feeling among the Roxboroughs, she lamented, "So one does the best they can do. You are aware that you have missed something of what life has to give. It's a sadness that never lets go."[56]

"Crossing over" was a proven strategy for navigating "chilly water"; at the same time, it raised concerns about how black families would remain whole when nearly white relatives moved away, formed new families, and started new lives. The 1926 article in *Opportunity* hinted at this dilemma, framing "this subtle migration" as "the most ambitious offensive ever launched by the sons of Ham," but worrying about "the deliberate annihilation of ethnic affiliation when physical appearance does not proclaim it."[57] Family members who brushed against or fully participated in the world of passing undermined black familial stability, leaving the very survival of some families hanging in the balance.

Caroline Bond Day used the language of social science to challenge the beliefs in racial inferiority held by eugenicists like Walter Plecker with the publication of her master's thesis, *A Study of Some Negro-White Families,* in 1932. An anthropology graduate student at Radcliffe working under the supervision of Ernest Hooten, Day began her study as an investigation into the results of racial intermixture. Hooten wanted to undertake the study, but he feared that blacks would be reticent to talk to a white researcher. Day was the ideal investigator. She was a mixed-race graduate of the Tuskegee Institute and an English and classical literature major at Atlanta University, where W. E. B. Du Bois had been her teacher and mentor.[58] She received a scholarship for advanced study at Radcliffe.

Day employed an unusual methodology. She collected the family photographs and genealogical information that comprised the lion's share of her evidence from relatives and members of her elite, racially ambiguous social circle. Day played on the desires of middle- and upper-class blacks to be acknowledged by whites. She conveyed the merit and larger significance of her "field work" by explaining that she was "compiling statistics about the better class of Colored Americans of mixed blood" and that she hoped her project would create a better understanding of "the lives and activities of our people."[59] To one hesitating friend, Day wrote, "you know there is a group of White people who absolutely do not believe that we have such a group as live, for instance, at Highland Beach," a resort town where elite black families vacationed on the Chesapeake Bay in Maryland.[60] Day included her own racial composition (7/16 white blood, 1/16

Figure 3.3. Caroline Bond Day, a Radcliffe-trained anthropologist who gathered and studied data on 346 racially mixed families.
Courtesy of the Schlesinger Library, Radcliffe Institute, Harvard University.

Indian blood, 8/16 black blood) and her family's genealogical chart in her project. Family members and friends—proud of the academic success of one of their own, honored to be asked to participate in a study bearing the prestigious Harvard imprimatur, but suspicious of the anthropological underpinnings of the project—were reluctant donors at first, but in the end, many allowed Day to examine their bodies and take their measurements using a caliper, a color chart, and a tape measure.[61] Several participants furnished Day with a precious cache of family photographs.[62] In all, Day collected the physical measurements as well as physiological and sociological information on 346 families and 2,537 mixed-race individuals.[63]

Writing in the peculiar language of race, genetics, and blood quantification of her time, Day classified her subjects into three groups—"a recessive type, leaning toward the Negro ancestral line;

an intermediate type; and a dominant type emphasizing the European characters"—and she reported that racially mixed people with three-eighths Negro blood or less showed no signs of having any black ancestry. As Hooten explained, "Swarthy skins, frizzy hair, and heavy features are conspicuously lacking from quadroons," and these racially ambiguous men and women could easily pass as white, "even before the experienced eye of the anthropological observer."[64] Day's study implied that it was very possible that many people who believed themselves to be white had black ancestry and that passing as white was not only possible, but also quite common.

But most importantly, Day demonstrated that racially mixed individuals were normal, well educated, and middle class, just like many white Americans of similar class backgrounds. Racial intermixture, contrary to the beliefs of eugenicists and white supremacists, did not result in mongrelization, but unremarkable, in fact, unnoticeable, differences between blacks and whites. As Day explained, "There is nothing mysterious or unnatural in the mixture of races and nothing extraordinary in the physical results of those mixtures."[65] Day presented a profile of her study's participants as happily married, college-educated homeowners living in nuclear families with just a few children. Many of the women were full-time housewives. These men and women enjoyed leisure activities including needlepoint, literature, and sports.[66]

Despite her groundbreaking work and her status as one of the first African Americans, male or female, to receive a doctoral degree in anthropology, Caroline Bond Day never found an institutional home as an academic, and her work was not reviewed by anthropological journals. Day did receive attention from white sociologists, including Louis Wirth at the University of Chicago and Herbert Goldhamer at Stanford University. Wirth and Goldhamer, impressed

Figure 3.4. Genealogical chart of the Day family's racial intermixture. This chart was published in Day's thesis, *A Study of Some Negro-White Families in the United States* (1932). Note the inclusion of the blood quantum of each individual.

by the comprehensive genealogies that Day assembled, included Day's work in an essay that they submitted for Gunnar Myrdal's landmark study, *An American Dilemma* (1946). But her project was published at a time when scientists were beginning to move away from biological understandings of race and toward theories of cultural relativism expounded by Franz Boas. As an outsider to the world of black male intellectuals, Day found that there were few positions available to her. She taught drama at Atlanta University until poor health forced her into retirement. In 1948, she died at the age of fifty-nine from heart complications.

On the other hand, Day's contemporary E. Franklin Frazier found institutional homes at the most prestigious black universities of his day, Fisk and Howard. Frazier was one of the first blacks to receive a PhD in sociology. He too built his scholarly reputation on an investigation of the black family, completing his dissertation, *The Negro Family in Chicago,* and earning a degree from the University of Chicago in 1932, where he studied under Robert Park, a founding father of the Chicago School of Sociology.[67] In 1939, Frazier published *The Negro Family in the United States* and won the John Anisfield Prize for the best book on contemporary race relations. With this publication and award in hand, Frazier became the nation's preeminent black sociologist.[68] He began teaching at Howard in 1934, became the chair of its Sociology Department, and remained there until his retirement in 1959. In 1948, he was elected president of the American Sociological Association, which made him the first black scholar to head a major academic organization.[69] Frazier garnered international acclaim when he was invited to Paris in 1949 to serve as chairman of a committee of scholars asked by the United Nations Educational, Scientific, and Cultural Organization (UNESCO) to formulate a definition of "race" in the modern world.[70]

Figure 3.5. From left to right: James Nabrit, Charles Drew, Sterling Brown, Rayford Logan, Alaine Locke, and E. Franklin Frazier at Howard University in 1950. E. Franklin Frazier was a pioneering sociologist who published the groundbreaking book *The Negro Family in the United States* in 1939. *Courtesy of the Moorland-Spingarn Research Center, Howard University.*

Even though Day and Frazier were writing at the same time, they had little contact with each other. Curiously, Frazier did not cite Day's work as foundational in his own arguments that attempted to dispel myths about black racial inferiority. Perhaps Frazier disliked Day for being part of the high society that he ferociously critiqued in *Black Bourgeoisie* (1957). Frazier's portrait of this community was unsparing and withering: an isolated, acutely status-conscious "society" that staged "a succession of carnivals"—cotillions, debutante balls, clubs, fraternities, sororities—"that compensated for their rejection by the white community" and sought "to achieve identification with upper-class whites by imitating as far as possible the behavior of white society."[71] As the managing editor of the *Pittsburgh Courier*, one of the black newspapers that Frazier criticized for doting on the black upper class, stated: "If you don't mind being cussed out, belittled, ridiculed and lambasted all at the same time, go ahead and read the book." But the editor admitted, "Yet, the more you read what Frazier is saying, the more you realize that his facts are pretty straight."[72]

Frazier was born in Baltimore, Maryland, in 1893. His father was a messenger who had never received any education, and his mother was a former slave. Frazier was teaching sociology at Morehouse College in Atlanta when a white mob forced him to leave after his 1927 essay "The Pathology of Race Prejudice" was published in *Forum* and drew parallels between southern racism and insanity.[73] In the late 1920s, Frazier joined a picket line outside of a movie house in Baltimore that featured D. W. Griffith's racist epic, *The Birth of a Nation*. A few years later, when Frazier was on a fellowship at the University of Copenhagen and a Danish theater showed *The Birth of a Nation*, Frazier's protests resulted in the removal of the film.[74] During his one year at Tuskegee, he declined to pay the city's voting tax because blacks were disenfranchised, and he refused to join his Howard colleagues in Woodrow Wilson's segregated inaugural parade. In Atlanta, he stormed out of a meeting of social workers upon discovering that the seating was segregated, and he insisted that a bank teller call him "Mister Frazier." If the teller would not comply with his wishes, Frazier would call him by his first name too. As he explained, "There was no power in heaven or hell that could make me call a white man 'mister' who did not put 'mister' to my name."[75] Frazier taught at Fisk University for five years, and while there, he locked horns with the power structure of the segregated South. Frazier lent his support to students who were striking against Nashville's segregation practices, and he investigated a local lynching.[76] At Howard University, Frazier's academic work aimed to reinterpret the black family in a way that would shed light on the plight of African Americans. *The Negro Family in the United States,* as the *Washington Post* explained, has become "basic reading for any serious student of the social problems that beset American cities."[77] The book drew on sociological and historical forces to explain racism and the social limits that African Americans faced.

The work of Caroline Bond Day and E. Franklin Frazier, while not specifically designed to study passing, opens a window onto this curious practice and offers evidence and insight into the social and psychological tolls of passing for those left behind.

Tactical or temporary passing—the practice of passing momentarily, with a particular purpose in mind—was born in the antebellum period as a means of securing one's freedom by passing as white to escape from slavery. It was reformulated primarily as "nine-to-five passing" during the Jim Crow years, enabling nearly white men and women to access employment reserved for whites only. On an undated questionnaire for Frazier's "A Study of the Negro Family," one respondent wrote "passes for white" as the occupation for both his brother and his uncle.[78] Caroline Bond Day bemoaned the difficulties of gathering information for her thesis because of the problems posed by "one or more [family] members who are 'passing' either entirely, or only temporarily for purposes of obtaining lucrative employment."[79] Passing worked as an effective strategy to expand one's employment opportunities, especially in white-collar professions.

When asked how many people in his community had "passed over into the white race," a man living in Ohio replied, "Yes, a lot of families left the community and went away from here and got positions and their children today wouldn't know they got a drop of colored blood in them. They did this because they couldn't get work no other way."[80] Leona Glover wrote that her grandfather moved from Chattanooga to Chicago, "passed into the other race and received a job as an engineer running from Chicago to Detroit."[81] Lloyd Harding Bailer's father had to relocate his medical office from downtown to Detroit's colored district after a misunderstanding occurred between the building's elevator operator and a black patient. The woman asked the elevator operator to take her to the doctor's office; when she was released on the wrong floor, she corrected herself and said that she wanted to see the "colored doctor." Soon afterward, Dr. Bailer was informed that his lease would not be renewed.[82] A participant in Caroline Bond Day's study who had "the straight hair of her mother, and rather small non-negroid features" prospered in a position as an assistant pharmacist in the Colodine Manufacturing Plant in Philadelphia where they did not employ Negro workers.[83] Outmaneuvering racially restrictive hiring practices and enjoying otherwise unfathomable professional success and upward mobility made passing an economically rewarding practice.

Given the strict segregation of employment opportunities, simply mentioning that a family member held a white-collar job became shorthand for passing for white. A woman wrote of a relative who was "working up in New York State passing as head manager of the largest paper factory in the country."[84] Family members signaled that a relative had a high-paying job by stating that he or she "works as white," and it could be assumed that a relative was passing if he or she worked in a particular field or in an all-white establishment. Mrs. J. A. Bass described her son's new life as a white man in Chicago by explaining, "He worked himself up at one of Walgreen's stores . . . and worked until he became the manager of the soda fountain."[85] Reverend Bass hinted that he had a stepsister who was passing by noting that she worked as a "head cook at the white 'Y' in Dayton."[86]

By "mak[ing] use of his light skin and good hair," the protagonist in Langston Hughes's short story "Passing" earned $65 a week and was next in line for a promotion to chief office secretary, a sharp contrast to the "colored boy porter who sweeps out the office."[87] In an essay, "Why, How, When and Where Black Becomes White," activist Mary Church Terrell described the discouragement that many colored men faced, with few trades open, "for a long time he knocks first at one door and then at another, which he finds can be opened only with a white man's hand."[88] Although this man "has always put it behind him, however, as a last resort, too contemptible and cowardly to be considered seriously," now he finds himself out of work, facing a "chronic" inability to secure a good position. Given its temporary nature as well as its material advantages, this type of passing was generally condoned, and sometimes even celebrated. Reformer Fannie Barrier Williams wrote, "Since 'passing' was the only means of gaining an equal opportunity . . . those who were willing to take the risk could scarcely be blamed, since they are certainly not responsible for the anomalous position in which they find themselves."[89]

Some family members enjoyed the subversive potential of passing as a practical joke and boasted of the achievements of relatives who successfully "got over" on whites. Henry Park was "the only colored fireman in New Haven," one family member bragged, adding, "he neglected to tell them he was Negro."[90] Similarly, Barrington Guy, the son of a wealthy black family in Washington, D.C., and husband of Clara Bruce, Mississippi Senator Blanche Bruce's granddaughter, conceded in 1939, "I never tried to pass. . . . Folks thought I was white and I didn't enlighten them."[91] One mother described a letter she received from her daughter who had changed the spelling of her last name from Bass to Bafs as she created her new identity as a white woman: "She wrote me that she was going out to get her a job the next day and I took it that she was going to pass for white, because she ended up the writing with a ha, ha."[92] Some blacks agreed with Langston Hughes's assertion that "as long as white folks remain foolish, prejudiced and racially selfish, they deserve to be fooled. No better for them!"[93]

Racially ambiguous men and women engaged in tactical passing to improve their economic lot, but they also used this form of passing to save themselves from the myriad humiliations of Jim Crow life. Yet another folly of American race relations was that by passing as anything other than African American, those who were racially indeterminate or even recognizably black could enjoy better treatment. After a tour of the Gettysburg battlefield during the summer of 1917, the nearly white African American novelist Charles Chesnutt and his family stopped for a meal. After a sharp exchange with the hostess, the restaurant's manager briskly approached the Chesnutts' table. Observing the altercation, Chesnutt's son instructed the family: "*Il faut que nous parlions français tout de suite.*" By speaking French and appearing as foreigners rather than as African Americans, the Chesnutts avoided the indignity of being ejected from the dining room.[94] Similarly, James Weldon Johnson delicately maneuvered through awkward circumstances in a cramped smoking car of a train traveling from Jacksonville to New York. A fortuitous turn of events, beginning with a comment about Johnson's Panama hat, led the passengers to misread Johnson's national identity and to assume that he was from Cuba. Once Cuban—still black, but no longer black American—Johnson relaxed, laughed, and shared a flask of whiskey with the white passengers.

But the fun of passing was usually short-lived; even "nine-to-five" and other forms of temporary passing required sacrifices and created anxiety that few could tolerate. In Nella Larsen's novel *Passing,* Clare Kendry marveled at why this practice was not more commonplace: "I've often wondered why more coloured girls . . . never 'passed' over. It's such a frightfully easy thing to do. If one's the type, all that's needed is a little nerve."[95] But passing required far more than "a little nerve," and after a few years of living "on the other side," even Clare Kendry would no longer believe her own words.

"Who Are Your People?"

In a memoir of her mother's life, Ronne Hartfield reflected on the expansive sense of black family feeling and captured an enduring theme: "It is said that colored people all over the world will ask each other upon first meeting, 'Who are your people?'"[96] Hartfield's question signaled the importance of locating black individuals within larger familial networks and sets of kinfolk. Day Shepherd, Hartfield's mother, lived in New Orleans in the 1920s and was encouraged but decided not to join a group of "octoroon" girls who were seeking white husbands. Shepherd was quite familiar with the practice of passing: her aunt passed to sell perfume as a counter girl in New Orleans, one of her brothers passed and married a white woman, and another brother passed to work as a foreman at the Link-Belt factory in Chicago.[97]

Shepherd, too, lived on both sides of the color line. At a bus station in Grenada, Mississippi, Shepherd was faced with an impossible situation when the operators at neither the colored nor the white booth would sell tickets to her. The man working at the colored booth believed that she was white, and the operator at the white booth took note of her brown-skinned children and assumed that she was black. In Chicago, Shepherd held a well-paying job working on the conveyor belts at the Automatic Electric Company. She did not volunteer any information about her racial background, and none of her coworkers, recent immigrants from Italy, Lithuania, and Poland, asked questions. As Hartfield explains, "This was the kind of tacit passing that allowed my mother to gain a foothold in Chicago in 1918 and 1919."[98] Despite Shepherd's intimate exposure to passing, she could not make sense of the familial dislocations that passing permanently necessitated: "In slavery days, people got cut off from their families and everything they knew like that, and that was sad, but then there was nothing they could do about it. But these passing people who choose to do that? I can't make any sense out of that at all. All they get in return for giving up everything is people can think they're white. People think I'm white anyway and I don't feel any different. I have my family and my true history. That means something."[99]

Shepherd's family relationships and her "true history" were more meaningful than the privileges of looking white. Passing meant letting go of one's people, or as Shepherd lamented, of "giving up any thoughts of ever seeing [one's] colored family again," something that she "could never conceive of in [her] mind." "How would anybody know who they were without their people?" she asked. Shepherd found comfort in her close-knit family: "We were lucky that all of our people lived right together on the Place, and you knew just how everybody was related to everybody else."[100] To Shepherd's mind, letting go of one's people was nothing less than letting go of one's self.

Shepherd's questions lay bare fundamental issues of identity. She locates the essence of one's personhood in one's familial relations and underscores the profound loss of self and the erasure of "true history" that permanent passing entailed. But the reality of modern American life made the kind of intimacy and closeness that Shepherd cherished increasingly difficult to sustain. Fewer family members "lived right together" in any one place, and it was increasingly uncommon that anyone "just knew how everybody was related to everybody else." Rather, passing and the disruption that it caused to many black families occurred in the midst of the unprecedented demographic transformations of a world in flux. Much of the black population was on the move and in the process of dislodging from the very communities that Shepherd eulogized.

For Caroline Bond Day, at every turn, the problem of passing surfaced and stymied her work of assembling coherent family trees. The handwritten note "Hugh is 'passing,'" the blank spaces, and the question marks left in the columns of questionnaires emblematized the difficulties that Day encountered as she sifted through the evidence for her study.[101] Tangled family histories, fuzzy lineages, and forgotten bloodlines made many of Day's questions difficult, if not impossible, for her subjects to answer. "I am sorry that I cannot answer all of the questions, as to the percent of blood," Annie Sims Lewis wrote to Day in 1927, "but to be perfectly frank, my father's mother had such a little I hardly know how to estimate it."[102] Another respondent, Alice McNeill, sent a similar message: "I've answered the questionnaire as well as I could. I do not know how to figure the proportion of negro blood (no 5) both of my fathers grand[fathers] were white . . . —the grandmothers being Negro—but what proportion I do not know, they never told their children much—mainly because they were ashamed of their illegitimacy. There is lots of information that we have lost due to that mid and pre-Victorian reticence."[103] Day's study trod on delicate family matters and few family members felt comfortable unearthing secrets that had been kept for generations.

Others appreciated the importance of Day's work but retracted their family photographs when the study went to press. Emma Milliston concluded an otherwise friendly letter with a curt declaration: "I wish to make it quite clear to you that under no circumstances would I like you to use any of my photos or my children singly or in group."[104] Many of Day's participants shared Milliston's reticence and discomfort about revealing their family histories. Describing her mother as a "closed book," Mama Penney explained, "Now Carrie dear about my ancestry, That's one of the hidden mysteries my mother kept to herself. My father I never knew but my grandmother gave me his name, Crosby. My mother's father was white." Penney offered no explanation about the nature of the relationship between her grandfather and her other family members, but the fact that it was a "hidden mystery" that her mother did not wish to share with others speaks to the sensitive nature of some interracial family ties. For Penney and many others, the effort required to "rake out those horrible ancestral skeletons" was simply too much to ask, especially for those who had done their utmost to "bury them long ago."[105]

Ever persistent in calling in favors from friends and family and eager to obtain the information necessary to complete her study, Day seemed, for the most part, untroubled by the demands that she placed on her respondents. Suspecting that the Percival family might be passing as white in Castile, New York, Day was no less determined to include them in her project. She wrote to assure them that their secret would be safe with her:

> Now, I know that you have a very interesting family history and so I am anxious for you to fill out as much of this blank for me as you will. At the same time, I am cognizant of your situation there in Castile. I presume that it is not generally known there that your family has colored blood, is it? And probably you may not wish any publicity concerning the information that you give me; therefore, if you prefer, I will not make any public use of the information which you give me, but will keep it for my private files.[106]

Day was mistaken. The Percival family elected not to complete Day's questionnaire, but not for the reasons that Day imagined. "We read and discussed the matter thoroughly," Mrs. Percival wrote to Day in 1928, explaining that her husband decided "he did not care to put himself or [his] family on record much as he appreciated your work." The family could not pass for white, Mrs. Percival reminded Day, but they chose not to draw unnecessary attention to their racial identity: "No, your idea of us was incorrect. We are known as colored and I would say, or can't exactly, we go for that, only we happen to be the only ones here. If you recall, my husband, he could not 'pass,' and would not, but does prefer to live apart and be just regarded as a man among men, rather than a 'race' man. As for myself, I made it known, when we first come to Castile, that I was of his race and settled the question once for all."[107] Many of Day's subjects opted out; those who were passing could not risk having family photographs published in a book on mixed-race families, whereas others claimed the right to define themselves as they wished, often relying on more subtle understandings of racial identity and rejecting categorization based on dubious anthropological methods.

Passing offered countless freedoms—from the pleasures of sitting in other sections of movie theaters besides the "buzzard roost," to the simple dignities of trying on a hat in a store without being compelled to buy it, to the elusive opportunities to "feel more like a man" or "to be treated like a lady." But passing—the anxious decision to break with a sense of communion—upset the collective, "congregative character" of African American life; it undermined the ability for traditions, stories, jokes, and songs to be shared across generations. Even the task of completing a family history became prickly, if not impossible. To be sure, not all family relationships were congenial, but once a relative decided to pass, meaningful touchstones and common experiences were lost. The fragmentation of one's identity and ancestral memory and the scattering of family relationships represent only a handful of passing's most troubling dilemmas.

The levity of "fooling our white folks" contrasted sharply with the high emotional stakes of passing as white. Passers could not be seen boarding buses headed to or from black neighborhoods, and they had to ignore black family members and friends in public. Passing may have begun as a joke to a woman who worked as white, but she later found that she could keep her job only "until she got so nervous that she had to stop."[108] Another woman described her experiences with the darker side of passing: she listened to white coworkers speak about blacks with bitter contempt, and she found herself teetering on a "state of nervous collapse," constantly fearing that her secret would be discovered.[109] With the ever-present fear of being exposed, the workplace became an anxiety-ridden site where those who were passing could never rest.

Family members were well aware of the significance of guarding the image of whiteness in the white workplace. Some family members used the tense racial dynamics of the workplace to their advantage. Confronted by his ex-wife and his recognizably black children at his job, a man who "worked as white" had no choice but to meet his ex-wife's demands for money. If he did not, she threatened to go to his white wife and expose his past.[110] The black ex-wife must have believed that her ex-husband was most vulnerable at his place of business—perhaps even more vulnerable than at his home—and that she had the upper hand and had the best chance of getting what she wanted from him there. A woman who participated in Day's study feared that her black ancestry would be revealed when Day's work was published. In a humble and earnest letter, the woman implored Day not to include her family's information. Losing her job was just the start of her worries:

> Dear Carrie, I'm very sorry to have to ask you not to use any of that record concerning me. But I made a sworn statement of my status as "w" and it was contested and I swore that there was no

> such record of me. Now if at any time it is found out I will be made to leave my job as well as some other things which will cause me serious embarrassments. Please Carrie on no condition use it for it will ruin my whole life. I can't write you all the details but will explain when I see you.[111]

Although some buckled under the fear of being discovered, others experienced a "strange longing" for black people and black culture, which is captured best in some of the fictional treatments of the phenomenon. Bored by her "pale life," Clare Kendry in Larsen's novel *Passing* is attracted to Harlem "as if by a magnet," as Nathan Huggins explained, because "there is something essential to Negro life—the gaiety, the warmth that she misses in her white world."[112] Clare finds the appeal of Harlem irresistible, and it is "this terrible, this wild desire" that prompts her reckless actions: she attends Negro balls, introduces black (yet passable) women to her unsuspecting white husband, and repeatedly jeopardizes her identity as a white woman.[113]

Huggins's statement risks reifying black life by suggesting that there is "something essential" to it; he romanticizes its "warmth" and "gaiety." Huggins is not alone. The historical record reflects equally broad overstatements about life within African American communities. In *Following the Color Line* (1908), journalist Ray Stannard Baker asked why more light-skinned blacks do not pass. He was given a variety of reasons, all of which referenced the jollity of black life. "Why, white people don't begin to have the good times that Negroes do," one man explained, adding, "They're stiff and cold. They aren't sociable. They don't laugh."[114] These comments are not universal truisms that can be taken at face value. At the same time, the sentiments behind these responses should not be dismissed entirely.

These expressions emphasize a belief in the effusiveness, effervescence, and conviviality of black life that sharply contrasts with white life as bereft of levity and laughter. The dimensions of racial identity—although sometimes imagined, amplified, and emotionally constructed—can be powerfully felt, nonetheless. These responses reveal the profound attachments that some blacks had to African American communities, notwithstanding the tendency to sometimes mischaracterize those attachments as inherent "racial" traits. Many blacks envisioned separating from their communities as psychologically and personally devastating. In some cases, feelings of loss were intolerable, leading some passers to eventually jettison their white identities and to return "home" to the black community. En route to Cincinnati in a luxurious, first-class cabin, one man's initial enthusiasm about passing waned when he began to ache for black fellowship. The man dined, smoked, and occupied a stateroom with white men. At first, he reveled in his secret, but soon, he was consumed by an unbearable loneliness: "In the evening he sat on the upper deck and as he looked over the railing he could see, down below, the Negro passengers and deck hands talking and laughing. After a time, when it grew darker, they began to sing—the inimitable Negro songs. 'That finished me,' he said, 'I got up and went downstairs and took my place among them. I've been a Negro ever since.' "[115]

A handful of options existed for passers who longed for black family and friends. Returning "home" was one possibility; convincing light-skinned relatives to pass was another. One woman explained an unexpected and emotional reunion between her father, who was of German and African American descent, and her aunt, who "went as white," dated white men, and became an actress. While her father was working as a bellhop, his sister came to the hotel as a guest. The two had not seen each other since childhood but immediately recognized one another. They wanted to embrace each other, but they had to restrain themselves. The sister arranged a secret meeting in her hotel room where she proposed that her brother "go as white" and travel with her. But the brother could not go along with his sister's plan; he did not want to lose his black friends or give up his status in high black society.[116]

Other inconvenient—and emotionally taxing—arrangements were possible. Recognizably black relatives could choose to work as maids in the homes of family members who were passing. Those who were passing could leave white family members behind and visit black relatives clandestinely, and passable blacks could visit with family members who lived "on the other side." Well versed in the demands and social limitations imposed by the Jim Crow regime, some family members accepted these terms to maintain relationships with relatives who no longer identified as black. Others may have been disappointed or ashamed of their family members' decisions and felt a sense of relief that they could save face when passers ended relationships with black relatives. Gene Thompson explained, "My mother's brother who lives in Philadelphia is a caterer who passes for white there and is married to a white woman. Very few people know this outside of the family; however, his actions do not present a very devastating problem to us for he has first severed all relations with the family and as a result we never hear from him or even know where he lives in Philadelphia." Although Thompson's mother's family did not condone the practice of passing and were "very touchy about the matter and freeze up if the matter is brought up even in front of the children," the uncle's decision not to "acknowledge either his race or his own family" shielded his relatives from the embarrassment had his story become public. As Thompson remarked, "I can not think of any other outstanding things which we keep locked up as best as we can from the curious tongues and ears of gossips."[117] For some families, it was best to keep the secret not only from whites but also from anyone inclined to spread scandalous information.

Family members and friends were likely to keep these matters in confidence, but on rare occasions, blacks betrayed those who were passing. Perhaps it was a larger sense of racial solidarity that compelled blacks to protect the identities of those who lived "on the other side." In a 1946 essay, "The World and the Jug," Ralph Ellison elaborated on the commonly held belief that blacks had a special "eye" to detect those who were passing: "Although the sociologists tell us that thousands of light skinned Negroes become white each year undetected, most Negroes can spot a paper-thin 'white Negro' every time."[118] Instances of exposure were unusual. As historian Williard Gatewood explained, "once individuals made the decision to pass permanently, most observers agreed that 'it took more than ordinary provocation for colored people to betray them,' because Negroes, of all colors, understood both why they did it and the bitter thralldom and humiliations that came with exposure."[119]

A woman who clerked at department stores in Chicago's Loop, however, described being betrayed more than once. First, she worked as a clerk at Mandel Brothers until she lost her job when a black man betrayed her. Undeterred, she worked as white again in a mail order house. A black postman knew that she was black and visited her desk each morning but never let anyone know her secret. But a black porter disclosed her racial identity when she would not speak to him after she accepted a higher position at Sears Roebuck. These betrayals suggest that though most blacks honored an informal code to protect the identities of those who passed, passers were also bound by particular protocols. And, given their precarious positions, passers could not afford to violate these conventions. When the woman's employers asked for her resignation, they informed her that they did not employ black people and they had mistaken her for "a dark-skinned white person."[120]

A "dark-skinned white person"? Perhaps the employers at Sears Roebuck knew that this woman was black (or at least that she was not white) but decided not to say anything about it. Perhaps this woman was a competent worker who arrived on time, conducted herself properly, met her employers' expectations as to how a white woman should act in the workplace, and therefore, never aroused suspicions. If she was friendly with her coworkers, dressed and spoke appropriately, what difference did her racial background really make? But, once someone called it to her employers' attention (as was the case with the physician who lost the lease to his office), once it became a public issue, her employers may have felt that they had no choice but to redraw the boundary that had been crossed. This story suggests that at times, passing may have functioned as an "open secret"; employers, neighbors, and friends may have suspected or even known that someone was not white, but as long as the passer behaved appropriately, the "secret" was kept.[121] Or perhaps as long as other markers of identity—particularly those of class and gender—remained stable, there was less urgency to expose racial transgressions.

For some who decided to "cross over," the secret could not remain open; the decision to pass required a brutal and absolute severing of familial relations. Ernest Torregano was born into a large black family in New Orleans in 1882. Sometime between 1902 and 1903, Torregano married Violet Perrett, and the couple lived in Torregano's mother's house in New Orleans. In 1904, the couple's daughter, Gladys, was born in her grandmother's house. When Gladys was less than one year old, her father took a job as a railroad porter on a line running between New Orleans and San Francisco. For the next year, Torregano continued this work and stayed with his wife and child when he had a stopover in New Orleans. He soon set up a residence in San Francisco but continued his visits with his family. During these trips, he told friends and family members that he was a warehouseman to prevent them from contacting him in San Francisco.[122] At some point after the 1906 earthquake, Torregano made two decisions: he would study law, and he would pass as white. He sent for his brother, Alfred, who was also able to pass. Torregano became a successful lawyer in San Francisco, and by 1915, he stopped visiting his wife and child in New Orleans, but stayed in touch with some of his black relatives. He maintained two addresses in San Francisco, one for his "white" legal establishment, and another where he could receive mail from his black family members. In 1915, his mother visited him in San Francisco. During that visit, his mother told him that his wife and daughter were dead. When his mother returned home to New Orleans, she informed his wife and daughter that he was dead. There was no further correspondence between Ernest and his wife and daughter, but Ernest did stay in touch with at least one of his sisters. On March 15, 1917, Ernest married a white woman named Pearl Bryant. Their marriage certificate indicated that both of Ernest's parents were white. Violet, believing that her husband was dead, remarried in 1922. Meanwhile, in San Francisco, Ernest Torregano's law practice flourished. He became an expert in bankruptcy law, and he joined the prestigious and politically powerful Lafayette Club.[123] His brother, Alfred, who could also pass, married a white woman and worked as a janitor in a department store.

When Ernest Torregano died in 1957, he left an estate valued at $275,000. His wife Pearl died in 1947, leaving his daughter Gladys, unknowingly, as the sole heir. At this time, Torregano's aunt shared critical information with her: Ernest was Gladys's father, and she had a rightful claim to the estate. When Gladys went to court, her uncle, Alfred, vehemently denied that he knew her or that she was related to Ernest. But once Gladys produced a birth certificate and affidavits from those who knew Torregano in New Orleans, the jig was up. Alfred admitted that he and Ernest had been passing as white, but he maintained that he had never heard of Gladys or her mother. Gladys knew that California law stated that a child would inherit an estate unless the child had been specifically disinherited. This led Gladys to believe that her father intended for her to inherit the estate since, as a lawyer, he was quite familiar with the law. Despite the overwhelming evidence in Gladys's favor, the court ruled against her. In accordance with a peculiar clause in Torregano's will, Gladys—Torregano's daughter as recognized by a parade of witnesses—received one dollar and the rest of the estate was granted to Alfred. Years later, when asked about her grandfather's decision to pass as white, Gladys's daughter stated, "It's something you learn to live with. We are neither proud nor ashamed. I doubt he would have reached such heights of importance if he had been known as a Negro."[124]

"Going as white" permanently created confusion as some family members disappeared across the color line, creating gaps in family genealogy. One woman explained, "My father's people, half of them pass for white so naturally I know nothing about hardly any of them."[125] For others, embarrassment and shame prevented an open discussion of family history: "Not much has been disclosed about the Patterson family. It is our guess that there were too many blood mixtures of which the immediate family is not any too proud to relate. . . . That this family has many skeletons is without a doubt true."[126] Merthilda C. Duhe wrote that her father used passing as a strategy to create a new life for himself; she knew little about him or his family because he left New Orleans and "deserted the family while they were very young and went over to the white side in Chicago."[127] Others expressed uncertainty about the racial backgrounds of their ancestors. One man questioned his grandfather's race and explained, "Father was always sensitive about that side of his family."[128] When asked whether her relatives in Detroit "go for colored or do they go for white," Mrs. Clemens responded, "I don't know, and I don't know what I am. We are 100 per cent American and that is all we can say."[129] Raymond Brownbow did not know much about his maternal grandmother, a mixed-race house servant who was "described as being very nearly white." As he explained, "I know very little about her, because it seems that my mother was and is a bit reluctant to discuss her. I remember my mother once telling me that she couldn't stand the remarks that people would make upon learning of her mother's mixed blood, and for that reason she refrained from talking much about her."[130]

Others had no choice but to rely on rumors and speculations as to the whereabouts of family members. The only information that Anthony Driver Chase could cobble together about his grandmother, Hester Ann, was that she was "light enough to pass for white and had long red hair which reached her waist"; her father was a slaveholder; and she had a brother who "went west, married a white woman and passed for white," and "it is rumored that he became wealthy."[131] Some family members were able to pass whereas others could not. One relative hinted that other family members passed by explaining, "Margot did not know much of her origin. It seems that her brown skin had been responsible for her separation from the rest of the family who were blonde."[132] Other families risked exposing relatives who had crossed the color line by providing too many details about their background. In response to sociologist E. Franklin Frazier's request for his family's history in 1932, T. S. Inborden explained, "I will say that I have not more than one sixteenth Negro blood in me if indeed that much. The rest is Mohawk and Caucasian. To publish this would cause a lot of talk and embarrassment. The first Governor of Texas was . . . perhaps half brother to my grandmother."[133] Others lacked critical information to piece together their family histories. Emblematic of the tensions created by passing, such omissions and doubts led to profound feelings of desertion, disconnection, and incompleteness. One man, describing his great uncle, explained, "I know of one brother, [the] father of a large family. They passed over into the other race and were finally lost to those who remained in the negro race."[134] Trying to make sense of an absent father who "looked like white," Pearle Foreman wrote, "The strangest thing was, no one ever told me about my father's people or from whence he came. I have not been able to find out any information concerning him, only that I resemble him in every respect."[135] Once family members "crossed over," they were usually lost, essentially dead to their families.

But the equation of passing to death too quickly dismisses both the ambiguity and the logic of passing, as well as the tolerance and understanding that family members extended to those who passed. Why else would a relative agree to work as a maid in a family member's home in the interest of continuing an untenable relationship in the Jim Crow era? As passing disrupted family life and made certain topics of conversation awkward if not impossible, it also called into question one's own identity and sense of personhood.

The question that Day Shepherd posed—"How would anybody know who they were without their people?"—suggests much broader and more intimate meanings of race and racial identity and reveals the interconnectedness of notions of self and family.

In every historical period, there are those who decide against passing, even though they are often mistaken as white. Fredi Washington first appeared as a chorus girl in *Shuffle Along* (1921), one of the most successful African American Broadway musicals, but she is best known for her role as Peola, a light-skinned black woman who breaks her mother's heart by choosing to pass as white in the 1934 film *Imitation of Life.* As *Esquire* magazine reported in 1935, the scenes between Peola and her mother stole the show: "The tragedy of the colored girl trying to pass for white completely overshadows the artificial little troubles concocted for the white folks: the audience leans intently forward whenever Louise Beavers (Aunt Delilah) or Fredi Washington (the daughter) is in the scene and simply relaxes even during the dramatic moments of the story proper."[136] In May 1935, Universal Studios reported that *Imitation of Life* was the largest grossing film of that year so far, which led many movie houses to return the film to the screen.[137]

Washington's appearance—her blue-gray eyes, white complexion, and light brown hair—and her compelling performance in *Imitation of Life* led some of her fans to presume that Washington had firsthand experience with passing.[138] Washington explained, "If I made Peola seem real enough to merit such statements, I consider such statements compliments and makes me feel I've done my job fairly way," but she was clear that her "private life is in no way similar to that of Delilah's daughter."[139] When the German philanthropist Otto Kahn saw Washington dancing at Club Alabam in Manhattan and suggested that she change her name and pass as French,

Figure 3.6. Fredi Washington, an African American actress, best known for her portrayal of "Peola" in the 1934 film *Imitation of Life.*

Photograph by Carl Van Vechten. Courtesy of the Van Vechten Trust. James Weldon Johnson Collection, Beinecke Rare Book and Manuscript Library, Yale University, New Haven, Connecticut.

she responded, "I want to be what I am, nothing else."[140] Washington was often asked why she chose not to pass. She would reply, "Because I'm honest, firstly, and secondly, you don't have to be white to be good. I've spent most of my life trying to prove that to those who think otherwise. . . . I am a Negro and I am proud of it." Washington would allow whites to speak disparagingly about African Americans and then shock them with the truth about her racial identity. In the presence of whites who assumed she was white too, Washington remarked, "I give them plenty of rope. . . . I let them talk, hang themselves, and then I quietly say, 'I'm Negro.'"[141]

Washington did pass as white occasionally. When she was traveling through the South with Duke Ellington and his band, she would go into ice-cream parlors and buy ice cream for the band members, who were excluded from restaurants. Whites called her a "nigger lover."[142]

Described as "honest, sincere, and fearless," Washington rarely held her tongue. She was a passionate spokesperson for blacks in theater and film, she founded the Negro Actors Guild in 1937, and she wrote a column called "Fredi Says" for the *People's Voice,* the progressive weekly published by Adam Clayton Powell Jr., the pastor and first black politician to represent New York in Congress.[143] She was an outspoken critic of black artists whose calls for equal rights were not loud enough. Washington perceived the struggle for civil rights as a lifelong battle: "I am here as a Negro—then that's the way I'll be and I'll fight until the day I die—or until there isn't anything left to fight against."[144]

In stripping away one's ascribed status, passing offers a sharper angle of vision onto the personal meanings of racial identity from the perspective of black individuals and communities. The communal politics of passing demonstrate the insufficiency of explanations of passing as a rebellious, individualistic practice and instead reveal the ways that race operated on the most private levels and in the innermost reaches of black communities. Passing—the vexed decision to break with a sense of communion and walk away from what was most precious about African American life—is a vehicle to recover and to concretize the most elusive and intimate meanings of African American group identities.

At the conclusion of a 1952 essay, Langston Hughes described the moment when he arrived at the Haus Vaterland in Berlin and two black waiters greeted him enthusiastically: "Hey now! What gives in Harlem?" This exclamation, uttered several thousand miles away from the "Race Capital," is reminiscent of the question, "who are your people?" as it suggests an elastic sense of connection and kinship, grounded in the sharing of something much more elusive than skin color or residence in Harlem. A similar experience occurred when Hughes was in Shanghai: riding in a rickshaw, he saw a "very colored man" in another rickshaw, traveling in the opposite direction. As the two made eye contact, the following exchange occurred: "As soon as we spied each other through the traffic in the busy street, he half rose and I half rose, and both of us yelled, 'Hy!' The rickshaw went on. I never saw him again the whole time I was in China. I never knew his name. But race had greeted race across space. And I remember his grin much more clearly than I remember the features of any of the [other] faces."[145]

To be sure, in these foreign contexts, it was skin color that allowed Hughes to make these connections and to recognize the waiters in Berlin and the "very colored" man in the rickshaw in Shanghai. But was it really *race* that "greeted race across space"? As the experiences of many of those who passed as white as well as many of those who were left behind reveal, race is so much more than this. Race functions as a proxy for a shared and expansive set of experiences, memories, jokes, stories, and songs. It was only because "race" was so much more than either biology or shared oppression that Hughes could find the grin on the "very colored" man's face so memorable.

4

Searching for a New Soul in Harlem

In a 1932 letter to Carl Van Vechten, Nella Larsen described a real-life exploit reminiscent of a scene in a Harlem Renaissance novel. In the company of Grace Nail Johnson, James Weldon Johnson's light-skinned wife, and without her own identifiably black husband, Fisk physicist Elmer Imes, Larsen easily passed as white:

> You will be amused that I who have never tried this much discussed "passing" stunt have waited until I reached the deep South to put it over. Grace Johnson and I drove about fifty miles south of here the other day and then walked to the best restaurant in a rather conservative town called Murfreesboro and demanded lunch and got it, plus all the service in the world and an invitation to return. Everybody here seems to think that quite a stunt.[1]

The "stunt" that Nella Larsen and Grace Nail Johnson pulled off in a restaurant outside Murfreesboro mirrors the decision of Irene

Redfield, the light-skinned protagonist in Larsen's 1929 novel, *Passing,* to "cool off" on the whites-only rooftop restaurant of the Drayton Hotel in Chicago. Irene disdained the practice of passing, but away from her neighborhood in Harlem and unaccompanied by her recognizably black husband and son, she took the elevator up to the hotel's roof, which she described as "like being wafted upward on a magic carpet to another world, pleasant, quiet, and strangely remote from the sizzling one that she had left below."[2] Neither Larsen nor Johnson desired to "live white" but rather decided to pass just long enough to enjoy lunch and good service in an all-white establishment. Perhaps those in the restaurant read Larsen and Johnson as white because of the car they drove, the clothing they wore, and the way they carried themselves. Given the assigned and inflexible roles for blacks and whites in the Jim Crow era, perhaps it was assumed that these two racially ambiguous women must be white simply because no right-minded black person would dare sit down and eat with whites, and certainly not in the "best restaurant" in town. And, even if someone had looked twice at these two women, it would have been impolite to scrutinize their racial backgrounds.

Passing has two sides. The delight of "fooling white folks" and prevailing over an unjust racial regime was often accompanied by the agony of losing one's sense of self and one's family. At the restaurant in Murfreesboro, Nella Larsen and Grace Nail Johnson did not wrestle with the weighty side of passing; instead, they reveled in knowing that they had won a small battle against Jim Crow.

The two sides of passing collided during the Harlem Renaissance in both the novels and the lives of many of the movement's most acclaimed authors. At the same time, a third side emerged. Similar to the Reconstruction era, the Harlem Renaissance opened up new discussions of racial ambiguity and new possibilities for racial identification. Late nineteenth-century literature often presented racially mixed people as liminal figures who were tormented by the racially degraded black society in which they lived and the white society into which they would never be accepted. These figures, described as "tragic mulattos," had limited options—they could embrace their African American identity and become race leaders, they could pass as white, or they could slump into despair and despondency.[3] The Harlem Renaissance, on the other hand, opened the possibility of an authentic and viable middle ground. A new opportunity for absolution arose by staking out a synthesis of black and white, or a "new race," in which black folk culture was foundational and restorative. Crafting an American version of *La Raza Cósmica* (1925), the treatise written by Mexican philosopher José Vasconcelos, some artists hoped that this "new race" might achieve W. E. B. Du Bois's famous aspiration of "merging two warring souls into a better one." The racial politics of the Harlem Renaissance promised to open new avenues to move beyond the double-barreled world of black and white. Passing had been a losing game historically, but it was no longer the only game for those who appeared racially indeterminate.[4] The Harlem Renaissance opened an alternative strategy for achieving racial wholeness, which dispensed with the tragic mulatto figure and allowed for the recognition of mixed-race identities.

The beginning of the twentieth century represented a period of tremendous social and cultural flowering for African Americans, even as the Jim Crow regime tightened in the South. A generation of black activists and artists emerged during the first waves of the Great Migration to embrace a new attitude toward blackness and to affirm black culture. The Harlem Renaissance ushered in transformations in African American life and presented African Americans as they had never been seen before—as artists, as intellectuals, and as fully formed individuals, not grotesque caricatures. Stalled political and economic progress led race leaders to see cultural advancement as a more powerful offensive in the fight against Jim Crow. Racial pride surged and Harlem became a "race capital," a cultural mecca that southern and Caribbean migrants, socialites and day laborers, drag ball queens and middle-class reformers all called home. Those who did not live in Harlem were drawn to it like a magnet, eager to experience its exuberant and often salacious nightlife, and to judge for themselves whether or not Harlem lived up to its billing as the "Nightclub Capital of the World." The Harlem Renaissance was nothing short of a cultural revolution. As Alain Locke roused his readers in *The New Negro* (1925), the manifesto of the movement, "We are witnessing the resurgence of a people. . . . Negro life is . . . finding a new soul."[5] At the same time as Locke voiced these enthusiastic pronouncements and as African American artists and intellectuals became more visible, passing became one of the most marketable and most popular themes in literature.

Indeed, the nation witnessed a veritable explosion of literary work on racial passing precisely at a moment when black artists celebrated blackness and racial pride. During the 1920s and the early 1930s, black and white authors alike found avid readers and enthusiastic audiences as a market for novels and plays about passing flourished. First published in 1912, James Weldon Johnson's novel, *The Autobiography of an Ex-Colored Man,* only became widely popular upon its rerelease at the height of the Renaissance in 1927.

Knopf's announcement that "the AUTOBIOGRAPHY is at once an intensely absorbing tale and a document of unusual value . . . a book that no one interested in the Negro can afford to overlook," struck a chord with readers in 1927 that it had not in 1912 when it had received scant attention. The blond-haired, blue-eyed Walter White, who had passed as white to investigate lynchings in the South, published *Flight* in 1926, the story of a light-skinned woman born in New Orleans. Both of Nella Larsen's major works, *Quicksand* (1928) and *Passing* (1929), addressed the theme of racial ambiguity. Jessie Fauset, one of the "midwives" of the Renaissance, wrote to Langston Hughes in 1924 to announce that her second book would tackle the topic of passing. She hoped that a strategic title might make the book appealing to black and white readers. As she explained, "I am going to call the book 'Philippa Passes,'—because that will carry the idea which I want carried to my colored readers and will carry a widely different idea to my white readers."[6] Fauset would rename her book *Plum Bun* and publish it in 1928. It became a best seller, receiving glowing reviews in the *New Republic* and the *New York Times,* and selling 100,000 copies within the first ninety days of publication. Black authors were not the only ones to capitalize on the popularity of the theme of passing. William Faulkner wrote of Joe Christmas's "parchment" skin in his 1932 novel, *Light in August,* and Edna Ferber penned the 1926 novel *Show Boat,* which was adapted as a musical in 1927. In the musical, leading lady Julie La Verne harbors a dark secret that is nearly revealed when one of the black characters puzzles over how Julie knows the lyrics of a song that only "colored folks" sing.

Literary critics and historians have studied the Harlem Renaissance extensively, resurrecting its lesser-known figures and deliberating on its dazzling personalities, its myriad goals, its vigorous debates, and its enduring legacies.[7] But the Renaissance also reveals an unprecedented historical moment when new conceptions of African American group identities were possible; when, in the aftermath of the Great War, national and ethnic identities were being reimagined. The Renaissance expanded notions of racial identity. Racial indeterminacy and hybridity emerged as new possibilities and alternative responses to passing. White-skinned African Americans could choose not to abandon their blackness but rather to embrace both sides of their putative racial selves.

Still, it was an unstable and transitory recourse and one laden with loss. Some writers like Jean Toomer disavowed a singularly black identity. Toomer would eventually abandon his insistence on racial hybridity and adopt a position of "racelessness" that, ironically, was not altogether different from passing. Unlike his grandfather, P. B. S. Pinchback, who during an earlier but notably different period of racial openness pleaded for a "white man's chance," Toomer appealed for an "American's chance," emphasizing his multiple racial origins and the subtleties and multivalence of his identity. Meanwhile, other artists, like Nella Larsen, struggled to negotiate an identity troubled by the absence of family bonds and by the intersections of race, gender, class, sexuality, and respectability. Langston Hughes used passing as a theme to satirize the illogic of race relations. At the same time, he hoped to connect his atypical upbringing with the experiences of the black masses, the inspiration for much of his work. These authors confronted the problem of racial indeterminacy in their own lives as well as in their fiction. Each experienced loss in grappling with the problem of fashioning an "unraced" personal identity in a racist society, struggling, as Toomer put it, "to name this reality adequately."[8]

These authors mark three distinct points on a spectrum. The choices that they made and the lives that they lived all circled around loss. Toomer chose ambiguity and a racially unmarked identity, yet lost the ability to be accepted for who he believed himself to be. Larsen emphasized the tragedy of passing and the pain of losing nurturing family connections. Hughes acknowledged the absurdity of racial categories in his writings, but chose to lose his mother and father in order to embrace black people and a black racial identity.

Jean Toomer: An American, Simply an American

Jean Toomer's racial identity—particularly whether he passed as white—has been the subject of long and lively debates. Some scholars have suggested that Toomer's grandfather, P. B. S. Pinchback, was white and claimed a black identity opportunistically, to take advantage of an auspicious moment for African Americans during Reconstruction. Others have argued that Toomer identified as black, but just long enough to produce his one and only novel, *Cane,* published in 1923. Toomer made several attempts to make sense of an indeterminate racial identity by speaking plainly, "When I live with the blacks, I'm a Negro. When I live with the whites, I'm white, or, better, a foreigner. I used to puzzle my own brain with the question. But now I'm done with it." Perhaps Toomer was "done with it" by the 1930s because he spent the better part of his early career groping in vain to find the appropriate language to explain it.

Toomer's nearly white skin and dark wavy hair made it difficult for anyone, including African Americans, to pin down his racial identity. In a letter dated April 23, 1923, Claude Barnett, an entrepreneur and founder of the Associated Negro Press, wrote to Toomer, asking him to clarify "who and also what [he is]." Barnett explained that he and some of his friends and colleagues had been debating Toomer's racial identity, and he hoped that Toomer could settle the matter once and for all. According to Barnett, Toomer's literary "style and finish" led some to believe that Toomer must be white, whereas others, including Barnett himself, felt that only someone who had "peeked behind the veil" could interpret black life so ably.[9]

Toomer responded with a detailed and knotty disquisition on his racial identity. He assured Barnett and his friends that they were not the first to raise questions about his background. "Inquiries of like nature" had arrived from all around the country and given that the "true and complete answer" was one of great complexity, Toomer did not expect it to be understood or accepted until after his death. To grasp Toomer's particular racial composition would require a sophisticated understanding of racial mixture, "tradition, culture and environment." Put simply, as the grandson of the black politician P. B. S. Pinchback, Toomer had undeniably "peeked behind the veil." By locating himself through his familial relationships—his people—he identified as black. Moreover, he had experienced black folk culture, which had transformed his literary work. Toomer became "body and soul, Negroid" after witnessing the undeniably "Negro" nature of "the old folk-songs, syncopated rhythms, the rich sweet taste of dark skinned life."[10]

In response to Barnett, Toomer attempted to explain his hybrid identity, fully aware that it might not make sense to his contemporaries. Toomer had lived on both sides of the color line. He was born into a sumptuous lifestyle in a wealthy white neighborhood and accepted into the white world of Washington as a result of his grandfather's political stature and wide social networks. When his

Figure 4.1. Portrait of Jean Toomer, poet and novelist during the Harlem Renaissance.

Courtesy of James Weldon Johnson Collection, Beinecke Rare Book and Manuscript Library, Yale University, New Haven, Connecticut.

grandfather's debts swelled and the family's fortunes declined, Toomer and his family moved to the thirteen hundred block of U Street, a black neighborhood near Howard University. Toomer attended a black high school—the prestigious Dunbar High School, which served the children of the black elite—and he encountered segregated aspects of the city. Toomer offered a complex statement of his racial identity, one that combined essentialized notions of race, including the "inherent gifts" that stemmed from the "Negro blood in his veins," with more experiential, aesthetic explanations.

Toomer's self-discovery was rooted in the black folk culture that he encountered in the backwoods of Georgia during his southern sojourn in the fall of 1921, when he worked as the acting principal of the Sparta Agricultural and Industrial Institute in Hancock County. The spirituals and work songs that he heard had shaken him to his very core, but he folded these cultural forms into his American identity, an identity that he described as stemming from both black and white people. "They were like a part of me," Toomer wrote to describe the songs that he identified with "so intensely" that he lost his own identity and found himself reborn in the "cane- and cotton-fields, and in the souls of black and white people in the small southern town." In this rural culture of Sparta, Georgia, in the melding of its black and white elements, Toomer experienced a homecoming. He found expression of his own soul, once bifurcated, now made whole: "My seed was planted in myself down there."[11] Toomer sought to fashion the raw materials of black rural life into a usable aesthetic that would renew his writing and infuse it with greater vitality.[12] He viewed black folk life as a wellspring of creativity and artistic innovation. The black peasantry offered simplicity and religiosity, and functioned as an antidote to the corruption and double-dealing that had compromised, if not altogether ruined, American society. He explained to Barnett that there is "no reason why [his] style could not have come from an American with Negro blood in his veins." Here, Toomer begins to sketch what would later become his vision of a new race, an American race, which embraced black folk influences as its most defining and regenerative elements.

Perhaps a black aesthetic, anchored in the rural South, could offer therapeutic healing and transform a desiccated America that had reached a cataclysm of its own making in the aftermath of World War I. The carnage and psychic devastation of the Great War coupled with the dizzying pace of technological advances laid bare the need for a self-satisfied and enervated Western world to experiment with new approaches and new ideas. For the first time, black artists performed on a national and international stage, and audiences received their performances enthusiastically as unique cultural contributions with a complex and compelling history all their own. By embracing black folk culture and black folk, artists and writers believed that they had found, as historian James Campbell writes, "an evangel, whose message would heal a wounded world."[13]

Around the time that Toomer responded to Barnett, he finished writing *Cane,* a modernist, experimental, and highly acclaimed novel and collection of poems. *Cane* was a swan song that mourned the inevitable passing of African American folk culture in the South. Toomer solemnly anticipated the assimilation of rural black folk into the "general outlines of American civilization, or of American chaos."[14] He expected some aspects of black folk life to continue to inflect the psychology of African Americans, but he knew that the richness of the culture that he experienced in Georgia was fleeting. And he was troubled by what kind of society would remain once the vitality and verve of the rural folks were gone. "One hundred years from now," Toomer wrote, "these Negroes, if they exist at all will live in art. They are passing. Let us grab and hold them while there is still time."[15] A son of Washington's fabled black elite who had been baptized in the Roman Catholic Church, Toomer had discovered a new self, a new body and soul that he believed could give him purpose and a more robust literary voice. The folk not only represented a resource that Toomer could mine to make his novels and poetry hale and hearty; the folk was a vehicle through which Toomer could suture his multiple identities. Toomer wrestled with the question, What constitutes racial identity? and his experiences in Georgia underscored the fact that racial affinity was made of much more than skin color. Skin color, according to Toomer, overdetermined and distorted racial identity. For Toomer, race was social and did not inhere in individuals but rather was created and experienced by groups of individuals. Race was also inherently mixed. Toomer claimed an American identity that, while rooted in black cultural forms like spirituals and work songs, could not extricate its black elements from its white components.

Toomer was right. The authentic black folk culture that he found in Georgia was passing. In "Song of the Son," a poem published in *Cane,* Toomer narrates this loss: "In time, for though the sun is setting on / A song-lit race of slaves, it has not set; / Though late, O Soil, it is not too late yet / To catch thy plaintive soul, leaving, soon gone, / Leaving, to catch thy plaintive soul soon gone."[16] The South was undergoing dramatic transformations by the 1920s as staggering numbers of African Americans fled the South and laid their hopes for better lives at the North's door during the post–World War I waves of the Great Migration.

Toomer worried that this loss would be exacerbated by the problem that other artists, particularly members of the middle-class black intelligentsia, steeped in a politics of respectability, "could not see it" and might even "be directly hostile" to black folk culture. In a 1922 letter to Lola Ridge, the editor of the literary magazine *Broom,* Toomer wrote of his deep disappointment in the "anemia and timidity (emotional) in folks" who were just a generation or two removed from slavery. Toomer was dismayed to find that these people, even though they were "full blooded" blacks, were "afraid to hold hands, much less love."[17] As the beauty, simplicity, and intimacy of rural culture disappeared, the higher strata of southern blacks expressed ambivalence, if not disdain, toward traditional forms of black culture. Toomer bemoaned the fact that the "Negroes in the town" derided spirituals by calling them "shouting." They preferred the faster-paced, urbane music that emanated from Victrolas and player-pianos. To Toomer's deep regret, the forces of modern life were too swift and too powerful for the folk: "The folk-spirit was walking in to die on the modern desert. That spirit was so beautiful. Its death so tragic."[18] This sorrowful passing is the foundation of Toomer's writing in *Cane.*

Toomer's authenticity as "body and soul, Negroid" and the artistic and emotional heft and inspiration that he drew from southern black folk won his work high praise. But in the literary world, it also lodged him as a Negro artist writing about distinctly Negro themes.[19] William Stanley Braithwaite wrote, "Jean Toomer is a bright morning star of a new day of the race in literature,"[20] and Countee Cullen described *Cane* as "a real race contribution, a classical portrayal of things as they are."[21] After reading one of Toomer's essays in the *Double Dealer,* Sherwood Anderson wrote to Toomer, "I liked it more than I can say. It strikes a note that I have long been wanting to hear come from one of your race. . . . Your work is of special significance to me because it is the first negro work that strikes me as really negro."[22] These commendations collapsed the intricate and multiracial identity that Toomer sought to cultivate. To these observers, Toomer was unquestionably gifted, but first and foremost, he was a Negro writer.

By the 1930s, Toomer would become more reticent, even hostile, to the notion that he was Negro, "body and soul." In this process of self-formation, Toomer wrestled with his ideas about race and with his understanding of his place in the world. He tried to carve out space for himself and a racial identity that was neither black nor white.

Toomer's frustration with the racial limitations that others placed on him reached a fever pitch in July 1930 when James Weldon Johnson wrote Toomer for permission to include some of his poems in a revised edition of *The Book of American Negro Poetry* anthology. The earlier version had been released before many of the younger writers of the Harlem Renaissance had come of age. Toomer offered a convoluted yet unequivocal response to Johnson's request. Toomer described the "various" and "mixed stocks" of which Americans are comprised and stressed that as complicated as the "matter of descent" might be, "we are all Americans." To Toomer's mind, racial divisions or "divisions presumably based on descents" had been overstated.[23] No poem of Toomer's would be published in Johnson's updated edition. Toomer was insistent that his poems did not belong in a Negro anthology because he saw himself as an American, not as a Negro. As Toomer explained, he recognized that "the negro art movement has had some valuable results," but "it [was simply] not for [him]." He wished to withdraw his name and his work "from all things which emphasize or tend to emphasize racial or cultural divisions."[24] Toomer hoped that Johnson and others would reach the same conclusion. Rather than defining poems as Negro or Anglo-Saxon, Toomer hoped that his work could be recognized as primarily a product of himself, and secondarily, as a product of America's long history of racial intermixture.

Toomer hoped to be known not as the first great "Negro" author, as his white publishers and colleagues insisted, but rather as a great American author. For a moment, Toomer believed that Sherwood Anderson, author of *Winesburg, Ohio,* might understand his predicament. *Winesburg, Ohio*—published in 1919, composed of twenty-two short stories, and set in a small town—shared *Cane*'s modernist and unconventional structure. Like Toomer, Anderson believed that black folk culture could be scoured as a source of artistic creativity. Toomer held Anderson in the highest regard, but Anderson's narrow view of Toomer's racial identity would ultimately disappoint him. In their early correspondence, Toomer spoke of being profoundly moved by Anderson's work. Toomer saw similarities in the content and the spirit of *Cane* and *Winesburg, Ohio,* and he was pleased to know that the appreciation was mutual: "I think that you touch most people that way. And when my own stuff wins a response from you, I feel a linking together within me, a deep joy, and an outward flowing."[25] This outward flowing, or Anderson's "Yea! to life" as Toomer called it, correlated with the impulses that Toomer had to write about the natural elements of rural life and to "reach for the beauty that the Negro has in him."[26] Just as Anderson perceived Toomer's writing as "really Negro," Toomer returned the compliment, praised Anderson, and expressed his indebtedness to him for "evok[ing] an emotion, a sense of beauty that is easily more Negro than almost anything [he had] seen."[27]

Despite this seemingly profound connection between Toomer and Anderson and despite the shared admiration for the emotional depth of each other's work, Toomer quickly became frustrated with

Anderson's misunderstanding of the complexity of his racial identity. After exchanging a few letters with Anderson, Toomer wrote to his close friend and leading light of the "lost generation," Waldo Frank, to explain this ideological conflict: "Sherwood Anderson and I have exchanged a few letters. I don't think we will go very far. He limits me to Negro. To try to tie me to one of my parts is surely to loose [*sic*] me. My own letters have taken Negro as a point, and from there have circled out. Sherwood, for the most part, ignores the circles. In direct contact I am certain that I would like him. . . . But I need something more."[28]

Toomer was equally frustrated by his publisher's decision to feature *Cane* as a "Negro novel." Horace Liveright, Toomer's publisher, was certain that he had hit upon an idea that would boost *Cane*'s sales. Liveright did not want readers to accidentally overlook Toomer's racial identity; instead, he wanted a "definite note sounded about [Toomer's] colored blood," so that the "real human interest value" of Toomer's work would be abundantly clear. There was certainly no reason to "dodge it," Liveright insisted, and instead, he suggested that a pamphlet that spotlighted Toomer's black racial identity be included with the review copies of *Cane.*[29]

Toomer was aggrieved by Liveright's plan, but worse still, he was stung and deeply disappointed in a man whom he believed understood him, a man whom he considered a friend. In a sharp-tongued response dated September 23, 1923, Toomer fumed, "My racial composition and my position in the world are realities which I alone may determine. . . . I expect and demand acceptance of myself on their basis. I do not expect to be told what I should consider myself to be." Especially unnerving was Liveright's suggestion that Toomer was "dodging" the matter. Toomer fired back, "Nor do I expect you as my publisher, and I hope, as my friend, to either directly or indirectly state that this basis contains any element of dodging. In fact, if my relationship with you is to be what I'd like it to be, I must insist that you never use such a word, such a thought, again." Toomer was hopeful that Liveright could market *Cane* to reach the largest audience possible and he welcomed his publisher to "make use of whatever racial factors" he wished in order to secure such a readership. While Toomer gave his consent for Liveright to "feature Negro," he made it plain that he should not expect him to do the same.[30]

Around the same time as Liveright unveiled his problematic proposal for *Cane*'s publicity campaign, Alain Locke decided to reprint stories from *Cane* in *The New Negro,* and Waldo Frank described Toomer as a "gifted Negro writer" in the preface to a revised edition. For Waldo Frank to pigeonhole Toomer as a "gifted Negro writer" must have been especially wounding since Toomer thought of Frank as his "surrogate" brother. The two had traveled together to Spartanburg, South Carolina, while both worked on novels about black life: Toomer was writing *Cane,* and Frank was working on *Holiday,* a protest novel against lynching. Frank's dark complexion and his association with Toomer allowed him to pass as black and to pose as Toomer's "blood brother." Toomer had written that "no one in this country (which means the world so far as *Cane* is concerned) but you my brother" truly understands "what my writing was about."[31] Toomer's inner circle, even his "blood brother," failed to understand him. To promote the book as a great Negro novel, written by a great Negro author, was not only to grossly oversimplify and flatten the complexities of a racial identity that Toomer earnestly tried to account for, but also, to Toomer's mind, to exploit the racial content of *Cane* for crass commercial purposes.

Toomer lamented that more fitting language did not exist for him to accurately and articulately express his ideas about his racial identity. Instead, he relied on phrasing about an "American identity," explaining, "As for me personally, I see myself as an American, simply an American."[32] Perhaps by describing himself as an American, Toomer believed that his identity would be more comprehensible to others. But Toomer's correspondence with Horace Liveright and Waldo Frank offers a far more revealing expression of the complex nexus that composed his identity. Here and elsewhere, Toomer made a claim for a different kind of identity, one that is racially ambiguous, multivalent, and interlaced. As Toomer explained to Jack McClure, editor of the *Double Dealer* magazine, he was "striving for a spiritual fusion analogous to the fact of racial intermingling." Such an endeavor—claiming to be the product of racial mixture rather than assuming a singularly black identity—had been "rough riding."[33] The "something more" that Toomer needed from Sherwood Anderson did not mean that Toomer endeavored to pass as white. Cautioning that he could easily be "loosed" if all of his "parts" were not acknowledged, Toomer made an effort to express a subjectivity that remained vexingly vague, ill-defined, and unrecognizable. Despite the openness and liberality of the racial politics of the Harlem Renaissance, Toomer found that he was constrained by the limits of racial thinking during this period.

To disavow a black racial identity did not necessarily mean to pass as white. Toomer's dilemma underscores a core problem of racially indeterminate identities—not only was the language to express a mixed-race identity nonexistent, but a person who claimed a racially indeterminate identity would likely be perceived as false and misguided, or as Liveright would have it, "dodging" his true identity. Toomer's complex racial identity was just as illegible to fellow artists during the Harlem Renaissance, immersed in a politics of racial either/or and of racial authenticity, as it is to contemporary critics.[34] As Henry Louis Gates has argued, "In a curious and perhaps perverse sense, Toomer's was a gesture of racial castration, which, if not silencing his voice literally, then at least transformed his deep black bass into a false soprano."[35] This line of thought—that Toomer was literally silenced after he disclaimed a black identity—seemed especially convincing since Toomer never published another work as celebrated as *Cane,* or as James Weldon Johnson explained, he "never worked further in the rich vein he had struck."[36] Gates's choice of strong sexual metaphors equated black to masculine and white to feminine and placed Toomer somewhere in the middle, betwixt and between. To be anything other than a "deep black bass" was to be intrinsically inauthentic. Racial inauthenticity (or "racial castration" according to Gates) also raised questions about Toomer's manhood. Emasculated as a (white) "false soprano," Toomer lacked the ardor and virility to produce another work like *Cane.* And Gates, by reinforcing the binaries that Toomer hoped to deconstruct, left no room for a racialized or gendered position between or beyond a "deep *black* bass" and a (white) "false soprano." Gates was not the only critic to perceive Toomer's racial "disidentification," to borrow literary critic Siobhan Somerville's term, as evidence of Toomer's immaturity, egotism, and personal confusion.[37] Many critics have pointed to the content of *Cane* and have argued that the work was not only a "swan song" for black folk culture but also a farewell to Toomer's black identity. *Cane* was a "parting gift," Alice Walker wrote, an emotional send-off to the Negro within himself.[38]

There is scant evidence to suggest that Toomer occasionally passed as white, however. There were rumors that he passed while a student at the University of Wisconsin.[39] He is listed as "white" on his marriage license, but this must be considered alongside other errors on the license, including the misspelling of his mother's maiden name. Perhaps Toomer did not want to be recognized as part of his storied family and mumbled his mother's maiden name to the clerk. Perhaps Toomer, already irked by racial categorizations, told the clerk that he was white, recognizing the folly of such classifications. Given that his fiancée Margery Latimer was white, Toomer may have thought that it would be easier to be listed as white on the marriage license. There are countless reasons why Toomer might have chosen a white identity at this moment. But since Toomer's father's name, Nathan Toomer, is listed on the marriage license, it is unlikely that Toomer was trying to obscure his racial origins since his father was known as a black man (though he occasionally passed as white). Moreover, a marriage license is a highly mediated record that reveals just as much about the licensing official, a powerful intercessor, as it does about one's self-identity. The clerk may have misread Toomer as white, particularly in the company of a white woman, and listed him as such.

Perhaps we should read Henry Louis Gates's recent assertion in the 2011 *Norton Critical Edition* of *Cane* that Toomer passed as white as a contemporary example of "ignoring the circles" that Toomer so desperately wanted Sherwood Anderson to see in 1923. Gates's evidence—Toomer's choice to live in Greenwich Village rather than Harlem and his refusal to send poems to James Weldon Johnson for *The Book of American Negro Poetry*—seems insufficient to prove that Toomer decided to leave behind a black identity. A more careful reading shows Toomer not as confused, racially misidentified, or frustrated with the limits of language, but rather struggling to convey a holistic self-understanding. As he explained to Waldo

TRIPLICATE

License Number 4301

STATE OF WISCONSIN
Department of Health—Bureau of Vital Statistics
CERTIFICATE OF MARRIAGE

PLACE OF MARRIAGE: County of ____ Township of ____ or Village of ____ or City of ____

I, Daniel Corrigan hereby certify that on the 30th day of October, A. D. 1931 at Portage in the County of Columbia, State of Wisconsin, Jean Toomer of Chicago State of Illinois and Margery Latimer of Portage State of Wisconsin were by me united in marriage as authorized by a Marriage License issued for that purpose by the County Clerk of ____ County and State of Wisconsin, numbered 4301 and dated the 28th day of October A. D. 1931.

We, the undersigned, were present at the Marriage of Jean Toomer and Margery Latimer as set forth in the foregoing certificate, at their request, and heard their declarations that they took each other for husband and wife.

Two Witnesses: ____

Signature of person officiating and P. O. Address: Name Daniel Corrigan; P. O. Address Manitowoc, Wis.

GROOM		BRIDE	
Name	Jean Toomer	Name	Marjery Latimer
Residence	Chicago, Illinois	Residence	Portage, Wisconsin
Age	36	Age	32
Color	White	Color	White
No. of Marriages	1st	No. of Marriages	1st
Birthplace	Washington, D.C.	Birthplace	Wisconsin
Nationality	American	Nationality	American
Relationship	None	Relationship	None
Occupation	Author and Lecturer	Occupation	Writer
Name of Father, Guardian or Curator	Nathan Toomer	Name of Father, Guardian or Curator	Clark Latimer
Maiden name of Mother	Nina Reichback	Maiden name of Mother	Laurie Bodine

If previously Married: Date of Marriage ____ To whom Married ____ Date of Death ____ Date of Divorce ____ Where Divorced ____ By what Court Divorced ____ To whom Divorce granted ____

Was a special dispensation issued? No

Date of Issue October 28 1931 — H. R. Tonjes, County Clerk.

Filed ____ 19__ Local Register.

Figure 4.2. Jean Toomer's marriage license. Toomer married a white woman, Margery Latimer. Note that Toomer is listed as white.

Courtesy of James Weldon Johnson Collection, Beinecke Rare Book and Manuscript Library, Yale University, New Haven, Connecticut.

Frank, "I actually do not see differences of color and contour. I see differences of life and experience, and often enough these lead me to physical coverings. I'm very likely to be satisfied with a character whose body one knows nothing of."[40] To Toomer's mind, race was superficial, simply a "physical covering"; life experiences were the foundational and defining factors in one's identity. Perhaps Elizabeth Alexander's poem "Toomer" comes closest to a deft articulation of the fragmented racial identity that Toomer tried to explain: "I did not wish to 'rise above' or 'move beyond' my race. I wished to contemplate who I was beyond my body, this container of flesh."[41] Toomer *did* express his thinking about race. The trouble was that most critics—past and present—have refused to take Toomer at his word. Despite Toomer's eloquent and unequivocal statements, his racial identity remained fixed by prevailing American racial categorizations.

To live a hybrid existence in a racially segregated world was certainly "rough riding," as Toomer told Jack McClure in 1922.[42] Toomer suggested this impossibility in a letter to Sherwood Anderson and wrote, "The Negro's curious position in this western civilization invariably forces him into one or the other of two extremes: either he denies Negro entirely (as much as he can) and seeks approximation to an Anglo-Saxon (white) ideal, or . . . he overemphasizes what is Negro."[43] Any other formulation was simply impossible. A choice must be made. Even Claude Barnett asked Toomer to pick one—he must either be black or white. Hardly at a loss for words to describe his racial position, Toomer's answer was an unequivocal *no*. His answer was not audible, either to his contemporaries or to many critics later. Even astute scholars such as W. E. B. Du Bois and James Weldon Johnson, as well as Toomer's closest friends, white and black, failed to comprehend him or the complexity of "race" as he envisioned it.

Hybridity and racial ambiguity were unworkable, even during the Harlem Renaissance, and therefore, the default option became passing as white. But it must be underscored that Toomer did not pass as a conscious act. Ultimately, Toomer disappeared from the black world and from the larger public and sought refuge in obscurity. He decided to study Eastern mysticism, Jungian psychology, and psychoanalysis. He joined the Society of Friends, and he became a follower of the spiritual leader George Gurdjieff.[44] As Harlem exploded into a bloody riot in March 1935, as the Great Depression ravaged the publishing world and created breadlines that wrapped around Harlem's once bustling streets, and as the Renaissance began to appear decadent, apolitical, and more of a fad than a meaningful movement, the option of claiming the kind of mixed-race identity that Toomer desired was dashed, not to appear again until the late twentieth and early twenty-first centuries.

Nella Larsen: "Everybody Has People. . . . Everybody"

Unlike Jean Toomer, Nella Larsen accepted racial categories. She had no choice. Race had overdetermined her life circumstances, severed her familial relationships, and heightened her emotional and professional insecurities. Larsen was lost in Harlem, but just like the protagonists in her novels, she seemed equally misplaced overseas, in Chicago, or in the South. For Toomer, the Harlem Renaissance represented the first hour of hope that his racial identity might be recognized. But Larsen's mixed-race identity—detached from the familial lineage and the personal attachments that would give it meaning—had been split into fragments. The emotional toll had been too high for Larsen to ruminate on her identity or to debate its content and value with others. Toomer believed that he would be made whole once his "parts" were recognized. Larsen's parts had been scattered too far to collect and reassemble into a coherent entity.

During the summer of 1927, Nella Larsen was at the end of her rope. In a letter to her friend and Harlem socialite Dorothy Peterson, Larsen complained, "Right now when I look out into the Harlem streets . . . I feel just like Helga Crane in my novel. Furious at being connected with all these niggers."[45]

Larsen's ambivalent relationship with African American identity has led some literary critics to argue that Helga Crane, the protagonist of Larsen's first novel, *Quicksand,* published in 1928, is a semiautobiographical character. Like Helga, Larsen lacked a stable home, which impinged on her ability to construct a coherent identity. Larsen's reputation as "the mystery woman of the Harlem Renaissance" had much to do with the fact that she was secretive about the details of her early life and was concerned that others, especially members of the black middle class, would perceive her family background as disreputable.[46] Her mother was white, and her father was a black man from the West Indies. When her parents' relationship collapsed, and her mother remarried a white man, Larsen's presence became ever more problematic to the new family, especially in the increasingly segregated city of Chicago. Discarded by her mother and sent away from her family to be among her own "people" at Fisk University, Larsen wrestled with feelings of abandonment, displacement, and anxiety as a result of the fragility of her primary familial attachments.[47]

Larsen's experiences reveal what happens when notions of race, self, and family—usually deeply entangled—burst apart. Unlike most African Americans, Larsen did not trace her ancestry to the American South or to the long history of Southern slavery, but rather to the Dutch West Indies and to Denmark. At a time when nearly 70 percent of African Americans lived in the South and when most African Americans in the North kept close ties with their southern kin and considered the South their ancestral "home," Larsen had no southern relatives, black or white. She had no knowledge of and no relationships with any black relatives, with the exception of her father who died when she was three.[48] It was best for Larsen to keep quiet about her Scandinavian roots and to refrain from speaking about her mother. Few would understand her ancestry because it could not be mapped onto any familiar racial genealogies.

Groups spelled trouble for Larsen. She remained an outsider and never truly belonged to any group, and certainly not to one with mostly African American members. Despite her mother's best efforts to send Larsen to a place where she might live happily among her own people, Larsen was expelled from Fisk for violating the dress code. As an assistant superintendent nurse at the Tuskegee Institute in Alabama, Larsen found the climate so stultifying and became so nauseated with the school's conservative leadership that she and the administration "parted with mutual disgust and relief."[49] Larsen finally settled into a comfortable place as the children's librarian at the lively 135th Street branch of the New York Public Library, where she would become part of a Harlem social circle that included Walter White, Dorothy Peterson, Carl Van Vechten, James Weldon Johnson, and Grace Nail Johnson. Still, she felt ill at ease among Harlem's "dicty" society women.[50] After the publication of *Quicksand* in 1928, Larsen was unprepared for her overnight stardom, and she worried whether she had done the right thing by accepting an offer from the Woman's Auxiliary of the NAACP to host a tea in her honor. She implored Van Vechten to come as she would "need all of [her] friends."[51]

Larsen married the prominent Fisk physicist Elmer Imes in 1919. Their marriage may have given her a temporary respite from the lack of emotional intimacy that she experienced during her childhood. The marriage would not last: Imes had a very public affair with a popular white administrator at Fisk, and a humiliated Larsen filed for divorce in 1933.[52] Her hopes that "it [could] be done discreetly in ten days" were thwarted when newspapers such as the *Baltimore Afro-American* carried headlines which cast blame on Larsen

Figure 4.3. Portrait of Nella Larsen. Larsen wrote two major novels during the Harlem Renaissance that explored racial and gender identity.
Photographed by Carl Van Vechten. Courtesy of the Van Vechten Trust. James Weldon Johnson Collection, Beinecke Rare Book and Manuscript Library, Yale University, New Haven, Connecticut.

in a headline that read, "Fisk Professor is Divorced by N.Y. Novelist: Friends Think Love Cooled While Wife Wintered in Europe."[53] Years before the demise of her marriage, Larsen struggled with deep feelings of professional insecurity as she wrote *Quicksand* (1928) and *Passing* (1929). In a letter to Carl Van Vechten dated July 1, 1926, she worried that *Quicksand* was "frightfully bad . . . too short . . . too thin."[54] When she began to write *Passing,* she lamented, "I am having the most hellish time . . . I've torn it all up and now face the prospect of starting all over again—if at all."[55]

"People" had always been a problem for Nella Larsen in real life and in fiction. Like her characters, Larsen bristled against racial stereotypes, especially those held by ostensibly liberal whites. In *Quicksand,* Helga became an exotic "ornament" and a "peacock" for her Danish relatives to put on parade during her visit to Copenhagen. Larsen wrote of her own experience charming a group of whites by performing an exaggerated black identity. Larsen described the incident to Van Vechten with her characteristic sardonic wit: "I went to lunch the other day with some people that I knew very little (fays). In the course of our talk it developed that they would have been keenly disappointed had they discovered that I was not born in the jungle of the Virgin Isles, so I entertained them with . . . stories of my childhood in the bush, and my reaction to the tom-tom undertones in jazz. It was a swell luncheon."[56] Larsen appeared to be most comfortable with Van Vechten, and she also enjoyed a friendship with a "nice young man who seems to have no feeling whatever about colour." But in the company of these white men, she grew tired of the stares of onlookers.[57]

For Larsen, racial and gender identities were mutually constitutive, both in her own life and in her novels; race inflected gender just as much as gender inflected race. Unlike Toomer, Larsen also had to address the relationship between racism and sexism and the difficulties that these problems posed in creating a stable sense of self.[58] Like Toomer, Larsen confronted "the impossibility of self-definition" and the difficulty in "nam[ing] the reality adequately." But unlike Toomer, who descended from an honorable lineage and had been raised in a secure family headed by his domineering grandfather, Larsen lacked the familial attachments, personal connections, and sense of "peoplehood" that Toomer experienced in Washington, D.C. Her miserable childhood left her in a state of racial confusion. For Larsen, early encounters of family trauma hindered the possibility of constructing a complete identity.

Similarly, the women in Larsen's novels see themselves through a glass darkly. Stifled by middle-class codes of respectability, those who challenge societal restraints do not fare well. *Quicksand* closes with Helga, once enamored with material things and boasting "impeccably fastidious taste in clothes," on her deathbed, the result of giving birth to four children. She made the unwise decision to move to a small town in Alabama and marry "the grandiloquent Reverend Pleasant Green," a man who "consumed his food, even the softest varieties, audibly," whose fingernails were always dirty despite the fact that he never worked with his hands, and who "failed to wash his fat body or shift his clothing."[59]

Larsen's second novel, *Passing,* also ends in tragedy. The circumstances of Clare Kendry's death are obscured by the limited angle of vision of the narrator. As Larsen writes, "one moment Clare had been there, a vital glowing thing, like a flame of red and gold. The next she was gone."[60] Clare openly flouted racial conventions, not only by passing as white but by recklessly returning to Harlem on "a wild desire" to escape her "pale life" and to be with "her people," a longing that she describes as a "an ache, a pain that never ceases."[61]

Irene Redfield, Clare's black friend in Harlem, pushed her out of an open window a few moments after Clare's white husband discovered that she has been passing and is, in fact, black. It was Clare's "faint smile on her full, red lips, and in her shining eyes," and her posture, "as composed as if everyone were not staring at her in curiosity and wonder, as if the whole structure of her life were not lying in fragments before her," that unhinged Irene.[62] Clare must remain white if Irene's world is to remain whole. For once Clare became racially untethered, Irene's carefully constructed life and her loveless but strategic marriage would surely hang in the balance. Earlier in the novel, Irene convinced herself that she kept Clare's secret out of a loyalty to the race: "She was caught between two allegiances, different, yet the same. Herself. Her race. Race! The thing that bound and suffocated her." But it is certainly not race that "bound and suffocated her." It is her fear of losing that which she prized most: her respectable middle-class life, her "manufactured conversations . . . the soft running sounds of inconsequential talk," and her fixed place in black society.[63] "Security," Irene believed, "was the most important and most desired thing in life."[64] And Clare, as Irene knew well, "was not safe . . . not safe at all."[65] Ultimately, Irene demonstrated her disinterest in the race and her ability to act far more impulsively than Clare.

Larsen suggests that there are no available avenues for women like Helga Crane, Clare Kendry, or Irene Redfield. Like Toomer, they have the appropriate language to "name their reality," nor do they have discerning listeners who will understand the complexities of their raced and gendered positions. They are suffocating; there is no space for self-fashioning, and there is no breathing room for these characters to appeal for a "new race." Instead, they are each strangled by an inflexible and unforgiving racialized and gendered

Figure 4.4. An advertisement for Nella Larsen's novel *Passing* (1929) that captures the major theme of the novel and its tragic conclusion. *Courtesy of James Weldon Johnson Collection, Beinecke Rare Book and Manuscript Library, Yale University, New Haven, Connecticut.*

regime. The reader can anticipate that their stories will not end happily.

In both *Quicksand* and *Passing,* characters convey a deep connection to a black racial identity and a yearning for one's people. As Irene implores Clare "to be reasonable" and stay away from Harlem, Clare explains why she cannot: "You don't know, you can't realize how I want to see Negroes, to be with them again, to talk with them, to hear them laugh."[66] In *Quicksand,* James Vayle explains to Helga that even though he experienced better treatment in France during World War I, he and the other African American soldiers were anxious to return to the United States: "He shook his head solemnly. 'I don't think anything, money or lack of money, keeps us here. If it was only that, if we really wanted to leave, we'd go all right. No it's something else, something deeper than that. . . . I'm afraid it's hard to explain, but I suppose it's just that we like to be together. I simply can't imagine living forever away from colored people.'" When Helga reminds Vayle that she is "a Negro too," he explains, "Well, Helga, you were always a little different, a little dissatisfied, though I don't pretend to understand you at all. I never did."[67]

Larsen was similarly "a little different, a little dissatisfied" and difficult for others to understand. It is likely that Larsen would neither have sympathized with Clare Kendry's longing for black people, nor understood James Vayle's connection to the United States. Missing the elements in her own experience that Vayle poignantly described, Larsen likely would have looked at Vayle quizzically, and finding that "the conversation had taken an impersonal and disappointing turn," she would have quickly but politely changed the subject.[68]

By the late 1930s, Larsen's friends had lost touch with her. The decade started off auspiciously—Larsen became the first black woman to win a prestigious Guggenheim Fellowship—but in the same year, she was accused of plagiarizing a short story titled "Sanctuary," which had been published in *The Forum* in January. Larsen had always been introverted and insecure. A charge of plagiarism, which impugned her ethics and principles as a writer, was simply too much to bear. The editors ruled in Larsen's favor, deciding that the similarities between Larsen's work and a 1922 short story by Sheila Kaye-Smith, "Mrs. Adis," had been a remarkable coincidence. But Larsen never recovered. Sidney Peterson noticed that her name was no longer on her apartment door. She did not attend her ex-husband's funeral in 1941, and she did not call anyone to inquire about his death. Around this time, her friends began to realize just how little they knew about her. Dorothy Peterson remarked that a letter that Larsen wrote to Van Vechten "is very interesting because it indicates a more intimate knowledge of her and her past than I ever had and I think that I was probably as close to her as anyone could be." Peterson knew that Larsen's father was from the West Indies, "at least she told [her] so," but she did not know that Larsen attended the University of Copenhagen, and she struggled to provide biographical data because she had "very little information . . . because there is so little about her that I am sure of."[69] Larsen would spend the remainder of her life working in obscurity as a nurse in New York. No obituary was published to memorialize her death in 1964.

The life and work of Nella Larsen offer a different lens on the lived experience of racial ambiguity. Race may have seemed just as illogical and arbitrary to Larsen as it did to Toomer, but it was too defining a factor for Larsen to dismiss it as simply a "physical covering." Larsen was well aware of the significance of race and the trauma that racial identities could cause; her skin color required a

Figure 4.5. Sidney Peterson, Nella Larsen, Dorothy Peterson (l. to r.), March 26, 1932. Socially isolated in Harlem, Larsen considered Dorothy Peterson to be one of her closest friends.
Courtesy of James Weldon Johnson Collection, Beinecke Rare Book and Manuscript Library, Yale University, New Haven, Connecticut.

painful separation from her family, one that troubled all of her subsequent attempts to fashion a sense of self. Race had torn Larsen from her family and set her on a path to be with people whom she did not recognize as her own. Soon after *Quicksand* was published, a reviewer surmised, "But always it is there—a wistful note of longing, of anxiety, of futile searching, of an unconscious desire to balance black and white blood into something that is more tangible . . . of a nervous fretful search for that will o' wisp called happiness."[70] For Larsen, attaining happiness was contingent primarily upon confronting the difficulties of living a life in the absence of reliable family ties rather than balancing black and white blood. In Larsen's world, black and white blood could not be balanced, making happiness elusive. Larsen's life emblematizes the disconnections, anxieties, and tensions that arise when one is hollowed out, without roots, without an anchor. Larsen reveals what is left of a racial identity when race is emptied out as a category of experience, when one has no people.

Langston Hughes: "A Typical Negro Boy"

"You, white man! You, white man!" This was hardly the greeting that Langston Hughes anticipated upon arriving on the west coast of Africa in 1923. Hughes had set sail for, as he described it, "My Africa, Motherland of the Negro peoples! And me a Negro! Africa! The real thing, to be touched and seen, not merely read out in a book." And, yet, as he explained, "It was the only place in the world where I've ever been called a white man. They looked at my copper-brown skin and straight black hair—like my grandmother's Indian hair, except a little curly—and they said, 'You—white man.' "[71] Hughes tried to explain the similarities in the oppressive conditions faced by Africans and African Americans, especially in the South. "I am a Negro, too," Hughes insisted. But his pleas for racial recognition did little to convince the Kru men whom Hughes worked alongside as a mess boy aboard the merchant ship the S.S. *Malone.* The Kru men laughed, shook their heads, and explained that the few colored people on the west coast of Africa tended to be missionaries who came "to teach us something, since they think that we know nothing," or colonial administrators who came to "help carry out the white man's laws." For these reasons, "the Africans called them all *white* men."[72] The label "white man" had little to do with skin color but instead described behavior and power relationships.

In contrast to Toomer and Larsen, Langston Hughes encircled himself with black people. Like Toomer, he was racially mixed (though both of his parents were light-skinned blacks), and like Larsen, he perceived himself as an unwanted child. But Hughes devoted his career to writing about the pleasure and pain of black life, and he measured his success by his reception among black audiences. The embrace of black people mattered most to him, even if it meant losing his mother and his father.

Hughes thought that "maybe [he] had been a typical Negro boy," despite the fact that he had an uncommon childhood.[73] His father was a lawyer who lived in Mexico City, and his mother was largely absent during his formative years. Hughes had "slept in at least ten thousand strange beds" over the years of being shuttled back and forth between Mexico City, Missouri, Kansas, and Illinois. Like Toomer, Hughes descended from a storied family. His grandmother had been the first black woman to graduate from Oberlin, and her first husband had been a free man who died while participating in John Brown's raid at Harper's Ferry. His granduncle was John Mercer Langston, a famous congressman from Virginia, elected in 1888, and later a minister to Haiti and the first dean of Howard University Law School. Similar to Nella Larsen, Hughes descended from a racially mixed background; his ancestry included almost an equal number of whites as blacks.

When Hughes wrote *Not Without Laughter* (1930), he wanted to capture a typical black family in the Midwest, so he created "aunts that [he] didn't have, modeled after other children's aunts whom [he] had known." His grandmother would not allow Hughes to play with black children, she strictly forbade the singing of spirituals, and when she was rejected by the local white Presbyterian church, she chose to stay home on Sunday mornings. One of his

Figure 4.6. Langston Hughes at the Grand Hotel in Chicago, February 1942. Hughes used passing as a theme throughout his writing to poke fun at racial categorizations.
Courtesy of James Weldon Johnson Collection, Beinecke Rare Book and Manuscript Library, Yale University, New Haven, Connecticut.

favorite jobs had been working behind the soda fountain at a cafeteria in a black neighborhood, a popular meeting place for newcomers from the South. He wrote, "And I never tired of hearing them talk, listening to the thunderclaps of their laughter, to their troubles."[74] Hughes heard bits of the blues while in Kansas City, and he heard shouts from a black minister's sermon when his grandmother died. Hughes relished the coming of southern migrants—"low down folks," as he affectionately called them—while his mother winced at their arrival. Indeed, by the 1940s, Hughes would lament that "Harlem just isn't nappy headed any more—except for the first ten minutes after the hair is washed. Following that the sheen equals Valentino's and the page boy bobs are as long as Lana Turner's."[75] Just as Jean Toomer's revered rural folks had given up spirituals for Victrolas, Hughes's beloved "low down folks" were no longer "low down" at all.

For Hughes, passing represented a sudden and traumatic breakup, the loss of one's people and one's identity. In a poem titled "Passing," Hughes captures glimpses of black life on a Sunday summer afternoon in Harlem—grandma's gospel hymns, the Dodgers on the radio, Harlem's residents attired in their "washed-and-ironed-and-cleaned-best." But the poem ends on a blue note: those who "crossed the line to live downtown" missed the pleasures of these sights and sounds.[76]

Hughes wrote about passing as a practical joke at the expense of whites, but more often, passing became a trenchant way for Hughes to identify the painful losses and sacrifices that occurred when the color line was crossed. Hughes felt a deep connection and a strong fidelity to black people. These feelings of loyalty and kinship may have been a response to his father's unapologetic hatred of blacks. In his autobiography, *The Big Sea* (1940), Hughes explained that his father "hated Negroes" and therefore, he hated himself too, for being a Negro. Hughes described the summer that he spent with his father as "the most miserable [he had] ever known."[77] Just like Nella Larsen, Hughes longed for attention and affection from his family, and he also felt lonely and abandoned. But unlike Larsen, Hughes spent a few short but enjoyable years with his aunt and uncle in Lawrence, Kansas, after his grandmother died. These family members were neither boastful nor bourgeois like most of Hughes's family, and as

Hughes explained, "There have never been any better people in the world. I loved them very much."[78] In contrast to Larsen, who had been discarded by her mother and who never found a stable or lasting home among her people, Hughes willingly sacrificed his relationship with his father to nestle himself more closely to black people.[79] Hughes wrote one of his most famous poems, "The Negro Speaks of Rivers," on his journey to Mexico, where he would reunite with his father. Struggling with the emotional distance that stretched between his parents and him, Hughes wrote the poem as both a repudiation of his father and a meditation on the beauty of black people. Reflecting on the long history of black people made Hughes's personal suffering more tolerable. Hughes left Columbia University after spending two semesters studying mining engineering (his father's idea). He never saw his father again, and he did not receive any more money from him. It was a small price for Hughes to pay.

Hughes relied on the theme of passing to poke fun at American race relations and the absurdity of the color line. In the short story "Who's Passing for Who?,"[80] Hughes expected an evening in the company of a well-meaning but dull white couple to be less about fun and more about sociology until the couple reveals that they are black and just temporarily passing as white. The evening takes an unexpected but delightful turn:

> Then everybody laughed. And laughed! We almost had hysterics. All at once we dropped our professionally self-conscious "Negro" manners, became natural, ate fish, and talked and kidded freely like colored folks do when there are no white folks around. We really had fun then, joking about that red-haired guy who mistook a fair colored woman for white. After the fish we went to

two or three more night spots and drank until five o'clock in the morning.[81]

Hughes's story captures the joys of being part of an inner circle where "self-conscious 'Negro' manners" could be dropped and where jokes, laughter, and conversation flowed freely. But as the revelry ended in the early hours of the following morning, the couple revealed even more startling news. Pulling away in a cab, the wife shouted back to Hughes and his friends: "Listen, boys! I hate to confuse you again. But, to tell the truth, my husband and I aren't really colored at all. We're white. We just thought we'd kid you by passing for colored for a little while—like you said Negroes sometimes pass for white." Dumbfounded by the woman's disclosure, which poked fun at widely held folk knowledge that blacks were especially attuned to the telltale signs of racial identity, Hughes writes that he and his friends weren't sure "*which* way they had been fooled."[82] Hughes told Carl Van Vechten that this was a story "about some Negroes who wanted to jive some white folks but got double jived themselves."[83]

Hughes reveled in the playful and subversive potential of the practice of passing. Although Hughes asserted that "as long as white folks remain foolish, prejudiced and racially selfish, they deserve to be fooled. . . . No better for them!," he also recognized the painful, human costs of passing.[84] Relocating to Chicago enabled a protagonist in Hughes's short story "Passing" to make the decision to "marry white and live white," yet he feared that a chance encounter with his brother or sister would ruin his plan. He wished that his siblings had stayed in their hometown of Cincinnati, and he worried that they might not be as "tactful" as his mother was when he passed her on the street without speaking while escorting his white girlfriend.[85]

Hughes had tremendous affinity for African Americans, especially southern migrants, whom he regarded as "the gayest and the bravest people possible."[86] His father hated blacks, believing that they were aimless and pitiable, so Hughes loved them unconditionally. His father disparaged Hughes's aspirations to become a writer and warned him not to stay in the United States "where [he] would live like a nigger with niggers," so Hughes lived most of his life as a writer in Harlem, the epicenter of the black world. Unlike Nella Larsen, who was sent away from her mother and lived a life without any people, Hughes interlaced his life with his people, even if it meant breaking away from his mother and his father. Receiving the Spingarn Award on June 26, 1960, Hughes accepted the honor "in the name of the Negro people: Without them, on my part, there would have been no poems; without their hopes and fears and dreams, no stories; without their struggles, no dramas; without their music, no songs."[87] Without the Negro people, he seemed to say, there would be no Langston Hughes.

The Harlem Renaissance—a momentary flirtation with racial openness—raised more questions about identity and racial categories than it could answer. At that moment in the developing story of identity, some African Americans questioned whether they were primarily American or African; artists or individuals; black, white, both, or neither. Jean Toomer, Nella Larsen, and Langston Hughes each came from mixed racial backgrounds. Each chose a different path. Toomer hoped to create an unmarked identity and to deconstruct racial categories by arguing that race could not adequately capture the multiple realities and the possibilities of his experiences. But despite his articulateness, he struggled to find

Figure 4.7. Langston Hughes accepts the Spingarn Award, July 26, 1960. *Courtesy of James Weldon Johnson Collection, Beinecke Rare Book and Manuscript Library, Yale University, New Haven, Connecticut.*

the language to communicate his ideas in a way that others could understand. Nella Larsen's tormented childhood caused by the absence of reliable primary attachments created multiple personal conflicts. An insecure racial identity was just one of a legion of troubles. Larsen's life and works also reveal the ways that race inflected gender and gender inflected race. Just like Larsen, many of her fictional protagonists were trapped at the intersection of their gender and racial identities and shared Toomer's frustration with the inability to "name [their] reality adequately." Langston Hughes was the most successful in presenting racial identity in a conventional way that was recognizable and understandable to his readers and that was consistent with societal notions of race. He simultaneously ridiculed racial categories and wholeheartedly embraced them. Where Toomer lacked the language, Hughes lacked the inclination. Working at the opposite end of the spectrum from Toomer, Hughes wished to be enveloped in blackness.

Reminiscent of the Reconstruction era in some ways, the Harlem Renaissance was a propitious moment. But ultimately, the possibility of reimagining race was thwarted by the prevailing ideas and attitudes of American society and the deep imprint racial thinking had made in the national consciousness. Despite the bright promises of the twenties, the racial order of the Jim Crow era was too sturdy; even the most eloquent artists could not break through. Conversations about the possibilities of mixed-race identities would fall on deaf ears until the beginning of the next century when new racial dynamics materialized.

5

Coming Home

Shortly after New Year's Day in 1932, the news of a lieutenant's fatal car crash created a commotion at the Presidio in San Francisco. Lieutenant William J. French was found on a desolate road near Gilroy, California, with his pistol nearby and a bullet wound to his head. The police ruled that his death was a suicide. But military personnel were far more startled by another revelation. An article on the front page of the *New York Times,* "Army Man's Suicide Reveals He Is Negro," reported that French had spent eighteen years "masquerading" as a white man. After his death, French's mother disclosed her son's racial identity, but she would neither comment on when her son decided to pass as white nor reveal any other details about his life. The *Times* noted that French visited his mother in Pasadena at Christmas and that "scores of Negroes" in that city knew that French was passing as white. The *Times* reported that French gave the Army eighteen years of "brilliant" service and distinguished himself during World War I as a commissioned officer who led white troops. French's relatives cautioned him against advancing too far in the military, and they tried to convince him that commanding white men was too risky. French chose not to heed these warnings. Maybe he had not expected to advance as quickly and as far as he did, and once the Army granted him the commission, perhaps he simply could not walk away from it. Maybe French worried that to decline such a promotion would arouse suspicions and attract unwanted attention. The last person to see French alive, Mrs. Gertrude McEnroe, was in the car with French at the time of the crash and claimed that French tried to kill her. McEnroe survived and later told officials that French had been on the verge of a nervous breakdown. It was McEnroe's opinion that French was driven to a state of insanity after years of fear and foreboding that his racial identity would be exposed.[1]

Lieutenant William J. French's successful military career and untimely death lay bare the tragic consequences of passing. But unlike most blacks who chose to pass permanently, French maintained a relationship with his mother. His visits to her house at Christmas were fraught with danger, yet still he went. Perhaps as a result of those yearly visits, other blacks in Pasadena learned that French was passing as white. French must have been in contact with the relatives who were uneasy about his strivings, who worried that he was too ambitious, and who urged him not to "attempt to carry his pose all the way to commanding white troops." French lived a life in the liminal space between the very separate worlds of black and white. Perhaps French was sustained by his Christmastime visits with his mother and his relationships with relatives and other blacks in Pasadena. Not one family member or friend broke the promise to protect his identity. But at some point, those promises were not enough; if McEnroe was right, French longed for more than military honors and Christmas holidays in Pasadena.

No one will ever know exactly what happened in the car on January 3, 1932, before it careened and crashed into a tree near Gilroy, California. No one will ever know the nature of the relationship between Mrs. Gertrude McEnroe and French, who was married to a white woman. Newspaper accounts do not explain why a truck driver stopped and rescued McEnroe from the wreck, but left French in the car. Reports about the case do not provide any answers to the question of why French allegedly tried to kill McEnroe. French's family members were uniformly silent about his personal life, his decision to pass, or any efforts that he made to bond his fractured identity into a more complete and satisfying whole. Without the silence of "scores of other Negroes," French's masquerade could have been foiled at any moment. But if McEnroe's assertion is correct—that French's secret drove him to an acute state of mental collapse and the desperate decision to take his own life—then the devastating and even deadly consequences of passing come into sharper view.

By the 1940s, the world of Jim Crow that had enveloped French was giving way to a new era with new possibilities. Less than ten years after French's suicide, Dr. Albert Johnston, a well-respected radiologist in Keene, New Hampshire, received notice of his acceptance as a lieutenant commander in the Medical Corps of the U.S. Navy. One year earlier, Johnston had been rejected due to "physical defects"; he was both overweight and slightly under the minimum height requirement to be granted a position as a commissioned officer.[2] But a dire need for more physicians, and especially radiologists, compelled the Navy to relax its standards and to reconsider applicants previously rejected for "organic defects" that would not interfere with the performance of their duties. The Navy reversed its prior decision and assigned Johnston to a naval medical specialist unit.[3]

Unlike the case of Lieutenant French, the Navy discovered Johnston's secret long before Johnston received his naval uniform. Only a few weeks after the letter of acceptance arrived, a naval intelligence officer visited Johnston at his home. During a short interview, the officer stated bluntly, "We understand that even though you are registered as white, you have colored blood in your veins." A naval background check uncovered that Johnston belonged to a black fraternity while he was in medical school. Johnston responded, "Who knows what blood any of us has in his veins?" A few weeks later, Johnston was informed that his post had been denied because of his "inability to meet naval physical requirements."[4] Unsettled by the Navy's discovery, Johnston carefully guarded his secret from his neighbors, friends, patients, and even his children. Six years later, however, the Johnstons told their children. In 1947, the family's story appeared in the popular periodical *Reader's Digest*. The Johnstons had come clean: the family had black ancestry and had been passing as white for nearly twenty years.[5]

The years between the suicide of Lieutenant William J. French in 1932 and the exposure of the Johnston family's racial identity in 1947 mark a critical turning point in the history of passing. By the late 1940s, many African Americans who had previously passed as white declared that they could no longer endure the emotional turmoil experienced by French and others. In the black press, testimonials of light-skinned blacks registered a palpable sense of relief that accompanied the disavowal of passing and a return to the race. Passing "passes out," a 1952 article in *Jet* magazine proclaimed, as a rearticulation of race consciousness emerged and joined hands with the civil rights movement.[6] These reports in the black press suggested that, similar to the Reconstruction era that followed the Civil War, America had been made anew in the aftermath of World War II. The racial dynamics of this period might allow one to live as black and be a citizen at the same time. Passing had been one of a limited number of strategies that opened doors for African Americans to participate more fully in American life. Perhaps in postwar America, passing would "pass out" and no longer be necessary, especially if postwar economic prosperity extended to African Americans. Perhaps light-skinned African Americans could claim a black identity and step out from the dark shadows that descended upon Lieutenant William J. French.

World War II and its immediate aftermath led mid-century Americans to reconsider the nation's democratic principles against the backdrop of unprecedented political, social, economic, and ideological changes. By the 1950s, the number of lynchings had decreased from hundreds to less than five; President Harry Truman had issued executive orders to desegregate the military and the federal civil service; and scientists jettisoned the belief that racial differences were based in biology, as the horrors of the Holocaust discredited assumptions about inherent racial inferiority. Even though the naval intelligence officer who interrogated Dr. Johnston in 1941 relied on an assumption that race was an invisible yet enduring essence that inhered in the blood, this logic was becoming outdated. During the 1940s, police forces, juries, baseball teams, public universities, and public accommodations were desegregated.[7] The black newspaper the *Pittsburgh Courier* announced a "Double V" campaign in 1941 that called for simultaneous victories against fascism abroad and racism at home. This campaign reflected a growing militancy among African Americans who believed that the valiant and willing military service of African American men entitled them to the guarantee of civil rights. A series of landmark Supreme Court cases opened primary elections to voters of all races (*Smith v. Allwright* in 1944) and declared racially restrictive covenants unenforceable (*Shelley v. Kraemer* in 1948). In 1954, the Court ruled that segregated schools were unconstitutional (*Brown v. Board of Education*). Between 1940 and 1956, black voting registration in the South increased by an astounding 624.5 percent.[8]

In the social sciences, Gunnar Myrdal's watershed 1,500-page sociological work, *An American Dilemma: The Negro Problem and Modern Democracy,* published in 1944, held that if white Americans would live up to the "American Creed"—liberty, equality, justice, and fair treatment for all—black Americans would enjoy fuller and more meaningful inclusion in the nation. Myrdal's work underscored the ideals of racial liberalism that emerged in the late 1940s. Racial liberalism coalesced around the New Deal belief that government intervention could ameliorate racial discrimination, that interracial contact was the antidote to individual prejudice, and that in the midst of the battle to win hearts and minds during the Cold War, it was in the national interest of the United States to portray itself as a racially progressive nation.[9] The interplay of social science research, federal action, civil rights pressure, and international scrutiny assured the vitality of civil rights as a national issue.

There was good reason for African Americans to feel particularly hopeful about the economic opportunities created by World War II. The 1940s marked the twentieth century's most economically equitable decade.[10] The demographic forces of migration and urbanization that occurred during the Jim Crow years consolidated black voting strength in the North and produced an embryonic black middle class that attained higher levels of income and education than an earlier generation could have imagined.[11] Economic inequality declined as the federal government created millions of jobs in the war industries and supported the growth of trade unionism. By the end of the 1940s, African American income equaled 60 percent of white income; it had been only 40 percent at the beginning of the decade. In Michigan and other highly unionized states that housed heavy industries, black income reached 90 percent of white income.[12]

In short, it was a season of hope. With African Americans once again taking their seats in Congress and on the federal judiciary, challenging racial mores, and pressing for more meaningful inclusion in the nation, Blanche Bruce and P. B. S. Pinchback might have recognized this period, aptly called the "Second Reconstruction," as remarkably similar to the first. The particular conditions and circumstances of postwar America left many to wonder whether passing was still a necessary practice. Maybe the painful loss of family and the alienation from a community were needless. The confluence of these changes suggested that in the postwar period, passing might no longer be obligatory to secure white-collar work, decent housing, or fair treatment.

But even in this season of hope, something was still amiss. The postwar period was rife with contradictions. Mass-marketed magazines including *Life, Look,* and *Ebony* worked as the agents of racial liberalism and disseminated photographs of the Johnston family as a symbol of peaceful and successful integration to readers around the country. But a closer look reveals that hospital trustees decided to oust Albert Johnston from his position, belying the magazines' cheerful assertions that once the town learned of the

Johnstons' racial identity, there "simply wasn't any" reaction. Racial liberals cheered the "message movies" released in the late 1940s that promised to tackle the problem of racism directly for the very first time. But the fractured reception of the 1949 film that presented the Johnstons' tale, *Lost Boundaries,* revealed national ambivalence and anxiety about the possibility of integration.[13] Although audiences around the country applauded the film for its stirring portrayal of racial inequality, city censors in Atlanta and Memphis banned it. The directors of *Lost Boundaries* and other "message movies," including the passing feature, *Pinky,* assumed that white actors would evoke more sympathy and draw larger audiences. These casting decisions drew the ire of black critics at a time when Hollywood made little room for black actors except in caricatured and stereotyped roles.[14]

Even sanguine news of rising black income and employment rates could not overcome hardened racial prejudice. The racial tumult experienced by many blacks, such as Betty and Donald Howard, ran counter to the ebullience of the postwar period. The Howards moved into Chicago's Trumbull Park Homes in 1953 after Chicago Housing Authority officials misrecognized Betty as a white woman. Betty had "not the slightest physical characteristics of a Negro," but the arrival of Betty's recognizably black husband, Donald, ignited nearly a decade of racial violence and neighborhood unrest. Mobs numbering in the thousands voiced unequivocal rejection of the idea of integration by breaking the Howards' windows and detonating ear-shattering explosives.[15] Even *Ebony,* a magazine firmly committed to presenting cheery accounts of black life, could not brighten the Howards' bleak story. A July 1954 article commented on Donald Howard's severe weight loss, his habit of chain-smoking, and the "terrific psychological toll" of the ordeal.[16]

Figure 5.1. Donald Howard looks on as his wife Betty and their children return to their apartment in the Trumbull Park Homes in Chicago. *Courtesy of the Claude Barnett Collection, Chicago Historical Society, Chicago, Illinois.*

Whether or not the practice of passing began to "pass out" in the postwar period is a subject for debate. The Howards' story, however, belies optimistic pronouncements about the irrelevance of passing and puts in plain view the frightening consequences of racial misrecognition in the postwar period. The events at Trumbull Park bring into focus a set of worrisome factors that challenged postwar commitments to racial liberalism and social inclusivity. Hardened social and economic barriers and the particularly explosive concern of housing left integrationist goals far from realized.

The post-1945 world, despite its inconsistencies and paradoxes, was strikingly different than the Jim Crow world that closed in on Lieutenant William J. French in 1932. French was trapped with no way out. But by the 1940s, more African Americans rejected passing and liberated themselves from the fear and anxiety of discovery. Racial discrimination persisted, and so did passing, but the promise of new economic possibilities coupled with a growing protest movement for civil rights led many to reconsider the choices they made about their racial identities. The arc of the Johnston family's story follows this logic precisely: at the beginning of the 1940s, the family was passing as white, but by the end of the decade, they had been exposed, grown tired of the masquerade, and decided to link their fate with other African Americans. By 1949, the family publicly declared that they would never pass again. Their story provides a blueprint to understand the transition from passing to a fuller embrace of black identity.

Albert Johnston was born in 1900. He straddled both sides of the color line during his early years. His father, who was lighter than Albert, had been raised on a farm in Michigan and descended from Northerners who had not been slaves. His mother, on the other hand, was from the Deep South; her parents had been slaves in Mississippi. The family lived in Chicago, and Johnston's father passed as white to work as a real estate agent. The family never invited black guests to their home. Johnston's father feared that the presence of black visitors would compromise his appearance and his employment. Albert Johnston went to public school in Chicago during the years before the Great Migration, when the schools were not segregated and only a few thousand African Americans lived in the city.[17] When Albert attended Wendell Phillips High School, a school that would become predominantly black by the 1920s, all of his friends were white, and he remembered only one black student in his graduating class.

Johnston's wife, Thyra Baumann, was born in 1903 in New Orleans. Her grandfather was a white man from Germany who married a black woman and served as the shipping commissioner of the Port of New Orleans. Thyra's father worked as a clerk in the post office at a time when the city was almost entirely segregated with the exception of federal offices.

The presidential election of 1912 would change the course of the Baumann family's life. Unusually large numbers of African Americans broke with the "Party of Lincoln" and cast ballots for the Democratic candidate, Woodrow Wilson. During the campaign, Wilson assured African Americans that he would advocate for racial justice and fairness. But once in the White House in 1913, Wilson dismissed fifteen out of seventeen black supervisors who held federal jobs. Throughout the country, blacks were segregated or dismissed from federal positions. Postmaster Albert Burleson of Texas made the case for segregation by complaining of "intolerable" conditions where whites were forced to work with blacks and share the same drinking glasses, towels, and toilets. White women recoiled at the affront of taking dictation from "drunken," "greasy," and "ill-smelling Negroes." The head of the Internal Revenue System in Georgia stated, "There are no government positions for the Negro in the South. They are to be in the cornfield."[18] President Wilson voiced no objections to segregation; in fact, he hoped that racial separation would help to reduce "friction" in federal departments.

Thyra's father quickly took notice of the pattern and the spread of segregation. He applied to transfer to the Boston post office. He hoped that in the North, he might find the just racial conditions that Wilson had promised in 1912 and thwarted only one year later in 1913.

The Baumanns passed as white, but unlike the Johnstons, they socialized with Boston's small community of black lawyers, doctors, dentists, and other professionals. Thyra took a job as a stenographer at the Mellins Food Company and put "white" on her application. Her white skin, light brown hair, and blue eyes made it easy for her to pass. When she applied for her next job, she followed her mother's instructions to leave the race part of the application blank and to "let them fill it out."[19] But in her new position, being white was not enough. The company had a policy of refusing employment to Catholics. To secure the job, Thyra passed as both white and Protestant.

Thyra's father was very particular about the men who dated his daughter. Being seen with a black man might cost Thyra her job. And even worse, marrying a black man was "going back" to the segregated life that Thyra's father had eagerly left behind in New Orleans. When the handsome black halfback on Brown University's football team invited Thyra to attend the Harvard-Brown football game, Thyra's father forced her to decline. When the young man wrote love letters to Thyra, her parents hid them from her. A broken-hearted Thyra wondered why she never heard from him again.

In 1923, Thyra spent two weeks in Chicago going on dates with the city's most eligible black bachelors, including Albert Johnston, a medical student at the University of Chicago. Albert was slightly darker than Thyra, but he could easily pass, and he did so to buy orchestra seats to see the Duncan sisters perform their signature roles in *Topsy and Eva,* a musical comedy derived from Harriet Beecher Stowe's classic, *Uncle Tom's Cabin.* One can only imagine how Albert and Thyra felt that evening, passing as white, taking their seats—the best seats in the house—to watch one of the most popular vaudeville duos in America. One can only wonder how they felt when Rosetta Duncan took the stage as Topsy in the most grotesque form of blackface and racial caricature. Indeed, in a review of *Topsy and Eva,* the *Sunday Advertiser* wrote, "When it comes to blackface art, the palm of accomplishment goes not, as you might suggest in the first three guesses, to Al Jolson, but to little Rosetta Duncan, co-star with her sister, Vivian . . . when it comes to applying the liquid burnt cork, she outdoes Jolson in every known direction." Rosetta Duncan outperformed Jolson largely because she "almost bathes" in the "ebony fluid," the reviewer explained. She was "practically immersed in color," with "only a narrow strip . . . minus makeup." Her hair was clumped in unkempt and unruly braids, sprouting from her head in every direction.

Sitting in the most comfortable seats in the theater, Albert and Thyra were far removed from the crowded balcony pejoratively known as the "nigger heaven," which was the only place for black viewers. It would not have come as a surprise to Albert or Thyra to see Rosetta Duncan go to "the limit in makeup in this part." *Topsy and Eva* was widely popular; it ran for forty-seven weeks in Chicago. Albert and Thyra knew what to expect. In this farce, Topsy appeared on the auction block and laughed heartily when no one would buy her because, as the auctioneer explained, "didn't nobody want poor Topsy," not even for a dime, a nickel or a cent.[20] When Eva asked, "Isn't *it* beautiful," or when Topsy crossed her eyes, stood on her head, and turned cartwheels to Eva's delight, Albert and Thyra may have felt ill at ease. Or maybe they enjoyed the performance. This couple—scions of Chicago's and Boston's light-skinned black elite—may have felt no kinship with Topsy, the incorrigible child and the laughingstock of the play. Maybe they had learned their roles so well that they knew when to laugh along with the white theatergoers who surrounded them in the orchestra.[21]

Even if Albert and Thyra found *Topsy and Eva* unbearable to watch, they certainly could not let it show. Loss was a prerequisite of passing. But the losses that passing demanded were not all the same for those who passed. Passing could mean the wrenching loss of one's family, but it could also mean the personal pain of losing one's dignity. It could mean laughing on cue at a minstrel show or constraining one's feelings and emotions and being unable to register disgust or outrage at a racist joke. For some, this was undoubtedly a bitter bargain. But for others, the connection with oneself and one's past had been lost long ago. Watching the spectacle of Rosetta Duncan playing the fool while drenched in "ebony fluid" may have meant little or nothing at all to this young couple.

A few days before they went to see *Topsy and Eva,* Albert proposed to Thyra at his fraternity house. Thyra was elated. Her parents were terrified. This love affair had transpired entirely while Thyra was in Chicago and far away from her family who lived in Boston.

Thyra's parents desperately needed to know what this young medical student looked like. To their great relief, he was light enough to pass, and he was a member of the right social circle. Thyra and Albert were married on Christmas day in 1924.

During his college years at the University of Chicago, Albert Johnston was not invited to the white social events, but he had a close group of black friends, and he was an active member of the black fraternity, Kappa Alpha Psi. Rush Medical College had a quota for black students; Johnston was one of two who were admitted. Neither Johnston nor the other black student was required to serve as junior intern at Presbyterian Hospital in Chicago because the administrators knew that the white patients would object. But before graduation, Johnston needed an internship at a prestigious hospital. Only four black hospitals accepted interns, and not one of these hospitals was acceptable to Rush. Johnston approached hospitals in liberal areas of the country in the hopes that he might be given a chance. He almost succeeded at Toledo, but once the doctors discovered that Johnston was black during the interview, he was told that it was not their policy to accept colored interns.

When Maine General Hospital telegrammed Johnston to express interest and did not ask any questions about race, Johnston kept quiet. He was hired. During his internship, he was feted at the Portland Club, and he danced and played tennis with the other interns. Yet he always worried that his racial background would be discovered. Later, some of the doctors told him, "When you first came, some of us thought you were a Filipino, or maybe Hawaiian or a Jew—we didn't know what you were."[22] If they did not know, he was not going to tell them.

After his internship at Maine General, Johnston began a medical practice in Gorham, New Hampshire, a rural hamlet at the base of Mount Washington. In the rolling hills of Gorham, Johnston delivered babies, pulled teeth, set a dog's broken leg, and treated the array of sicknesses and diseases that afflicted Gorham's residents. The quintessential country doctor, Johnston was sometimes paid in cash and sometimes in butter, eggs, or various types of produce.[23] The neighbors were very selective about who could move into the neighborhood. As Johnston explained, "only the best people lived there—no Jews or Catholics, for example." The Johnstons appeared white and Protestant, and thereby "just right."[24] When Thyra arrived, the women in the town taught her to light the coal stove and encouraged her to enroll the children in the church's cradle class. A Catholic woman from New Orleans would become a devout Congregationalist in New England.

At first glance, Gorham seemed calm and idyllic, the perfect home for a young family. But tensions—racial, ethnic, and religious—roiled beneath the peaceful veneer. The older Yankees looked upon the newly arriving French Catholics from Canada with disgust. A Ku Klux Klan klavern was assembling. Albert claimed not to be worried. The Klan, Albert believed, was intolerant of Jews, but they seemed to treat Abe Stahl, the only Jewish resident in Gorham, with respect. Maybe Thyra's southern roots caused her greater alarm. She was particularly concerned about her children and what would happen when they grew up. Albert tried to reassure her by saying, "Let's just saw wood and see what happens."[25]

It is hard to believe that Albert was not more distressed, even panicked, as his neighbors and patients formed a Klan in the seemingly placid town of Gorham. He must have known that these honest and hard-working folks could turn on him at any minute. He was a black man who was intimately involved in their lives. He delivered their babies, cared for their children, examined their wives, and buried their dead. The Klan, founded in 1866 in Pulaski, Tennessee, had been dormant since the 1870s, when the federal government launched a series of investigations that led to the passage of the Enforcement Acts of 1870 and 1871 and prosecutions under that law. As Congress listened to the arresting testimony, the federal government discovered what black men and women in the South knew too well: the Klan had terrorized and intimidated African Americans, coerced their economic dependency, and attempted to reinstate the social customs of antebellum America in the name of preserving white supremacy. The Enforcement Acts buttressed the Fourteenth and Fifteenth Amendments by protecting the rights of African Americans to vote, to hold office, to serve on juries, and to receive equal protection under the law. The federal government effectively prosecuted Klan members and disbanded the organization in the 1870s.[26] But in 1915, a second Klan rose, this time on the top of Stone Mountain in Atlanta, Georgia, and found a large and sympathetic base in the Midwest and the Northeast. By the end of the 1920s, the "Invisible Empire" was hardly invisible: membership swelled from three million to eight million, and the organization exerted enough political muscle to control the state legislatures in Colorado and Indiana. Klansmen were elected mayors in Portland, Maine, and Portland, Oregon.

Even as a Klan gathered in Gorham, the Johnstons felt safe. They made close friends and became actively involved in the town's civic life. Albert was elected to the school board, the Rotary Club, and the Masonic Lodge.[27] Thyra was selected to be the president of the White Mountain Junior League of the Congregational Church, she served two terms as president of the Gorham Women's Club, and she played bridge and hosted parties and teas. But they never relaxed entirely. Their lives seemed anchored in Gorham, but Albert and Thyra decided to rent their house because they feared that their racial identity might be revealed if they decided to buy. If their background were discovered, they reasoned, they would not have the burden of a house to sell. With only a rental agreement, they could leave town on a month's notice, assuming that they would have that much time.

When a rambling three-story house with seventeen rooms, two parlors, and a reception hall went on the market, the Johnstons took a risk and bought it. The house, shaded by ancient elm trees, sat high on a hill and overlooked all of Gorham. Soon the Johnstons' new home was the social hub of the town: the Congregational Church planted its Christmas tree in the yard and held the annual Christmas social at the house, and the Johnstons entertained Gorham's residents at an elegant New Year's reception.

We will never know what the residents of Gorham would have done if they had found out about the Johnstons' racial identity. They never did, despite rumors. There was the day when Albert Jr. teased the family's French-Canadian maid who responded by calling him a "little picaninny."[28] There was the time when Thyra's father, who looked white, visited Gorham and a man approached him and pointed to Thyra. "See that lady down there?" he asked. "Well, they say she's a real mulattress. But now, funny thing is, her husband's darker'n [than] what she is."[29] Thyra's father insisted that man was mistaken; "that lady" was his daughter and therefore she was certainly not "a real mulattress." The man took Thyra's father's word for it. Thyra and Albert did not know whether to be worried or reassured. The man seemed more curious than hateful.

Perhaps this was an encouraging sign of how the other residents might react if the family's racial identity were discovered.

Old friends in Boston kept the Johnstons' secret, even if they disapproved of the practice of passing. The Johnstons went to Boston for visits, but they never took their children with them. The milieu of Boston's light-skinned black elites would be unfamiliar to the children who lived in an entirely white world. Only the most rare occasions brought the children into contact with black people. A black drifter stayed overnight in the Gorham jail and Albert Jr., along with the other curious children, went to the jail in the morning to get a glimpse of a black man.[30] Perhaps a black cook or housekeeper might accompany a family who visited Gorham for the summer. With so few blacks in the town, the Johnstons' black friends in Boston understood that they would never be invited to Gorham. Over time, the Johnstons lost those friends. When Dr. Johnston received an offer to take a one-year postgraduate course at Harvard Medical School, there was no cause for worry. As Thyra explained, "our colored contacts are mostly weaned away now. . . . And, if I run into any of them on the street when I have the children, well, I can handle that."[31] Only Thyra's mother knew, and they could trust her to keep their secret.

The year in Boston passed by without much trouble for Thyra and Albert, but their son Albert Jr. encountered prejudice from those who thought he was Jewish. Because of his darker complexion, he was called a "kike." When the family returned to Gorham, Albert Jr. made the honor roll, joined the ski team, played the piano, and was recommended for the prestigious Mount Hermon School in western Massachusetts.[32] At Mount Hermon, Albert Jr. faced anti-Semitism again. He had trouble with a roommate who announced that he hated Jews. The roommate made a habit of asking, "What *are* you? A kike or a Greek or what? No? Well, I bet you've got some nigger in you."[33] During this time, Albert Jr. did not know that he was black. Perhaps he felt the sting of these slurs and began to see himself through the eyes of others long before his parents told him the truth.

Dr. Johnston's postgraduate studies at Harvard created an opportunity at the leading hospital in Keene, New Hampshire. The family was reluctant to leave Gorham, especially when they were beginning to trust their neighbors, but this was a position that Johnston could not refuse. In the fall of 1939, the family moved 160 miles south to a three-story brick house sheltered by majestic elm trees on a large corner lot. Moving to Keene and living among strangers stoked fears about the "colored thing," but in Keene as in Gorham, Thyra and Albert became intimately involved in the town's social and civic life.[34] Thyra joined the Ladies Medical Auxiliary and took part in a variety of civic and volunteer organizations.[35]

Class and gender identities remained intact while racial boundaries were crossed. Race and gender are never isolated, disparate, or distinct categories, rather they are always linked, interrelated, and intersectional. Despite their skin color (which was brown enough to cast doubt on their presumed whiteness), the family's presentation of their class and social status enabled their acceptance by Keene's white residents. Albert was an esteemed radiologist, and his wife was the archetypal housewife and mother. Thyra's role in the Johnstons' masquerade was equally, if not more, important, than her husband's. White women were ensconced in the home; black women were tethered to the work force. White women were the homemakers; black women were the housekeepers. Thyra—through her absence from the labor force, her gracious hosting, her efficient

Figure 5.2. Portrait of the Johnston Family in their home in Keene, New Hampshire.
Courtesy of the Archive Center at the Historical Society of Cheshire County, Keene, New Hampshire.

homekeeping, her dedication to Keene's civic causes—played the role of an upper-middle-class white woman to the hilt. As one observer noted, the Johnstons enjoyed a lifestyle in Keene "that would have been impossible if they had given themselves merely the *label* Negro."[36]

But in the early 1940s, it all came to an abrupt end. Two unrelated events altered the direction of the Johnstons' blissful lives in Keene: an offhand comment made by Albert Jr. and Dr. Johnston's decision to enlist in the Navy. At Mount Hermon, Albert Jr. befriended a popular black student, Charlie Duncan, the son of the actor Todd Duncan, who starred in *Porgy and Bess.* When Albert Jr. was home from school, he made a careless remark to his parents: "Everyone liked Charlie, even if he *was* colored." This unthinking praise of his son's only black friend infuriated Dr. Johnston, and at this particular moment, he felt that he could no longer continue the pretense. Albert and Thyra had raised their sons and daughter as white children who rarely even heard the word "Negro."[37] Was not Albert Jr. saying what any white man in the early 1940s might say if he formed a new friendship with a black person? Yet something about this comment, or perhaps the cavalier way that Albert Jr. said it, offended Dr. Johnston to the point that he was willing to risk the life that he and Thyra had so carefully constructed over twenty years. Even as his wife cried out to him, "No! No! Don't do it! Don't ever do it!"[38]

Albert Jr. was preparing to go on a date when he heard his father say, "Well, you're colored." He remembered that a "funny sensation" ran through his body.[39] He stopped getting dressed. He asked if his mother was colored too, even though he already knew the answer. His mother and father were black as were his four grandparents, but they all could pass as white. Albert and Thyra explained what passing was, and they assured their son that they were not ashamed of being black, but rather that passing as white was the only way that Dr. Johnston could practice medicine. Now that Albert Jr. knew the family's secret, he would have to keep it. The younger children did not know yet, and if such startling news spread around town, the consequences would be calamitous for Dr. Johnston and his flourishing medical career. Instead of getting ready for his date, Albert Jr. spent the evening learning how, why, and when his family decided to pass. The stories spilled out from his mother and father; they interrupted and talked over each other as one filled in the details that the other had forgotten.

From Portland to Gorham to Keene, Albert and Thyra had been stalked by the constant fear that their racial identity would be discovered. They had guarded their secret with great care, and they had made great sacrifices. They lost friends. They fell out of touch with relatives who could not pass. As Albert Jr. recalled, "During all these years my mother and father had a few colored contacts in New York and Boston but never had colored friends as guests . . . because of fear of discovery."[40] Dr. Johnston may have remembered that his father, a "white" real estate agent, would not allow any black guests at his house. Thyra had not been allowed to date any men who looked black. Passing not only required looking white, but also meant keeping one's distance from black people.

More puzzling was Dr. Johnston's decision to apply to enlist in the Navy as a medical officer. The Navy urgently needed radiologists, so perhaps Dr. Johnston assumed that the naval standards might be relaxed. Or as Thyra suggested, perhaps the naval intelligence officer had visited their home to make sure that Dr. Johnston did not look "really black." Regardless, Dr. Johnston had to know that he would be subjected to an exhaustive investigation. He had lived as a black man while he was in college at the University of Chicago. He must have known that his membership in a black organization, the Kappa Alpha Psi fraternity, would be quickly and easily uncovered, as it was by the naval intelligence officer who visited Johnston at his home in 1941.

Perhaps by 1941, Dr. Johnston had grown tired of passing, or he no longer could tolerate attending medical conventions and nodding his assent when his colleagues said that Negroes did not have the "brains" or the values of white doctors. Perhaps the stress and the sacrifice had become too much to bear and Albert and Thyra wanted their children to live lives free of the secrets that had beleaguered them.

When the younger children were told that they were black, they understood why they had never known their own relatives the way that other children did. They understood why they only knew Aunt Nette, their mother's sister, who looked white, and why their parents whispered when they talked about race relations. Albert Jr. had difficulty in school after he was told, and he tried to find solace by traveling across the country with an old friend from Gorham. He visited many of his black relatives and learned that some blacks lived just like the white families in Gorham and Keene. He also found other relatives who were passing. He planned to visit an aunt and uncle in Los Angeles but upon his arrival, he discovered that they had divorced; his uncle had "gone over to the other side," married a white woman, and was passing permanently. Like the Johnstons, Albert Jr.'s uncle had to sever all ties with his black friends to maintain his new life. Albert Jr.'s aunt was stung by the divorce, but she never betrayed her ex-husband's secret. When she called to tell him that his nephew was in town, he refused to see Albert Jr. He may have felt that he could not trust his ex-wife's word that Albert Jr. was light enough to pass, or he feared that his nephew might expose him before his white wife and white friends.[41] Regardless, Albert Jr. would never meet his uncle. Passing made some relationships impossible. This was one of them.

Picturing Integration

It is curious why the Johnstons waited six years to tell their children about their racial identity. They may have felt that 1947 was a more auspicious time to declare that they had black ancestry than 1941. Given the economic, social, and political changes that occurred in the wake of World War II, the Johnstons may have read the postwar period as a dawn of a new era in race relations.

The story spread quickly around town after the Johnstons told their children. In 1947, *Reader's Digest* published an article about the family, and by 1949 millions of Americans could see photographs of the Johnstons on the pages of mass-marketed magazines like *Life, Look,* and *Ebony.* These magazines put passing in the national spotlight and brought it to its largest audience. *Life,* known as "America's Favorite Magazine," was possibly the most influential American magazine of the twentieth century. One study found that half of all Americans older than the age of ten had seen one or more copies of the magazine in 1950 (just a year after *Life* published the Johnstons' story).[42] In the words of its founder, Henry Luce, *Life*'s mission was to be the "Show-Book of the World," to educate and entertain its twenty million primarily white, urban and suburban, middle-class readers by opening a window "to see life, to see the world, to eyewitness great events, to watch the faces of the poor and the gestures of the proud."[43] *Life*'s coverage of the Johnstons coupled the magazine's embrace of the nuclear family and postwar domesticity with its commitment to racial liberalism. *Life* normalized the Johnstons, presenting their story as one of human interest, far removed from the battlegrounds of politics and crises over desegregation. White readers could look and see just how similar the Johnstons were to their own families. The Johnstons' class status and conformity to traditional gender roles and ideals about family values also made them a source of pride for *Ebony,* whose founder and publisher, John H. Johnson, promised to deliver the "happier side of Negro life" to its readers and focused its content on black "firsts," celebrities, and consumerism.[44]

Life and *Look* acted as the emissaries of racial liberalism and promoted the idea of an integrated society before the fact of one existed, casting the Johnston family and their tolerant neighbors as symbols of the dawn of a new era in American race relations. These magazines proudly announced that the residents of Keene embraced the Johnstons, even though they were a black family who had passed as white. In February 1949, *Look* reported with delight, "The Johnstons, a leading family in Keene, N.H., last spring let the world know that they were Negroes. The reaction? There was none." *Look* editor William Houseman described the magazine's investment in depicting peaceful integration and wrote to Albert Johnston Jr. that the "most important message" of the article was that "the Johnstons of Keene, New Hampshire, have passed through such a remarkable experience without altering their lives one single bit." *Look* presented the Johnstons as ideal neighbors: they were "the proprietors of one of the happiest hangouts in the little town of Keene," and, most importantly, the family "is one of the most socially accepted and prosperous in the town."[45]

Life and *Look*'s splashy photographs of Keene as a newly but peacefully integrated community offered visual certainty of the town's acceptance and featured each family member in a placid interracial setting. *Look* pictured the Johnstons' daughter, Ann, playing cards encircled by white friends and assured its readers that she is still the "most popular girl in her high school class." *Ebony* showed the Johnstons entertaining "European-born" guests in their elegant living room, and *Life* featured Albert Johnston Jr. sharing a room with two white students at the University of New Hampshire. Although most of the photographs featured the Johnstons in social situations, other pictures placed Dr. Johnston in professional settings, supervising other doctors, discussing x-ray film, and treat-

Figure 5.3. The Johnston family home in Keene, New Hampshire. This home was the social hub of Keene.
Courtesy of the Archive Center at the Historical Society of Cheshire County, Keene, New Hampshire.

ing white patients.[46] The photographs visually corroborated the optimistic text of the articles and gave a national readership a rare first look at the lives of residents of an amicably "integrated" town.

Although the photographs foregrounded the Johnstons, the articles lavished praise on the white residents of Keene for their "compassion" and "open-mindedness." The "real heroes" were the sympathetic and kindhearted white friends and neighbors who embraced the Johnstons after discovering their racial ancestry.[47] The article "New Hampshire Neighborliness Crosses the Color Line," published in the *New Hampshire Sunday News,* commended the town's "tolerance, transcending racial bias and color lines to accept a Keene family as neighbors, though they have Negro blood."[48] Echoing earlier observations that there was "no reaction at all," the articles insisted that race simply did not matter to the kindhearted folks of Keene. The same article noted that Dr. Johnston's patients "trusted him and respected him as a doctor. And that, for Keene, was enough."[49] The local newspaper, the *Keene Sentinel,* gushed with pride when it described a Sunday morning in which the parishioners invited Dr. Johnston to ring the church bells. The *Sentinel* described that idyllic moment as symbolic of "the world as it should be."[50] The 1949 film *Lost Boundaries* staged the town's acceptance in similar ways, and newspapers responded with equal praise: the *Boston Record* found that the "unanimously generous, understanding reaction of the neighbors" offered the film's viewers "profoundly stirring sequences."[51] Reminiscent of Myrdal's attention to "what goes on in the minds of white Americans," the authors of these articles underscored the role of liberal whites as agents of change.[52] These articles overstated the impact of integration on whites and presented integration as a generous act of white sacrifice and benevolence. Little if any inquiry was directed toward the attendant effects on blacks.

Ebony shifted the focus back to the Johnstons and offered a more cautious analysis of Keene's acceptance of the family. Although featuring a similar collage of interracial photographs, *Ebony* carefully noted, "always accepted and considered white by the community, the Johnstons are now exposed as Negroes—all voluntarily on their part. To date their status in the small town of Keene, NH is unchanged."[53] *Ebony* voiced more skepticism about the town's reaction and anticipated that the disclosure of the Johnstons' racial identity would eventually cause trouble for the family. A critical assessment of the reaction of the New Hampshire community led to *Ebony*'s report that "proud though they are of Keene's liberality toward Negroes, some residents of the city wonder whether it is because so few colored people live there that acceptance of Negroes is not a problem." *Ebony* interviewed Felix Eckhardt, a white resident of Keene and a friend of the Johnstons, who supported this claim by observing, "Majority groups in nearly every city are willing to accept members of a minority readily, as long as there are not too many of them to assimilate. Perhaps Keene could accept even this situation, but since it has not come about, there is no sure way to tell."[54] Keene residents had no cause to fear a "black invasion"; Albert Johnston Jr. counted only six black families living among Keene's 13,800 residents.[55] Still, George Miller, one of the few black residents, unequivocally defended Keene's progressive image. Proudly stating that he had never encountered any social or professional discrimination, Miller described Keene as "one of the most liberal cities in the world."[56]

The Limits of Racial Liberalism

Even in the purportedly progressive town of Keene, racial liberalism proved ambiguous. Although *Life, Look,* and *Ebony* circulated the Johnstons' story as an encouraging sign of successful integration, Thyra Johnston recalled that when word got around Keene that the family was black, "good friends sent many cards, letters, flowers and called. . . . We weren't quite sure whether they were congratulating us or condoling with us."[57]

The media's celebration of the town's neighborliness and wholehearted acceptance of the Johnstons cloaked a fractious political battle that occurred at Elliot Community Hospital. The board of directors tried to oust Johnston from his position shortly after they discovered his racial identity in 1947. After a contentious six-year battle, the board was successful. On July 5, 1953, the hospital trustees terminated Johnston's contract. Johnston described a "most harmonious relationship" with the hospital's board of trustees before he revealed his racial background. Indeed, Dr. Johnston offered confirmation of the town's tolerance and declared, "If I wanted to be militant about our family's new status, it would be just like Don Quixote fighting windmills."[58] Over the course of his thirteen-year career in Keene, he had played a major role in attracting new patients and increasing the yearly income of the radiology department.[59] But, in fact, this friendly relationship soured after the *Reader's Digest* article was published. In a letter to Louis de Rochemont, the producer of *Lost Boundaries,* Thyra Johnston spoke candidly about "the stink going on among some of the board of directors at the hospital to 'oust' [Johnston] out of the hospital."[60] Thyra told de Rochemont about an incident in which Johnston confronted a trustee who "had the nerve to practically admit it was a color issue," convincing Thyra that the doctors at the hospital would "stoop to any means to get him out." Seeing the dispute as one of both race and class, Thyra blamed the "malicious jealousy" of a small clique known as the "Court Street Gang" and speculated that things might have been different if she and Dr. Johnston had been "friends of theirs" or "had joined their country club."[61] Thyra remained confident that "there are more people in Keene who are not prejudiced, as is this little clique that are trying to instigate trouble for us."[62]

After the release of *Lost Boundaries* drew national attention to the family's story, local branches of the NAACP asked the Johnstons to speak on the subject of integration. These branches saw the Johnstons as uniquely situated to advance a civil rights agenda and to denounce racial inequality.[63] Johnston's earlier rejection from the Navy provided additional fodder for the NAACP. Lillian Jackson, president of the Baltimore branch, asked Johnston to speak about his experiences with the Navy and noted that "the day is fast dawning when a man's position in life will not depend upon the color of his skin, but upon his ability alone."[64] Johnston's professional and socioeconomic credentials also heightened his appeal. As an upper-middle-class physician, Johnston was well poised to be an NAACP spokesman. The sensationalism of the story attracted large audiences. NAACP members were eager to have a look at the Johnstons and judge their appearance for themselves. If these members subscribed to *Ebony,* they would have been familiar with articles that played with the curious nature of passing by asking readers to identify "Which is Negro?" and "Which is White?" from a collage of photographs of racially ambiguous men and women. Both the NAACP and *Ebony* relied on the fascination with passing within the black community to sell magazines and to draw large turnouts to the Johnstons' speaking engagements.

While he lived as a white man, Dr. Johnston had fallen silent on issues of race for almost twenty years; when he finally spoke before the Baltimore branch of the NAACP in September of 1949, he had much to say. He offered an especially scathing critique of the failure of the nation to fulfill its promises to blacks: "The U.S. stands before the entire world as a hypocrite because of the racial equality it preaches and the arrogant bigoted white racial superiority it practices. . . . Even an imbecile doesn't believe the tommy-rot about racial equality as practiced by the U.S. government." Johnston proposed an aggressive program to improve race relations that emphasized interracial interaction "on a social basis." Drawing on his own experiences, he explained that only "when one person through intimate social contact understands another, his weaknesses, and virtues, prejudice breaks down."[65]

Johnston's speeches coupled messages of race pride with explicit critiques of racial discrimination. Reflecting a nascent racial consciousness and speaking about the resilience of the black community, he identified himself with his audience and expressed pride in "our race" that has "undergone and is undergoing so many humiliations, brutalities, injustices and suppression," but still had the "patience and fortitude and still is unequalled in its ability to be happy and joyous in the presence of fear, humiliation and—for most of us, poverty." While Johnston's middle-class upbringing sheltered him from many of the hardships that he described, he spoke candidly about discrimination, noting the irrationality and inexplicability of prejudice during a time when the nation needed the skills of its entire population: "Nature does not give talents according to color, and the Lord only knows how many Edisons have spent their life mopping floors because of the lack of opportunity to develop latent talents. No country can present their full strength without using the labor, the genius, and culture of all its people."[66] Johnston ended his speech by linking racial progress with national interests: echoing the racial rhetoric of the Cold War period, he called for the immediate passage of legislation to "abolish this very un-American racial persecution" and implored the government not to "bow for political expediency to the minority of racial bigots" but rather to "conscientiously support such vital legislation in the interest of national security."[67] Hitting all the right notes, Johnston connected personally with his audience and made an impassioned plea for the country to live up to its democratic principles.

Dr. Johnston also offered a more sobering portrayal of the series of events that led to his dismissal from the hospital to NAACP audiences and in an article published in the *Keene Sentinel.* Recanting his previous statement that he would be "like Don Quixote tilting at windmills" if he said that he had experienced any trouble, as early as November 1949, Johnston stated that he believed that "racial discrimination or personal animosity" was the underlying motive behind the effort to terminate of his contract.[68] Johnston suspected that "somebody was knifing [him] shortly after the information got around that [he] was a Negro."[69] A chance meeting confirmed Johnston's suspicions when, early in 1949, Johnston was accidentally introduced to the new radiologist who would replace him. Johnston stated that he built the department fivefold in seven years. "You can imagine my shock," Johnston told the *Keene Sentinel;* "I had been in Keene since 1940 and I had built up the department considerably. I was on the best terms with everyone and had no idea what was being planned. It was all done very quietly."[70] The hospital trustees denied Johnston's allegations and argued that he had neglected his duties at the hospital by opening a private practice. Johnston offered a different explanation: in June 1949, his decision to open a private office was for "self protection, for the time when they might pull the rug out from under me."[71] The debate continued and in a front-page article of the *Keene Sentinel* on June 12, 1953, hospital official Charles Kingsbury denied that Johnston's dismissal was related to his race; Johnston countered Kingsbury's argument and stated that he "has no doubt he was fired because he is a Negro."[72] After his dismissal, Johnston continued a successful private practice in Keene until 1966, when he and Thyra left Keene and retired in Hawaii.

Passing Goes to Hollywood

If *Life, Look,* and *Ebony* magazines gave passing its largest readership with splashy photographs and optimistic prose, the silver screen brought these pictures and stories to life, making the agony of those who passed palpable, even heart-rending to national audiences. Although some moviegoers were moved to tears, others never had the opportunity to see the film at all. Southern censors banned *Lost Boundaries,* claiming that it was a threat to public health and a violation of the laws of segregation. Some black critics cheered at the film's rare dramatic depiction of an intact, refined, upper-middle-class black family, but others fumed at the decision to cast white actors in the Johnstons' roles.

Ralph Ellison was perhaps the most vocal critic of *Lost Boundaries* and other "message movies" of the late 1940s. To Ellison's mind, pulling black humanity out of the wreckage of the racist epic *The Birth of a Nation* (1915) was a tall order: "In the struggle against Negro freedom, motion pictures have been one of the strongest instruments for justifying some white Americans' anti-Negro attitudes and practices."[73] An exasperated Ellison argued that rendering whites the "true protagonists" of the film was an inexcusable affront. Even the advertising for *Lost Boundaries* directly addressed white audiences and evoked white sympathy by asking, "Would You Condemn the Carters for Living Their Lie?"[74]

In a critique of *Lost Boundaries* and other message movies, Ellison observed, "obviously these films are not about Negroes at all; they are about what whites think and feel about Negroes." By broaching the issue of racial prejudice, Ellison explained, the filmmakers had fallen upon the "eggshell ice," but they simply were not "heavy enough to break it." The power of the narrative and the effort at exposing racial prejudice was blunted by the hesitation and lack of courage of the directors, resulting in "a defeat not only of drama, but of purpose."[75] Perhaps the most troubling scene in *Lost Boundaries* occurred when Albert Johnston Jr., devastated by the revelation

Figure 5.4. Advertisement for *Lost Boundaries* (1949), the film that tells the Johnstons' story. This image captures the folk mythology that racial identity was legible on one's fingernails and hands.

Courtesy of the Archive Center at the Historical Society of Cheshire County, Keene, New Hampshire.

of his black ancestry, traveled to Harlem to gain a better understanding of black people and black culture. The film presents Harlem through a series of terrifying images: violence and crime erupted on every street corner, and in a frightening dream sequence, Albert Jr.'s mother's pleasing smile suddenly morphed into a frowning and hardened black face. *Lost Boundaries* presented passing not as a choice, but as a logical strategy to escape the dysfunction and disorder of black life.

Albert and Thyra Johnston, on the other hand, recognized the importance of white identification and sympathy, not only to the box office success of *Lost Boundaries* but also to the film's potential to change racial attitudes. The Johnston family was very satisfied with the production. In a letter to the director, the family wrote: "'Lost Boundaries' is a perfect portrayal of the emotions and reactions of our family. We congratulate you on producing such a realistic and dramatic presentation of one of America's dilemmas."[76] Still, anticipating a backlash from the black community over the all-white cast, Thyra wrote to express her support of the casting decisions: "Colored folks are very touchy. . . . I say, one thing at a time, and the risk of getting 'Lost Boundaries' filmed at all was quite an undertaking. Had you known of its guaranteed success, no doubt you could have used colored actors, and yet I do think the impact would not have been half so forceful."[77] The production company preempted some protest by strategically casting Canada Lee, a well-known black actor and an outspoken civil rights activist, in a minor yet visible role.[78] Regardless of this last-minute addition to the cast, Thyra's letter and the producer's decisions echoed Gunnar Myrdal's assertions that racial progress was contingent on a combination of white benevolence and white action. Canada Lee parroted

Myrdal and other racial liberals when he described the film's greatest asset as its "subconscious tug on the heart."[79]

The *Baltimore Afro-American* noted the film's value in making "some people think, who are not otherwise easily reached."[80] The *Atlanta Daily World* praised the film, stating that *Lost Boundaries* had "evok[ed] unanimous praise from hardened critics. . . . The explosive race subject has been presented intelligently and in a manner the most ignorant will approve."[81] A February 1947 editorial in *Ebony* argued that a "legion of decency for negroes in movies" was needed because "Mammy-minded, plantation-prejudiced movies . . . [had] done more to disrupt peaceful race relations and set back Negro progress than a fistful of Bilbo speeches in Congress."[82] African American audience reaction to the film was decidedly mixed: some laughed at the melodrama and the caricatures of black life in Harlem, whereas others hoped that the film would appeal to the moral conscious of liberal whites, in Myrdalian fashion, and advance the cause of race relations.

The film concludes with a sermon that calls for Christian love and forgiveness—forgiveness, that is, of the Johnstons for their sin of racial transgression and not for the long history of racial discrimination that led to the decision to pass and that implicates both the small New Hampshire town and the nation. In keeping with the documentary style of the film, a real clergyman delivers the sermon in a scene shot on location in Portsmouth, New Hampshire, not far from Keene, at a church whose congregants were cast as extras.[83] Ultimately the Johnstons are absolved—but not because their neighbors believe that no real difference separates them. Instead, the racial trespass can be pardoned because the neighbors, just as the newspapers reported, were extraordinarily charitable and public spirited. Once again, the frame shifts away from the black characters to focus on white charity and benevolence. As the sermon concluded, few churchgoers pondered the actual conditions that animated the practice of passing in the first place.

The board of directors of Elliot Community Hospital was not the only group to object to racial passing. In 1949, a film reviewer for *Variety* predicted the obstacles that *Lost Boundaries* would face in southern theaters, noting that the themes portrayed in the film were "virtually guaranteed taboos in large sectors of the South."[84] Christine Smith, the city censor in Atlanta, immediately banned *Lost Boundaries,* stating that it "contained inferences throughout which created preachments against long-standing customs that also were part of the laws of the South."[85] Segregation, Smith reminded northern critics, "is a matter of law in the South—not just a matter of prejudice." Lloyd Binford, chairman of the Memphis Board of Censors, bluntly stated, "We don't take that kind of picture here."[86]

Binford had a long history of censoring films that he believed clashed with the "Southern way of life" or offered even the slightest suggestion of the southern bugbear of social equality. In 1943, he ruled that city and county movie screens could depict blacks only in roles of subservience. During the same year, the Memphis Board of Censors passed a resolution that ordered that "no moving picture shall be exhibited . . . in which an all negro cast appears or in which roles are depicted by negro actors or actresses not ordinarily performed by members of the colored race in real life."[87] This ruling rejected even hackneyed portrayals of blacks in musicals such as *Cabin in the Sky* (1943). But *Lost Boundaries* levied a more direct attack on racial inequality and posed twinned problems for the censors: the film depicted blacks as professionals, and it displayed a level of interracial interaction and intimacy that vexed even the most liberal southern audiences. As Walter White noted, the film depicted the Johnstons as "what they were—he an excellent and industrious physician, she a superlative housekeeper and church worker, quite different from the prevailing notion of Negroes as stupid, lazy and ignorant."[88] White had argued that improving the representations of blacks in American culture was a key battlefront in the struggle for racial equality. For white racial attitudes to change, blacks must be depicted as rounded, complex, and multidimensional human beings, not flattened, grotesque caricatures. But Binford saw positive portrayals of black life as "inimical to the public welfare" and bristled at the depiction of "social equality between whites and Negroes in a way that we do not have in the South."[89]

The specter of social equality haunted Southerners long before *Lost Boundaries* was released.[90] Small fissures in the Jim Crow system created widespread panic, especially during World War II, when the demands of war mobilization produced new spatial arrangements and placed blacks and whites on the same assembly lines, on the same workbenches, and in the same break rooms and bathrooms in integrated war plants. Southern newspapers charged President Roosevelt's Fair Employment Practices Commission (FEPC) with working "to see that Negroes are put in all sorts of positions where they . . . may associate with white men and white women who work in similar capacities, and thus to break down social barriers."[91] Eugene "Bull" Connor, Commissioner of Public Safety in Birmingham, wrote letters to Roosevelt censuring wartime employment organizations for preaching "social equality" and "stirring up strife."[92] Mississippi senator and segregationist Theodore Bilbo feared that workplace integration would inevitably lead to whites "entertaining Negroes" and warned against "associating with the Negro on equal terms," which would only result in "mongrelizing and contaminating the best blood on earth."[93]

The postwar period did little to quell southern anxiety. The interplay of wartime gains, more aggressive demands of the NAACP and other black organizations, and the government's formal commitment to civil rights made it clear that times were changing. When a strong message on civil rights served as the centerpiece of President Truman's 1948 State of the Union address, black leaders lauded the platform as "Lincolnesque" and the "greatest freedom document since the Emancipation Proclamation." In response, thirty-five southern delegates stormed out of the 1948 Democratic Convention, waved Confederate flags, organized the Dixiecrat Party, and nominated Strom Thurmond for President.[94] Contempt for government action still simmered one year later when *Lost Boundaries* was released, and alarm over threats to the racial status quo guided the decisions of southern censors.

Christine Smith argued that *Lost Boundaries* violated an Atlanta city ordinance that "governs the exhibit of pictures which are obscene, lewd, licentious, profane, or will adversely affect the peace, health, morals and good order of the City." Although Smith admitted that the film was not in particular "lewd, obscene, licentious or profane," she and the other members of the censorship board voted unanimously to ban the film, arguing that its exhibition would "create dissension and strife between the members of the white and colored races, and would be likely to cause disorders, disturbances and clashes between the races."[95] While Smith had approved other films that also dealt with race, she was especially rankled by this film's transparent depictions of the absence of racial segregation and distinguished *Lost Boundaries* based on its "outright pleas for breaking of segregation."[96] Some liberals such as Alexander Miller, director of the Atlanta Anti-Defamation League, supported Smith's ruling. Miller excused Smith's actions by noting that she "does have certain laws and regulations which she must follow."[97]

Binford also appeared inconsistent when he allowed the message movie *Home of the Brave* (1949) to play in Memphis but rejected *Lost Boundaries.* Binford read a distinct difference between the two films: *Home of the Brave* dealt with the association of blacks and whites in the military and the horrors of war; it dramatized interactions and experiences that "could happen," implying that the Johnstons' (true) story could not happen. The *Washington Post* countered Binford's attempt to deny the actuality of the story and described *Lost Boundaries* as a "real life drama" that was "no novel" but rather that offered "the stark truth, names, places and all."[98] Still, *Lost Boundaries* would never play in theaters in Memphis or Atlanta.

In response to the decision to ban the film in Atlanta, Albert Johnston Jr. wrote a letter to the editor of the *Atlanta Constitution* and spoke directly to Southerners: "I do not believe Mr. de Rochemont had any intention whatsoever of trying to 'preach' against the traditional Southern ideology of the so-called 'Negro Problem.' It is understandable why Miss Christine Smith and the Atlanta Censorship Board at first decided to ban the film. 'Lost Boundaries' is the first major film produced on the social aspect of the 'Negro problem' in the United States, and naturally, it must have been quite difficult—if not impossible—to determine how audiences would react." Albert Jr. soft-pedaled the film's messages to assuage southern fears about its intent.[99] Theater owners around the country, including those in southern cities such as New Orleans, Charlotte, Richmond, Miami, and Dallas, reported packed houses when the film was released. Newspapers in New Hampshire heaped praise upon the film and urged "every American to see it."[100] Theater owners in some cities reported varying amounts of audience participation, ranging from "sincere hissing to equally sincere applause." Critics argued that film producers should not object to receiving negative reactions, but should object to "the fact that [some] audiences are not given a chance to react at all."[101]

Has Passing Passed Out?

In July 1949, at the weekly luncheon of the New York Press Club, Albert Johnston announced that if given the chance, he would not pass again.[102] Two years earlier, Johnston had described a deep sense of relief and a "great burden lifted from [his] shoulders" after he publicly disclosed his racial background.[103] Johnston was not alone in disavowing passing. During the late 1940s and through the 1960s, the black press published numerous testimonials of African Americans who decided to give up on passing and catalogued the countless psychological advantages of embracing a black identity. Focusing on the collective pride that African Americans experienced when they returned to the race, rather than shame or disadvantage, the testimonials reflected the growing protest spirit and racial affinity of the burgeoning civil rights movement.[104]

In the 1950 essay "I Refuse to Pass," Janice Kingslow described how she made peace with a decision to retain her dignity by turning down "a chance that millions of American girls have dreamed of."[105] Struggling to find work as an actress to support her ailing mother, Kingslow was charged $20 more for rent than her white neighbors, she was personally insulted by white actors who did not want to share the stage with her, and she struggled to find roles other than maids and servants.[106] Presented with the proposal to change her name and pass for white, Kingslow considered the advantages:

> Then like a dream of paradise came the final temptation. If I accepted this offer I could go anywhere I wanted. I could do anything I wanted, without question. No saleswoman would ever again refuse to sell me a dress. No hotel clerk would refuse me a room. No head waiter would deny me a table. No man would ever look at me again the way that producer had when I told him I was a Negro. The sharp stabs which hurt so much each time they happened would be ended forever. I would be free at last from the unremitting hour to hour, day to day burden of prejudice.[107]

Then, Kingslow considered the sacrifices that passing would entail: "This meant stripping my life clear of everything that I was. . . . Conscience wrestled with dreams of fame and money, and conscience won." After negotiating the advantages and disadvantages of passing, Kingslow described her sense of belonging along with a collective identification with the struggles of other African Americans: "I myself might escape the burden of prejudice by living a lie. But what about other Negroes? Was I ready to admit I wasn't strong enough to endure what they had to bear?"[108] In a reversal of the worry of selling one's birthright for a mess of pottage or "choosing the lesser part," Kingslow reiterated the desire of many African Americans to "knit spirit and soul together" and remain in the race.

Black actor Herb Jeffries was presented with a similar yet more elaborate proposition. Jeffries was a superstar among black moviegoers, known as the "Bronze Buckaroo." Cowboy star Buck Jones encouraged Jeffries to travel to South America for a year to learn

Spanish and later return to the United States as Jones's newly discovered Spanish star. Jeffries told *Life* magazine, "I was almost tempted because by then I'd learned how things are stacked against you as a Negro. But . . . I suddenly asked myself just what the hell I had to run away from, or be ashamed of. So I turned Buck down."[109] Earlier in Jeffries's career, a movie producer, unaware of his race, offered him a role opposite the white actress Hedy Lamarr. When Jeffries explained that he was a black man, he could not take the role, the movie producer asked incredulously, "Why do you want to be a Negro? You could be anything!"[110] Jeffries responded by stating, "I decided some time ago that the Negro people need all the good, intelligent, unbelligerent representatives they can get in this world, and I'm trying to be one." *Life* praised Jeffries for his honesty and integrity, for "scrupulously elect[ing] to 'pass' for nothing but what he is—a light-skinned Negro."[111]

In the 1950s, journalistic accounts of recrossings of the color line pointed to economic opportunities to explain the "end" of passing. *Jet* magazine optimistically predicted that "as race barriers fall, the thousands of Negroes who 'passed' to find decent employment [will] 'return' to their race."[112] The white press, including *U.S. News & World Report,* also cheerfully announced "an era of progress for U.S. Negroes," in which "America's nearly 19 million Negroes are making economic progress that would be hard to match anywhere in the world."[113] One article specifically noted advances in professions such as medicine that "show increasing numbers of Negroes—twice as many as there were in these fields 18 years ago."[114] In 1944, the *Chicago Defender* had identified medicine as "the most Jim Crowed profession in American life," but by 1950, the American Medical Association passed resolutions urging medical societies to remove racially restrictive membership provisions. During the early 1950s, the *Journal of the National Medical Association* printed a number of articles that praised the collapse of racial barriers in medical societies and registered efforts to integrate hospitals.[115] Times had changed. Albert Johnston's prospects would have been much brighter had he applied for internships in 1950 rather than in 1928.

Ebony and *Jet* hoped to beckon blacks back into the fold by depicting the economic ascendancy and the social well-being of the black community. The mission of *Ebony* to "create a windbreak that would let [blacks] get away from 'the problem' for a few moments and say 'Here are some Blacks who are making it'" could easily be repurposed to reacquaint blacks with the material benefits of postwar African American life.[116] The oversized images and overstated successes on the pages of *Ebony,* excoriated by sociologist E. Franklin Frazier in *Black Bourgeoisie,* were tailored toward middle- and upper-middle-class blacks, *Ebony*'s target demographic and its advertisers' leading consumers. The achievements of this group (displayed through regular stories that emphasized "the first, the only, the best") and their enjoyment of the accoutrements of middle-class status—automobiles, washing machines, and televisions, for example—appeared on the pages of the magazine and enabled readers to see racial progress.[117] The 1952 *Jet* article "Why 'Passing' Is Passing Out" noted, "most economically-sound Negroes who could 'pass' prefer being high-class Negroes to low-class whites."[118] Glossy pictures of blacks attending exquisite society balls, taking expensive vacations, and relaxing in well-appointed homes reminded readers that African Americans were living "the good life" too. These magazines hoped to offer a convincing argument that the time had come to eschew the "false uplift" of passing and to participate in more honest forms of class mobility available to African Americans in the postwar period.[119]

"Post-passing" narratives called for a renegotiation and reconciliation with black identity. For some, the end of a racial masquerade meant disentanglement from the psychological burdens of negotiating a divided identity and freedom from the complex and emotionally draining bargaining processes that passing entailed. In "I'm Through with Passing," published anonymously in *Ebony* in March 1951, the author predicted that although many of her friends would pass "without a moment's hesitation just to be free from color problems, poor-paying jobs and all the other vicious injustices that all too often go with being a Negro," she had a different perspective after experiencing the darker side of passing. Listening to white coworkers speak about blacks with bitter contempt, teetering on a "state of nervous collapse," and living in constant fear that her secret would be discovered, she felt relieved to be "through with passing." No longer did she have to worry about returning coworkers' social invitations or getting sick on the job and being taken home by a coworker who would discover that she lived in a black neighborhood. She could now enjoy a life free from "all the hiding, all the dodging, all the miserable lies that turned [her] life into a confused, frustrated existence."[120] Others, feeling sheepish and dishonest about turning their backs on their people, refused to pass and instead chose to cast their lot with fellow African Americans, come what may.

Passing, or racial invisibility, seemed especially incongruous with the upsurge of civil rights activism during this period.[121] The testimonials published in the black press in the 1950s expressed a changing, but not entirely new, sensibility. Its antecedents can be traced to the Reconstruction era, but the desire to live "openly, honestly and without deception" has been a familiar desire for many racially ambiguous people. The salience of changing material conditions (if only rhetorically) should not be discounted, but it must be noted that something more transformative was also at work.

"Making History and a Race"

During the 1960s, racial politics had changed course once again. Black identities were affirmed and passing was rejected. Black was beautiful. Large Afros were in; chemically straightened hair was out. The chant of "black power," the surge of black pride and black unity, and the revival of black nationalist movements rendered passing dissonant with the times. Blending in with the white world seemed no longer economically necessary, politically advantageous, or socially desirable.[122] Attention shifted to black history and black art. In 1968, the *Chicago Defender* created a contest called "How To Build Black Pride" that invited readers to submit ideas about how to increase self-respect and self-love in the black community. Readers recommended the eradication of the "white image" from the thoughts and actions of black people.[123] Black parents were charged with "bequeathing" black pride to their children. In an urgent appeal for authenticity, the *Defender*'s readership suggested that the damage done by the hegemonic white image could be reversed by simply "being ourselves."

To be sure, passing continued, just as it had in every previous era. But in this racial climate, passing was no longer discussed in magazines, no longer the subject of popular films, no longer an above-the-fold story in the *New York Times* or the *Atlanta Daily World*. The racial winds had shifted. By the 1970s, many African Americans perceived passing as either a relic of the past or the worst form of racial treachery.

Rather than asking if passing "passed out," more specific questions should be posed about how the confluence of the political, social, and economic currents of the postwar era guided the decisions that light-skinned blacks made about their racial identities. Many chose to opt out of passing; once "home," some enjoyed greater economic opportunities because of a booming postwar economy, but most delighted in the pleasure of racial fellowship and the freedom from the anxiety of being discovered. Others, like actor Herb Jeffries, spoke of accepting individual inconveniences in order to closely align themselves with the larger struggles of African Americans. Although this is a recurrent historical theme—early in the century we heard the Ex-Colored Man lament in 1912 that he had "chosen the lesser part" and had failed to devote himself "to work so glorious" as that of Booker T. Washington and others "who [were] making history and a race"—these concerns were amplified in the context of the midcentury civil rights movement. The dichotomy of "getting ahead vs. making history" posed by film scholar J. Ronald Green in his discussion of the filmic style of passing juxtaposes the painful trade-offs that passing required with its assurance of economic gain.[124] "Getting ahead," as many of the examples of "working as white" indicated, was both the most obvious and the most morally justifiable reason for passing.

"Making history" was a much more rigorous pursuit, open only to those who identified as black. It was far too risky to make history while passing; few who passed would invite the kind of scrutiny that becoming famous demanded. During the civil rights movement, one did not have to be a race leader to make history as new potentialities emerged for the heroic involvement of everyday people. At that moment, passing struck the wrong notes and had too many hallmarks of false advancement. Similar to the Reconstruction era, when to be black was to be "somebody," whereas to be white was to be "nobody," the postwar years marked an analogously transformative age when passing as white meant confinement to a nontransformative role. As J. Ronald Green argues, "That choice also bypasses the mission of one's group, and in that sense, it is to pass out of history."[125] Passing out of history had been desirable at times—Ellen Craft and countless other racially ambiguous runaway slaves hoped to pass out of the history of slavery, and years later, Lieutenant William J. French hoped to pass out of the constraints of life under Jim Crow. But this was no longer a legitimate or logical desire in the postwar period. Not at a time when it was clear that history was about to be made.

Epilogue: On Identity

> It is difficult to obtain the desired facts when making a study of a family such as mine. My family has a mixture of races that would produce confusion in any genealogical tree. Its history is colorful, to say the least.
>
> The social stigmas of the times have spread a dark haze, like unto a huge smoke cloud, around so many of my ancestors that it has been practically impossible for me to trace the line back but a few generations with any degree of clarity or assurance of truth.
>
> —ANONYMOUS, E. FRANKLIN FRAZIER PAPERS

The woman who wrote this family history claimed to be certain of only two things: her mother was a colored woman born in Virginia around 1875, and her father was a white man born in Virginia in 1865.[1] Her family adhered to the social conventions of the Jim Crow South and lived in a black neighborhood. In their father's company and beyond the neighborhood limits, the children could easily pass as white. As one daughter explained, "When we went places with our father and left our mother at home, we could go wherever we wished without question as to race."[2] The children relished these holidays and their father, "staggered" by his children's blond-haired, blue-eyed beauty, enjoyed bringing them along wherever he went. Perhaps these days were holidays for him too. He spent most of his life straddling the color line in similar ways as blacks that passed as white. "His working world belonged to the white race," his daughter explained, but after work, he returned to a black neighborhood and spent his evenings with his black wife and seven mixed-race children.[3] Family life continued this way, peacefully and uneventfully, until the father's final wishes conflicted with the life that he lived, casting doubt on his self-identification, and leaving troubling questions for his wife and his children. His daughter puzzled over his last request: "There is one thing surrounding my father's death which has always caused me to feel that he had not reorganized his scheme of life to fit into a world with his colored wife and half-white children." Despite years of discord and estrangement from his white relatives, he made arrangements to be buried in a plot in the white family's cemetery. In death, he wished to be white. When his children visited his grave with their mother, his daughter wrote that white mourners stared at them as if to ask why they had "invaded their sacred territory."[4] The phenomenon of passing gave the lie to the notion of "sacred territory," even during decades of legalized segregation when racial categories were presumed to be inviolable. But it also left family members struggling to reckon with painful and sometimes unanswerable questions.

A history of passing opens a window onto the complexity of the human experience. This practice offers a vehicle for understanding a set of actions that would otherwise vanish from the historical record. A study of passing must take account of the absurdities of the American racial situation: the illogic of the one-drop rule, the possibility of changing one's racial identification by walking across a state line, the reliance of nineteenth-century judges on "experts" including hairdressers and foot doctors to determine racial identity in the courtroom, and the belief that race could be revealed through a look in the eye or a bluish tinge on the fingernails. In Langston Hughes's story, "Who's Passing for Who," the revelation that the couple is white after all pokes fun at widely held folk knowledge that blacks were especially attuned to the signs of race and could, borrowing Ralph Ellison's words, "spot a paper-thin 'white Negro' every time."[5] This presumption led the owners of segregated movie theaters in Washington, D.C., to hire black "spotters" to eject passers who took their seats in the white sections rather than the balcony, colloquially known as the "nigger heaven."

If the lesson from Hughes's story is that black folks could be fooled too and that white folks could do the fooling, then race amounts to little more than a skilled performance and a clever enactment of a role. Sometimes passing was characterized as a joke or a trick. Similar to the Uncle Remus tales of Brer Rabbit and the stories of numerous slave tricksters in African American folklore, passers "fool[ed] . . . white folks" by trading on racial ambiguity to skillfully maneuver out of a position of weakness, to live out the fantasy of "getting over," and to successfully improve their lot.[6] Self-help and self-determination were enduring and fundamental American values, but this racial sleight of hand unnerved and alarmed those who believed in the visibility and certainty of race.

Passing reveals the vagaries of race and the farcical nature of racial categorization, but it also produces much more intimate understandings of race and identity, not only as ambiguous analytical tools or social categories, but also as relationships between people. Identity is a series of networks and a set of connections. A question posed by anthropologist James Clifford in *The Predicament of Culture* underscores identity's relational quality: "What if identity is conceived not as [a] boundary to be maintained but as a nexus of relations and transactions actively engaging a subject?"[7] Boundaries are unreliable and easily crossed, but networks and connections inside the boundaries remain foundational to one's identity.

The film *The Return of Martin Guerre* (1982) elucidates this point. In the film, a clever impostor, Pansette, is welcomed into a family and a village by claiming to be Martin Guerre, an unhappy peasant who abandoned his wife, his child, and his land nine years earlier. The villagers took note of the obvious physical differences between the new Martin and the old, but Pansette's dazzling memory and his intimate knowledge of Martin's personal life reassured even the most dubious. Pansette's immediate recognition of Martin's sisters, uncle, and neighbors, his vivid reminiscences of youthful pranks and games played fifteen years before, and his easy recall of the most private details of Martin's marriage seemed to provide indisputable evidence of his identity. Who else but the "real" Martin Guerre could know where he left the white hosen before he fled from the village? Or the number of masses needed to break the spell and free him from the humiliation of impotence?[8] Along the way, Pansette must have had accomplices. He likely overheard gossip about Martin and his family. Presumably, neighbors, family members, and even Martin's wife, unwittingly or not, helped

Pansette to fashion his new identity and eventually, to become a more authentic Martin than Martin himself. When the real Martin returned to reclaim his wife, his property, and his identity, he performed poorly, bungling the answers to questions about his past. With family cooperation and collaboration, Pansette was able to make Martin's life his own.[9]

As in the story of Martin Guerre, those who passed as white remind us that identity is not simply inscribed in one's person. The history of passing enables us to imagine racial identity as an active and close association between people, as a historically contingent relationship that changed in response to various interactions, and in the context of different social spaces. Pansette's gambit foundered before the reappearance of the real Martin in the dramatic finale of *The Return of Martin Guerre.* This man, as some family members and villagers concluded, could *not* be Mathurin Guerre's son—not after violent quarrels with his uncle over his inheritance and his astonishing lack of gratitude for the protection that his family received during his long absence. The deterioration of Pansette's relationships signaled the disintegration of Pansette's identity. His last hope lay in his claim to be the husband of the honorable Bertrande de Rols, for who could corroborate the missing man's identity with greater certainty than his own wife? But as a virtuous woman, Bertrande could not afford to stand by the side of the accused man. She had her own identity to preserve. If this man was neither Mathurin Guerre's son nor the husband of Bertrande de Rols, then just who was he? Who were his people? He had none. And without people, he was nothing more than an impostor subject to a fitting punishment: arrest and execution.

The decision to pass created a profound sense of loss: kin were rejected, networks were disbanded, and connections were broken.

Ronne Hartfield observed that colored people all over the world immediately ask, "Who are your people?" when they meet each other for the first time, which suggests just how traumatic losing one's people could be. To be sure, there were new people to gain and new relationships to enjoy on "the other side," but some experienced the loss of one's family of origin like a phantom limb dangling from the body or clenched in a painful position. The family members were physically gone yet vivid memories remained. Intermittent reminders and distorted sensations of their presence persisted.

In stripping away one's ascribed status, passing offers a sharper angle of vision onto the personal meanings of racial identity from the perspective of African American communities. For black family members, racial identity aligned with familial affinity, and as such, race became much more about a sense of belonging and completeness, styles of living, memories, stories, desires, and even myths.

The most important lesson that can be drawn from a history of passing, then, is a deeper and more meaningful understanding of the ways that race is lived and experienced. With only a quick glance, contemporary eyes may view passing as an unconscionable act, the ultimate metaphor of racial and familial abandonment, and the very worst kind of "selling out." If we recall Frazier's excoriation of what he observed as a self-hating and apathetic black middle class, we can imagine how his critique might have been amplified when directed at those who turned away from African American life altogether.

But by dwelling too long on the theme of race shame, we may overlook the equally compelling theme of race pride. For it was a sense of race pride (and sometimes a desire to dissociate from the shame of passing) that was apparent in rhetorical devices used by racially ambiguous men and women who immediately identified themselves as black to avoid confusion or embarrassment. In 1872, Robert Harlan made his racial identity known to reporters at the Republican National Convention by announcing, "I look as if I am on the other side, but I am entirely on the dark side."[10] During his short lifetime, Charles Drew, a surgeon and blood plasma pioneer, was known to make a habit of placing himself squarely within the African American community. Lenore Drew, Drew's wife, explained that because "[Drew's] skin was so white, people assumed he was white. Instead of waiting for them to find out [he was black], he would say, 'When those of us who are Negroes' or some other phrase. He'd let people know right away."[11] Tensions between the feelings of race shame and race pride are best summarized by film scholar J. Ronald Green's formulation of the dichotomy between "getting ahead vs. making history."[12] Passing was a useful strategy for getting ahead, but it was no way to make history. A number of testimonials published in the black press in the 1950s attested that when a sense of race pride outweighed feelings of race shame, when one worried about the consequences of "choosing the lesser part" or "selling [one's] birthright for a mess of pottage," making history became a far more honorable pursuit than simply getting ahead.

Still, passing's most urgent and most emotionally freighted questions were not about effective strategies for "making history." Instead, passing broached more personal and intimate themes and underscored an expansive sense of racial affinity. Day Shepherd's question—"How would anyone know who they were without their people?"—lays bare fundamental concerns about identity and expresses puzzlement about the familial dislocations that passing required.[13] In the end, passing offers an intimate look at the convoluted and vexing history of race and racial identity in America. By ordering the disavowal of what many found precious about African American life, passing reveals the most private and the most personal meanings of African American identities.

Mixed-Race Identities in the Twenty-First Century

The long history of passing reveals that older racial formations never give way entirely. Shards and fragments of past racial regimes remain visible in contemporary ones. Even in historical moments widely heralded as turning points, when the nation seems to pivot and reverse course, the past still can be seen in the present. This observation does not suggest that nothing is new, but rather that new arrangements are never wholly free of some elements of the old. Racial ideologies are plastic, and they are quick to adapt and reproduce under new social structures. The past is stubborn. Time never begins again. As our present moment unfolds, we are often left to wonder if we have seen this movie before.[14]

Without question, racially ambiguous people in the twenty-first century are living through a very different moment than those who lived in the 1920s or the 1820s. The racial dynamics of the new millennium have created an array of choices that were inconceivable and unavailable to mixed-race people in the past. In the 1920s, Jean Toomer wondered why he had to choose a racial identity. His appeal for a hybrid identity and his statement that to "tie me to one of my parts was to loose [*sic*] me"[15] fell on deaf ears.[16] Toomer was marked, whether he liked it or not, as "a great Negro writer," even by close friends who he assumed knew better. When he resisted this title, refused to publish his poems in James Weldon Johnson's anthology, moved to Greenwich Village, and became a follower of the Russian spiritual leader Georges Gurdjieff, it was assumed then (and is now, among some scholars) that he had chosen to pass for white. In Toomer's time, there were only two options for racially ambiguous people: pass as white or live as black. Regardless of how eloquently Toomer argued for hybridity, his idea never gained traction. The racial constraints of the Jim Crow era would not allow it.

By the beginning of the twenty-first century, the racial landscape had changed and new choices and possibilities emerged. In 2003, Halle Berry became the second African American actress in film history to accept an Academy Award. In her tearful speech, Berry, who is mixed race, accepted the Academy Award by paying tribute to underappreciated African American actresses. She wholeheartedly embraced a singular black racial identity at the Oscars, but afterwards, she had access to a number of racially unmarked roles. After his historic election as the first African American president in 2008, Barack Obama checked "African American" on the 2010 census but chose not to identify himself as "the black president."[17] This decision may have been a personal choice, or it may have been guided by political expediency. Obama had to perform a racial balancing act. First, critics voiced concerns about Obama's sense of racial kinship because he is not a descendent of slaves and the most influential figures in his life have been white, including his mother and his grandparents. To counter these doubts, Obama sprinkled rhetorical flourishes throughout his speeches, and he dazzled observers with his basketball skills. His wife, Michelle, who has a recognizably black American family history, has helped Obama to shore up his racial bona fides. By the twenty-first century, African American success in the White House and beyond hinged on one's ability to claim a black racial identity, but to transcend it at the same time.

This choice—identifying as black but embracing hybridity—is not entirely new. By recognizing both sides of his racially mixed heritage, Obama embodied the qualities of the "The Future American" that both Toomer and Charles Chesnutt had envisioned in the early twentieth century. To be sure, the conditions of the late twentieth century and the early twenty-first century made this approach more possible and more legible to others, but it was not without constraints—there continues to be resistance to the notion of a hybrid identity—or historical antecedents.

Passing and the acceptance of racial hybridity function as the two most discernible points on a spectrum of possibilities for those who are racially indeterminate. We might also think of passing and living with hybridity as two interrelated sides of the same coin. In each historical period, passing and hybridity have been possible responses to particular circumstances. The conditions of the twenty-first century allow for a greater acceptance of hybridity. Obama can find his "people" in his grandfather's service in General Patton's army and in his father's homeland in Kenya. He can celebrate his mother's family while also enjoying the "comfort, the firmness of identity that a name might provide," when he is recognized as his father's son by a British Airways official at the Kenyatta International Airport in Nairobi.[18]

Beginning in the 1990s, American society began to move toward the end of the spectrum that recognized hybrid identities. This change was reflected not only in personal attitudes and experiences but also in federal racial classifications. In 1993, multiracial activists challenged the one-drop rule and argued that mixed-race people should be officially recognized on the 2000 census. In 1997, the U.S. Census Bureau's policy changed for the first time in almost eighty years to allow individuals to "mark one or more" categories. Numerous mixed-race organizations, magazines, college classes, and websites appeared and began to garner greater public attention.[19]

Suddenly, mixed-race men and women were in vogue. A 2003 article in the Style section of the *New York Times* named a new crop of Americans "Generation E. A." (an abbreviation for "ethnically ambiguous"), and noted the marketing power of this group. The article observed that casting calls for blond-haired, blue-eyed actors had dwindled and were replaced by calls for actors of color, such as one for a CBS soap opera that requested: "Light complexioned African-American. Could be part Brazilian or Dominican."[20] According to the *New York Times,* the look of racial ambiguity was especially profitable for companies that marketed products to a younger set. Linda Wells, *Allure* magazine's editor-in-chief, explained the fixation on racial hybridity: "Five years ago, about 80 percent of our covers featured fair-haired blue-eyed women, even though they represented a minority. . . . Uniformity just isn't appealing anymore."[21] New marketing priorities were the result of societal and demographic changes caused by increased levels of immigration and interracial marriage. Interracial marriage increased tenfold between 1960 and 1990 (from approximately 150,000 to 1.5 million); the number of mixed-race children born to these marriages skyrocketed from approximately 500,000 to 2 million.[22]

As mixed-race author Danzy Senna explained, America had entered the "Mulatto Millennium." In a futuristic parody of the same name, Senna describes her surprise when she wakes one morning to discover she was "in style . . . that mulattos had taken over. They were everywhere—playing golf, running the airwaves, opening restaurants, modeling clothes, starring in musicals with names like *Show Me the Miscegenation!* The radio played a steady stream of Lenny Kravitz, Sade, and Mariah Carey. . . . Pure breeds (at least black ones) are out; hybridity is in." Senna had previously identified as a black girl, "an enemy of the mulatto nation," who frowned upon those who described themselves as racially mixed. This stance on race was largely because of Senna's upbringing in the 1970s in Boston where "mixed wasn't an option. . . . No halvsies. No in between."[23] Senna chose not to claim a mixed-race identity, but her experience of Boston in the 1970s was remarkably similar to Toomer's experience of Harlem in the 1920s: few Americans—black or white—were comfortable with the concept of hybridity. But by the late 1990s and the early 2000s, much had changed.

The friendly embrace of hybridity in the twenty-first century neither signals the achievement of a "postracial" age nor supports the colorblind thesis that race no longer matters. On the contrary, the increasing acceptance of hybridity underscores just how germane race continues to be to contemporary American society. Some scholars have argued that the chorus of support for a mixed-race movement corresponds with worrisome setbacks to civil rights legislation. A mixed-race movement could vitiate the solidarity needed to press for racial justice. The championing of a multiracial category on the U.S. census by conservatives has done little to quell this alarm. Some have argued that the addition of a multiracial category coupled with the elimination of affirmative action programs in an overall effort to eradicate racial categories will increase racial harmony. But if racial accounting is interrupted or terminated, compensatory programs, including affirmative action, would be threatened.[24] The claim that without the state's action and intervention the nation would be colorblind is erroneous. Race is reproduced all around us, at every level of society, including in our everyday lives. The state must then be involved to redress the historical and ongoing inequalities that racism has produced. Nations such as France and Brazil that have adopted official policies of "race blindness" are rife with racial disparities. We are left with a paradox:

race must be acknowledged in public policy decisions because attempts to get rid of race result in a deeper entrenchment of racism and racial inequality.

Perhaps passing, as traditionally understood, has "passed out" in the twenty-first century. But underneath, the core issues of race and identity remain. Hybrid identities are still racialized identities. Racially ambiguous people are racially marked and still must negotiate the terrain of a racist society. Personal choices about how to live with race continue to be tested and contested over time, correlating and shifting with historical circumstances and social structures. New opportunities bring new limitations. Each generation must navigate the social currents and racial realities of its own making.

NOTES

ACKNOWLEDGMENTS

INDEX

Notes

PROLOGUE

Epigraph: Mary Church Terrell, "Why, How, When and Where Black Becomes White," n.d., unpublished manuscript, ms., box 102–3, folder 128, p. 1, Mary Church Terrell Papers, Moorland-Spingarn Research Center, Howard University, Washington, D.C. (hereafter Terrell Papers, MSRC). Terrell borrows this phrase from a friend who "wishes to show what little effort is required to bring a certain thing to pass." Terrell notes, "But falling off a log is really a difficult feat compared with the ease with which colored people in this country are sometimes transformed into white."

1. James Weldon Johnson, *The Autobiography of an Ex-Colored Man* (1912; repr., New York: Dover Publications, 1995), 100.
2. Kenneth Robert Janken, *White: The Biography of Walter White, Mr. NAACP* (Chapel Hill: University of North Carolina Press, 2006), 3–4.
3. Quoted in Werner Sollors, *Neither Black nor White yet Both: Thematic Explorations of Interracial Literature* (Cambridge, Mass.: Harvard University Press, 1997), 147.

4. Thomas Jefferson to Francis C. Gray, Esq., March 4, 1815, in Thomas Jefferson and Henry Augustine Washington, *The Writings of Thomas Jefferson: Being His Autobiography, Correspondence, Reports, Messages, Addresses, and Other Writings, Official and Private: Published by the Order of the Joint Committee of Congress on the Library, from the Original Manuscripts, Deposited in the Department of State* (Washington, D.C.: Taylor & Maury, 1854), 436–437. My thanks to James Campbell for pointing me to this letter. For exceptions to this rule, see Ariela Gross, "Litigating Whiteness: Trials of Racial Determination in the Nineteenth Century South," *Yale Law Review* 108, no. 1 (1998). Legal scholars, including Cheryl Harris, Randall Kennedy, Ariela Gross, Paul Lombardo, and Daniel Sharfstein, have considered the complex interactions and mutually constitutive relationships between racial identity and the law. Along with historian Peggy Pascoe, these scholars have described the efforts of judges and juries to rely on slippery physical characteristics to place racially ambiguous litigants into unstable racial categories. See Cheryl Harris, "Whiteness as Property," *Harvard Law Review* 106, no. 8 (1993); Randall Kennedy, *Interracial Intimacies: Sex, Marriage, Identity, and Adoption* (New York: Pantheon Books, 2003); Ariela Gross, "Litigating Whiteness"; Paul Lombardo, "Miscegenation, Eugenics, and Racism: Historical *Footnotes* to *Loving v. Virginia*," *UC Davis Law Review* 21, no. 2 (1988); Daniel Sharfstein, "The Secret History of Race in the United States," *Yale Law Journal* 112 (April 2003) and "Crossing the Color Line: Racial Migration and the One-Drop Rule, 1600–1860," *Minnesota Law Review* 91, no. 3 (2007). Also see the work of historian Peggy Pascoe, "Miscegenation, Law, Court Cases, and Ideologies of 'Race' in Twentieth-Century America," *Journal of American History* 83, no. 1 (1996).
5. Charles Chesnutt, "What Is a White Man?" *Independent* 41 (May 30, 1889), 5–6.
6. James Baldwin, *Tell Me How Long the Train's Been Gone* (New York: Dial, 1968), 61.

7. Literary critic Cheryl Wall writes that passing novels "symbolize the oppression of blacks, the irrationality of prejudice, or the absurdity of concepts of race generally." See Cheryl Wall, "Passing for What? Aspects of Identity in Nella Larsen's Novels," *Black American Literature Forum* (Spring–Summer 1986): 98. Irene Redfield, the narrator of Nella Larsen's novel, *Passing,* is right, then, to dismiss the notion that racial differences could be detected by examining "finger-nails, palms of hands, shapes of ears, [and] teeth" as "silly rot." See Nella Larsen, *Passing* (New Brunswick, N.J.: Rutgers University Press, 1986), 150.
8. "Saw Murphy Date Miss U. Co-eds," *Pittsburgh Courier,* October 6, 1962, 25.
9. "Negro Passing as White Reveals His Ole Miss Career," *Washington Post,* September 26, 1962, A4.
10. A constellation of scholarship exists on racial mixture, racial hybridity, white racial formation, the social construction of race, and passing that speaks to the larger theme of identity. For recent works on passing, racial ambiguity, the social construction of race, and miscegenation, see Daniel J. Sharfstein, *The Invisible Line: Three American Families and the Secret Journey from Black to White* (New York: Penguin, 2011); Michele Elam, *The Souls of Mixed Folk: Race, Politics, and Aesthetics in the New Millennium* (Palo Alto, Calif.: Stanford University Press, 2011); Peggy Pascoe, *What Comes Naturally: Miscegenation Law and the Making of Race in America* (New York: Oxford University Press, 2009); Martha Sandweiss, *Passing Strange: A Gilded Age Tale of Love and Deception Across the Color Line* (New York: Penguin, 2009); Elizabeth Smith-Pryor, *Property Rites: The Rhinelander Trial, Passing, and the Protection of Whiteness* (Chapel Hill: University of North Carolina, 2009); Baz Dreisinger, *Near Black: White-to-Black Passing in American Culture* (Amherst: University of Massachusetts Press, 2008); Ariela Gross, *What Blood Won't Tell: A History of Race on Trial in America* (Cambridge, Mass.: Harvard University Press, 2008); Kathleen Pfeiffer, *Race Passing and American*

Individualism (Amherst: University of Massachusetts Press, 2003); Renee C. Romano, *Race Mixing: Black-White Marriage in Postwar America* (Cambridge, Mass.: Harvard University Press, 2003); James M. O'Toole, *Passing for White: Race, Religion, and the Healy Family, 1820–1920* (Amherst: University of Massachusetts Press, 2002); and Gayle Wald, *Crossing the Line: Racial Passing in Twentieth-Century U.S. Literature and Culture* (Durham, N.C.: Duke University Press, 2000).

Several memoirs have been written about racial identity and passing: Bliss Boyard, *One Drop: My Father's Hidden Life—A Story of Race and Family Secrets* (New York: Little, Brown, 2007); Ronne Hartfield, *Another Way Home: The Tangled Roots of Race in One Chicago Family* (Chicago: University of Chicago Press, 2004); and James McBride, *The Color of Water: A Black Man's Tribute to His White Mother* (New York: Riverhead, 1996).

11. Whiteness studies produced by David Roediger, Alexander Saxton, Matthew Jacobson, George Lipsitz, Shelley Fisher Fishkin, and many others have traced the convoluted course by which European immigrants became white and, borrowing from W. E. B. Du Bois's classic history *Black Reconstruction* (1935), explored the "psychological wage" that accrued to those with white skin. See David Roediger, *The Wages of Whiteness: Race and the Making of the American Working Class* (New York: Verso, 1991). Also see David Roediger, *Working toward Whiteness: How America's Immigrants Became White, The Strange Journey from Ellis Island to the Suburbs* (New York: Basic Books, 2006); Alexander Saxton, *The Rise and Fall of the White Republic: Class Politics and Mass Culture in Nineteenth-Century America* (New York: Verso, 2003); Matthew Jacobson, *Whiteness of a Different Color: European Immigrants and the Alchemy of Race* (Cambridge, Mass.: Harvard University Press, 1998); George Lipsitz, *The Possessive Investment in Whiteness: How White People Profit from Identity Politics* (Philadelphia: Temple University Press, 2006); and Shelley Fisher Fishkin, "Interrogating 'Whiteness,' Complicating

'Blackness': Remapping American Culture," *American Quarterly* 47, no. 3 (1995): 428–466.

For criticism of whiteness studies, see Eric Arnesen, "Whiteness and the Historians' Imagination," *International Labor and Working Class History* 60 (Fall 2001): 3–32; Barbara J. Fields, "Whiteness, Racism, and Identity," *International Labor and Working Class History* 60 (Fall 2001): 48–56.

12. See Glenda Gilmore, *Gender and Jim Crow: Women and the Politics of White Supremacy in North Carolina, 1896–1920* (Chapel Hill: University of North Carolina Press, 1996): 61–118; Evelyn Brooks Higginbotham, "African American History and the Metalanguage of Race," *Signs* 17, no. 2 (1992): 251–274; Barbara Welke, "When All the Women Were White, and All the Blacks Were Men: Gender, Class, Race, and the Road to *Plessy*, 1855–1914," *Law and History Review* 13, no. 2 (1995).
13. Cheryl I. Harris, "Whiteness as Property," *Harvard Law Review* 106, no. 8 (1993): 1709–1791. Harris has formulated the equation of "whiteness as property" to examine whiteness as both a form of privileged identity and a "property interest" that could be "experienced and deployed as a resource." Otto H. Olsen, *The Thin Disguise: Turning Point in Negro History:* Plessy v. Ferguson; *A Documentary Presentation (1864–1896)* (New York: Humanities Press, 1967), 83.
14. Olsen, 83.
15. Kathleen Pfeiffer, *Race Passing and American Individualism* (Amherst: University of Massachusetts Press, 2003), 4. Pfeiffer connects "passing *as* American individualism and vice versa."
16. I borrow the term "psychic rudder" from Adam Green's discussion of black families in Chicago during the Great Migration. See Green, *Selling the Race: Culture, Community, and Black Chicago, 1940–1955* (Chicago: University of Chicago Press, 2007), 149.
17. Steve Cheseborough, *Blues Traveling: The Holy Sites of Delta Blues* (Jackson: University Press of Mississippi, 2001), 22. My thanks to James Campbell for pointing me to this quote.

18. "Is Passing for White Comfortable?" *Baltimore Afro-American,* May 24, 1947, M-8.
19. Stuart Hall, "Introduction: Who Needs 'Identity'?," in *Questions of Cultural Identity,* ed. Stuart Hall and Paul du Gay (London: 1996), 1–17.
20. Benedict Anderson, *Imagined Communities* (London: 1991), 7; Green, *Selling the Race,* 209. Here, Pierre Bourdieu's concept of "habitus" is also helpful as a term used to describe "a set of collective and virtually pre-conscious dispositions that societies create within individuals"; these cultural dispositions, based on past experiences, shape the ways that individuals interact with their social world. See Daniel Wickberg, "What Is the History of Sensibilities? On Cultural Histories, Old and New," *American Historical Review* 112, no. 3 (2007), http://www.historycooperative.org/journals/ahr/112.3/wickberg.html, para 23.
21. See Michael Omi and Howard Winant's classic work, *Racial Formation in the United States from the 1960s to the 1990s* (New York: Routledge, 1994).
22. See Walter Benn Michaels's discussion of "why race is not a social construction" in "Autobiography of an Ex-White Man," *Transition,* no. 73 (1997): 122–143. I disagree with the notion that if race is not a social construction, it must be rooted in biology. What one passes away from is not an essentialized, biological blackness, but rather a set of experiences and a way of being in the world that is subject to individual experiences and is always undergoing change. Passing is not a tribute to essentialism, as Benn Michaels argues on page 137, but rather an act that reveals the multiple ways that individuals lived with race.
23. Mary Keller and Chester J. Fontenot Jr., eds., *Re-cognizing W. E. B. Du Bois in the Twenty-first Century: Essays on W. E. B. Du Bois* (Macon, Ga.: Mercer University Press, 2007), 146.
24. Charles Chesnutt, "The Future American," *Boston Evening Transcript,* August 18–September 1, 1900. This essay was published in

three parts. Jean Toomer to James Weldon Johnson, July 11, 1930, box 4, folder 119, Beinecke Rare Books and Manuscripts Library, Yale University, New Haven, Conn.

25. See Walter White, *A Man Called White: The Autobiography of Walter White* (Athens: University of Georgia Press, 1995). On Langston Hughes's tumultuous relationship with his mother and father, see Langston Hughes, *The Big Sea* (New York: Hill and Wang, 1993); James T. Campbell, *Middle Passages: African American Journeys to Africa, 1787–2005* (New York: Penguin, 2007), 188–225.
26. Ralph Ellison, "Change the Joke and Slip the Yoke," in *Shadow and Act* (New York: Vintage, 1972), 55.
27. See Karen Halttunen, *Confidence Men and Painted Women: A Study of Middle-Class Culture in America, 1830–1870* (New Haven, Conn.: Yale University Press, 1982), xv. Literary critic Werner Sollors explains, "In the American imagination, however, passing may also have emerged through its connection with literature of masquerading and with traditional social satire upon the upstart; hence passing has not infrequently remained allied with such themes as the *parvenu,* cross-dressing, double, rebel and victim. . . ." See Sollors, *Neither Black nor White yet Both,* 256.
28. Quoted in Erika Lee, *At America's Gates: Chinese Immigration during the Exclusion Era, 1882–1943* (Chapel Hill: University of North Carolina, 2003), 162.
29. For further discussions of these forms of passing, see Marcia Graham Synnott, *The Half-Opened Door: Discrimination in Admissions at Harvard, Yale and Princeton, 1900–1970* (Westport, Conn.: Greenwood Press, 1979). Synnott explains that statisticians who profiled Jewish students at Harvard in the 1920s were convinced that they could not rely on last names for "a positive identification" given the likelihood that a Jewish name had been changed. See Synnott, *Half-Opened Door,* 94–95.

    For more on Loreta Janeta Velazquez, see Elizabeth Young, "Confederate Counterfeit: The Case of the Cross-Dressed Civil

War Soldier," in Elaine K. Ginsberg, ed., *Passing and the Fictions of Identity* (Durham: Duke University Press, 1996), 181–185. A more recent example of cross-dressing is the case of Lauren Cook Burgess who sued the United States Department of the Interior in the 1990s when it was discovered that she was attempting to impersonate a male soldier in the 21st Georgia Infantry: "Although her disguise—which included binding her chest, wearing her hair short, and speaking with a husky voice—was convincing on other occasions, during a reenactment at the Antietam Battlefield Park in August 1989, Burgess was unmasked, reputedly spotted after leaving the women's bathroom." See Young, "Confederate Counterfeit," 181.

I borrow the terms "putting hair up" and "letting hair down" from George Chauncey, *Gay New York: Gender, Urban Culture, and the Making of the Gay Male World, 1890–1940* (New York: Basic Books, 1994): 6–7.

30. Mezzrow is quoted in Gayle Wald, *Crossing the Line,* 53. Norman Mailer gave voice to a similar sensibility in the essay, "The White Negro: Superficial Reflections on the Hipster," which appeared in *Dissent* in the fall of 1957.
31. Nelson Mandela, *Long Walk to Freedom: The Autobiography of Nelson Mandela* (New York: Little, Brown, 1994), 121.
32. Pierre L. van den Berghe, "Miscegenation in South Africa," *Cahiers d'Études Africaines* 1, no. 4 (1960), 72. More recently, see Eusebius Mckaiser, "In South Africa after Apartheid, Colored Community Is the Big Loser," *New York Times,* February 15, 2012.
33. Mandela, 152. My thanks to J. P. Daughton for guiding me to this case.
34. "Race in South Africa, Still an Issue," *Economist,* February 4, 2012.
35. "Racial democracy" refers to the myth that there is no racial discrimination in Brazil, a country of mixed descent. In 1933, Gilberto Freyre, a sociologist and writer, introduced the idea of Brazil as a racial democracy in his work, *Casa Grande e Senzala* (The Masters and the Slaves), which portrayed Portuguese slavery

and colonialism as relatively benign and predicted that blacks, whites, and Indians would eventually form a superior Brazilian race. See France Winddance Twine, *Racism in a Racial Democracy: The Maintenance of White Supremacy in Brazil* (New Brunswick, N.J.: Rutgers University Press, 2005), 6; Nicolas Bourcier, "Brazil Comes to Terms with Its Slave Trading Past," *Guardian,* October 23, 2013. Also see "Skin Color Still Plays a Big Role in Ethnically Diverse Brazil," *All Things Considered,* National Public Radio, September 17, 2013, http://www.npr.org/2013/09/19/224152635/skin-color-still-plays-big-role-in-ethnically-diverse-brazil; Luisa Farah Schwartzman, "Does Money Whiten? Intergenerational Changes in Racial Classification in Brazil," *American Sociological Review* 72, no. 6 (2007), 945. Also see G. Reginald Daniel, *Race and Multiraciality in the U.S. and Brazil: Converging Paths?* (University Park: Pennsylvania State University Press, 2006).

Cuba has a similar system of multiple "in-between" racial designations. See Umi Vaughan, "Shades of Race in Contemporary Cuba," *Journal of the International Institute* 12, no. 2 (2005); Robert Zurbano, "For Blacks in Cuba, the Revolution Hasn't Begun," *New York Times,* March 24, 2013; Leonardo Padura, "Race in Cuba: The Eternal 'Black Problem,' *The Root,* July 27, 2010.

36. Schwartzman, 942. Schwartzman is quoting from a 1994 study by Nelson do Valle Silva. This study was challenged when scholars suggested that socioeconomic status led the interviewers to classify the respondents differently, not that the respondents thought of themselves as lighter or darker based on their class position.

Racial ideologies are not sealed off within the nations where they are produced; they circulate and migrate across national borders. For example, Claude McKay, a luminary of the Harlem Renaissance, was undoubtedly influenced by his experiences in Jamaica before he arrived in the United States in 1912.

37. Ibid. For more on Brazilian national identity, see *Brazil in the Making: Facets of National Identity,* ed. Carmen Nava and Ludwig

Lauerhass Jr. (New York: Rowman & Littlefield, 2006); Twine, *Racism in a Racial Democracy*; and Donna Goldstein, "'Interracial Sex' and Racial Democracy in Brazil: Twin Concepts?," *American Anthropologist* 101, no. 3 (1999): 563–578.

38. Jennifer L. Hochschild and Brenna M. Powell, "Racial Reorganization and the United States Census, 1850–1930: Mulattoes, Half-Breeds, Mixed Parentage, Hindoos, and the Mexican Race," *Studies in American Political Development* 22, no. 1 (2008): 59–96. Southern politicians argued for the inclusion of the mulatto category on the census in order to advance the claims of white supremacy made by race scientists that mulattoes were less fertile. John C. Calhoun hoped to prove that emancipation led to insanity and other forms of regression in free blacks. Others saw it as a form of surveillance and control over the growth of a worrisome population. Whig Senator William Seward of New York saw the growth of mixed-race people as a sign of "progress" and believed that the census could be used to track just how much "progress" had been made. Other Northerners planned to use the census data on the growth of the mulatto population to make the case for abolition as the only remedy for the moral degeneration of the South. See Hochschild and Powell, "Racial Reorganization," 53–54.

39. Arnold Hirsch, "Massive Resistance in the Urban North: Trumbull Park, Chicago, 1953–1966," *Journal of American History* 82, no. 2 (1995): 523.

1. WHITE IS THE COLOR OF FREEDOM

1. "Black Matt: How a Slave Sold His Master," newspaper clippings, 1859–1862, "On Slavery," scrapbook 24-S-4, no. 12, Cromwell Family Papers, Moorland-Spingarn Research Center, Howard University, Washington, D.C. (hereafter Cromwell Family Papers, MSRC, Howard University). Italics in the original.

2. P. Gabrielle Foreman and Cherene Sherrard-Johnson, "Racial Recovery, Racial Death: An Introduction in Four Parts," *Legacy* 24, no. 2 (2007): 160–161.

3. Quoted in Elaine Ginsberg, ed., *Passing and the Fictions of Identity* (Durham, N.C.: Duke University Press, 1996), 1. Also see Werner Sollors, *Neither Black nor White yet Both: Thematic Explorations of Interracial Literature* (Cambridge, Mass.: Harvard University Press, 1997), 255–262.
4. William Still, *The Underground Railroad: A Record of Facts, Authentic Narratives, Letters, &c., Narrating the Hardships Hair-breadth Escapes and Death Struggles of the Slaves in Their Efforts for Freedom, as Related by Themselves and Others, or Witnessed by the Author; Together with Sketches of Some of the Largest Stockholders, and Most Liberal Aiders and Advisers of the Road* (1871; repr., Chicago: Johnson, 1970): xi–xii.
5. Ira Berlin, *Many Thousands Gone: The First Two Centuries of Slavery in North America* (Cambridge, Mass.: Harvard University Press, 1998), 7–8. Berlin writes, "In slave societies, by contrast, slavery stood at the center of economic production, and the master-slave relationship provided the model for all social relations: husband and wife, parent and child, employer and employee, teacher and student. From the most intimate connections between men and women to the most public ones between ruler and ruled, all relationships mimicked those of slavery" (8). As Frank Tannenbaum has written, "Nothing escaped, nothing, and no one" (Tannenbaum quoted in Berlin, 8). In societies with slaves, Berlin writes, "Although most planters appeared to presume people of African descent were slaves—since they were purchased from slave traders—no law yet enshrined African slavery in either Maryland or Virginia, and the laws that referred to black people were scattered and miscellaneous" (32). Berlin also refers to this as "sawbuck equality" (66).
6. Quoted in Daniel Sharfstein, "Crossing the Color Line: Racial Migration and the One-Drop Rule, 1600–1860," *Minnesota Law Review* 91, no. 3 (2007): 620. Also see Ariela J. Gross, "Litigating Whiteness: Trials of Racial Determination in the Nineteenth-Century South," *Yale Law Journal* 108, no. 1 (1998).

7. Karen Halttunen, *Confidence Men and Painted Women: A Study of Middle-Class Culture in America, 1830–1870* (New Haven, Conn.: Yale University Press, 1982): xv.

   Parental worries about the consequences of young men leaving home are captured in a letter written by John H. Rapier to his son: "I am fearful bad company have been thine Ruination. I hope John that will not be your case when Boys get out of the Syte of thine Father and Mother they forget all the advice thine Best Friends can give them." See John H. Rapier Sr. to John H. Rapier Jr., December 28, 1858, box 1, folder 39, Rapier Family Papers, MSRC (hereafter Rapier Family Papers, MSRC, Howard University).
8. Halttunen describes the excitement that attended the arrival of a stranger in a town during the colonial period: "In the small towns of colonial America strangers were the exception rather than the rule. Most inhabitants knew the other members of their community, and the arrival of a stranger was a special event that initiated certain traditional responses. Ship captains often reported the names of newcomers; inhabitants were expected to inform the authorities whenever they gave lodgings to a stranger; and certain large towns appointed special officials to watch for unknown visitors." See Halttunen, *Confidence Men and Painted Women,* 34. The period between 1820 and 1860 demonstrated the fastest rate of urban growth in all of American history. The proportion of people living in cities rose by 797 percent whereas the national population increased only 226 percent. Such rapid population growth rendered "traditional ways of 'coding' or identifying strangers . . . impossible, as an urban area with a population of roughly eight thousand to ten thousand or more" (35).
9. David Waldstreicher, "Reading the Runaways: Self-Fashioning, Print Culture, and Confidence in Slavery in the Eighteenth-Century Mid-Atlantic," *William and Mary Quarterly* 56, no. 2 (1999): 252. According to Waldstreicher, because very few people had extensive wardrobes, describing one's clothes was often as good as

describing the man or woman" (252). This strategy, however, was doomed to fail when slaves jettisoned tattered "negro shoes" and purchased, borrowed, or stole "free men's" clothing. Different styles of clothing also offered opportunities for different forms of passing. In the case of "a Mullatto Negroe named Tom, about 37 Years of age," his master "has been informed that he intends to cut off his watch-coat, to make him Indian stockings, and to cut off his hair, and get a blanket, to pass for an Indian" (172).

10. Quoted in Brenda Stevenson, *Life in Black and White: Family and Community in the Slave South* (New York: Oxford University Press, 1996), 305.
11. W. Jeffrey Bolster, *Black Jacks: African American Seamen in the Age of Sail* (Cambridge, Mass.: Harvard University Press, 1997), 10. Berlin defines Atlantic creoles as "cosmopolitans, shrewd traders of African birth but African and European ancestry who were skilled in intercultural negotiations" (Berlin, *Many Thousands Gone,* 17–28).
12. Bolster, *Black Jacks,* 26. Similarly, historian William B. Hart has described the fluidity of the frontier in the eighteenth century and the kinds of possibilities that emerged for "cultural appropriation and identity alteration" and writes that "contact between these European Americans and persons of Indian ancestry and of African descent led to almost limitless possibilities for social innovation and cultural transformation." He also notes the ways that racialized categories broke down when an individual could assume more than one identity. He offers the example of Eve Pickard, who was identified as a mulatto but had familial ties to the Mohawks. After she was accused of stealing land, a "white crime," she and her behavior were recategorized as white. See William B. Hart, "Black 'Go-Betweens' and the Mutability of 'Race,' Status, and Identity on New York's Pre-Revolutionary Frontier," in *Contact Points: American Frontiers from the Mohawk Valley to the Mississippi, 1750–1830,* ed. Andrew R. L. Clayton and Fredrika J. Teute (Chapel Hill: University of North Carolina Press, 1998), 88–114.

13. Graham Russell Hodges and Alan Edward Brown, eds., *Pretends to Be Free: Runaway Slave Advertisements from Colonial and Revolutionary New York and New Jersey* (New York: Garland, 1994), 13.
14. Ibid., 6.
15. Ibid., 88–89.
16. Waldstreicher, "Reading the Runaways," 247. But the system was falling apart all over, and not just because of runaway slaves. As Waldstreicher writes: "The interests of masters who owned runaways sometimes clashed with an arguably greater public interest in having a flexible, skilled, and increasingly mobile labor force. As long as labor was cheap, many farmers and master artisans did not care whether it was bound or free, white or black, or some ambiguous combination of all these" (256).
17. For a sampling of different opinions as to when the consolidation of a racialized slave society emerged, see Berlin, *Many Thousands Gone;* Edmund Morgan, *American Slavery, American Freedom: The Ordeal of Colonial Virginia* (New York: W. W. Norton, 1975); Kathleen Brown, *Good Wives, Nasty Wenches, and Anxious Patriarchs* (Chapel Hill: University of North Carolina Press, 1998).
18. Waldstreicher, "Reading the Runaways," 257.
19. By the mid-seventeenth century, policing the movement of indentured servants and slaves became an anxious project. Legal historian Sally Hadden writes that in the aftermath of an aborted slave rebellion in 1649, slaves traveling beyond their plantation were ordered to carry a signed pass. See Sally Hadden, *Slave Patrols: Law and Violence in Virginia and North Carolina* (Cambridge, Mass.: Harvard University Press, 2001), 11, 15–16, 27.
20. Henry Bibb, *Narrative of the Life and Adventures of Henry Bibb, an American Slave, Written by Himself* (1849; repr., Philadelphia: Historic, 1969), 135.
21. Just as literate slaves were sometimes less valuable in the market, so were light-skinned slaves. For example, one slave advertised as "about thirty-five years of age, light complexion—tall—rather

handsome-looking, intelligent, and of good manners," was only valued at $1,000. It was explained that "if he had been a few shades darker and only about half as intelligent as he was, he would have been worth at least $500 more. . . . The idea of having a white father, in many instances, depreciated the pecuniary value of male slaves, if not of the other sex." The belief was that "rebellious blood" coupled with a "considerable amount of intelligence" essentially ruined a slave. On the other hand, very light skin could raise the value of a female slave exponentially. Historian Walter Johnson has discussed the spectacular amounts paid for "fancy girls." Walter Johnson, *Soul by Soul: Life Inside the Antebellum Slave Market* (Cambridge, Mass.: Harvard University Press, 1999), 113–115, 154–155.

22. Still, *Underground Railroad,* 423–424.
23. Hodges and Brown, *Pretends to Be Free,* xxix.
24. Jill Lepore, *New York Burning: Liberty, Slavery, and Conspiracy in Eighteenth-Century Manhattan* (New York: Random House, 2005), 124.
25. Hodges and Brown, *Pretends to Be Free,* 121, 178–179.
26. Billy G. Smith, "Runaway Slaves in the Mid-Atlantic Region during the Revolutionary Era," in *The Transforming Hand of Revolution: Reconsidering the American Revolution as a Social Movement,* ed. Ronald Hoffman and Peter J. Albert (Charlottesville: University Press of Virginia, 1995), 199–200. Smith also explains that "running away was primarily a male activity"; masters expected female slaves to return after visiting relatives on other plantations and were reluctant to spend money on advertisements or rewards for female slaves. For this reason, Smith notes, female fugitives were rarely advertised. Domestic work and child-care responsibilities limited enslaved women's mobility as well as their familiarity with the surrounding area. It is also possible that enslaved women expected to face more difficulties finding employment and passing as free. Enslaved women had to fear sexual

exploitation while on the run, which also may have discouraged them from making attempts at escape. For enslaved mothers, running away with a child was especially risky (13–14, 210–211).

27. Still, *Underground Railroad,* 443.
28. Hodges and Brown, *Pretends to Be Free,* 47.
29. Jill Lepore, *New York Burning,* xi. Alexander, Lepore explains, was not thinking of chattel slavery as he wrote, but rather liberty of the press and tyranny as a form of slavery.
30. Hodges and Brown, *Pretends to Be Free,* xxvi–xxvii.
31. Ibid., 75.
32. Ibid.
33. Hadden, *Slave Patrols,* 112.
34. Hodges and Brown, *Pretends to Be Free,* 222–223.
35. Ibid., 91–93.
36. *Pennsylvania Packet and Daily Advertiser,* Wednesday, September 7, 1785, posted by Ronald Seagrave on http://dinwiddiecountyhistory.blogspot.com/2007/08/forge-slave-pass-certificates-of.html.
37. Newspaper clippings, 1860–1862, "On Slavery," scrapbook 24-S-4, no. 1, Cromwell Family Papers, MSRC, Howard University.
38. Berlin, *Many Thousands Gone,* 99. Berlin's emphasis.
39. Quoted in Debby Applegate, *The Most Famous Man in America: The Biography of Henry Ward Beecher* (New York: Three Leaves Press, 2006), 6. Also see Mary Niall Mitchell, "'Rosebloom and Pure White,' or So It Seemed," *American Quarterly* 54, no. 3 (2002): 391–392.
40. William Craft, *Running a Thousand Miles for Freedom: The Escape of William and Ellen Craft* (Baton Rouge: Louisiana State University Press, 1999), 4–6. Historian Mary Niall Mitchell offers an example of a husband who sold his wife into slavery near Beaufort, South Carolina, and quotes the author of the *New York Tribune:* "The selling of wives is not uncommon in South Carolina . . . especially when their health is broken down and they are unable to do hard work." See Mitchell, "'Rosebloom and Pure White,'" 376. Mitchell

also describes fears that beautiful young girls would be sold into slavery: "Ellen's face, the narrator explained, was 'more than pretty, for it was downright beautiful, with its rosebloom and pure white and the dark, lustrous eyes and well-shaped mouth.'" On the auction block, men came to scrutinize Ellen's white face and body. "High bids are expected," the auctioneer announced, "for it isn't every day such an angeliferous loveliness comes to the hammer." Ellen's story ended happily, with a last-minute rescue by Quaker friends who were able to prove her British citizenship, but her story functioned as a cautionary tale that demonstrated to readers the slight distance between "a white woman's purity and the abominations of slavery" (377).

41. Bibb, *Life and Adventures of Henry Bibb,* 60.
42. Newspaper clippings, 1863–1865, scrapbook, 24-S-6, "On Slavery," v. 4, Cromwell Family Papers, MSRC, Howard University.
43. Mitchell, "'Rosebloom and Pure White,'" 395. Mitchell discusses the power of photography as a "truth-telling medium," coupled with the production and widespread distribution of *cartes de visite*, small photograph cards that were patented in Paris in 1854 by the French photographer André Adolphe Eugène Disdéri. These small cards became enormously popular. Their small size allowed them to be easily traded among friends and family. The circulation of images of the brutality of slavery on *cartes de visite* enabled northern white audiences "to see what slavery really looked like."
44. Sidney Kaplan, "The Miscegenation Issue in the Election of 1864," *Journal of Negro History* (July 1949): 279–343; Ronald G. Walters, "The Erotic South: Civilization and Sexuality in American Abolitionism," *American Quarterly* (May 1973): 185. Some abolitionists went as far as Elijah Lovejoy and claimed, "One reason why abolitionists urge the abolition of slavery is, that they fully believe it will put a stop, in a great and almost entire measure, to that wretched, and shameful, and polluted intercourse between the

whites and the blacks, now so common, it may be said so universal, in the slave states."

45. Gross, "Litigating Whiteness," 111, 148. Two racially ambiguous litigants, Abby Guy and Alexina Morrison, won their cases, in part because the judge instructed the jury that "every presumption, consistent with reason, should be indulged in favor of freedom" (135).

46. Craft, *Running a Thousand Miles for Freedom,* 16. Ellen Weinauer writes, "The issue of emasculation certainly circulates in *Running a Thousand Miles for Freedom,* in which not just the slave owner but also the slave-wife poses a threat. On their run for freedom, Ellen and William play out the roles of master and slave. Their charade thus emblematizes the relations of proprietorship at work in the roles of husband and wife. In this case, however, those roles are reversed; the slave-wife becomes white 'master,' and the husband becomes once again a slave." See Ellen Weinauer, " 'A Most Respectable Looking Gentleman': Passing, Possession and Transgression in *Running a Thousand Miles for Freedom,*" in Elaine Ginsberg, *Passing and the Fictions of Identity,* 51.

William Craft writes, "My wife's first master was her father, and her mother his slave, and the latter is still the slave of his widow. Notwithstanding my wife being of African extraction on her mother's side she is almost white—in fact, she is so nearly so that the tyrannical old lady to whom she first belonged became so annoyed, at finding her frequently mistaken for a child of the family, that she gave her when eleven years of age to a daughter, as a wedding present. This separated my wife from her mother, and also from several other dear friends. But the incessant cruelty of her old mistress made the change of owners or treatment so desirable, that she did not grumble much at this cruel separation." See Craft, *Running a Thousand Miles for Freedom,* 3–4. Although Ellen first shrank from the idea of running away, William writes that she agreed to the plan, believing that "God is on our side."

47. Quoted in Weinauer, "'A Most Respectable Looking Gentleman,'" 41.
48. Craft, *Running a Thousand Miles for Freedom,* 19.
49. See Craft, *Running a Thousand Miles for Freedom,* 21; Weinauer, "'A Most Respectable Looking Gentleman,'" 37.
50. Craft, *Running a Thousand Miles for Freedom,* 19.
51. Ibid., 29. Craft writes, "When the gentleman finds out his mistake, he will, I have no doubt, be careful in [the] future not to pretend to have an intimate acquaintance with an entire stranger" (29).
52. Lindon Barrett, "Hand-Writing: Legibility and the White Body in *Running a Thousand Miles for Freedom,*" *American Literature* 69, no. 2 (1997): 315–336. On the other hand, some characters in literature "darken up" in order to escape from slavery. P. Gabrielle Foreman and Cherene Sherrard-Johnson have argued that "passing for black" allowed some protagonists to "escape without being seen"; it provided "additional veils." See Foreman and Sherrard-Johnson, "Racial Recovery, Racial Death," 159–160. For a discussion of desk clerks and their responsibilities at hotels as well as the larger concept of hospitality, see A. K. Sandoval-Strausz, *Hotel: An American History* (New Haven, Conn.: Yale University Press, 2007), 203–227. Sandoval-Strausz discusses the Crafts' escape on p. 222.
53. Craft, *Running a Thousand Miles for Freedom,* 24–25.
54. Ibid., 33. Craft's emphasis.
55. Ibid., 29. Traveling with an obedient servant raised Ellen's stature. For example, William wrote that when they arrived at "the best hotel, which John C. Calhoun, and all the other great southern fire-eating statesmen made their head-quarters while in Charleston," the proprietor of the hotel made him "stand on one side, while he paid my master the attention and homage he thought a gentleman of his high position merited" (27). For William, already the slave of a white man and now the slave of his otherwise dutiful wife, the success of the disguise required the crossing of

multiple boundaries, some that he may have found more unsettling than others. William made attempts to recover Ellen's "true womanhood" by insisting on her discomfort while she was dressed in gentleman's clothing: "My wife had no ambition whatever to assume this disguise, and would not have done so had it been possible to have obtained her liberty by more simple means" (19).

56. Bibb, *Life and Adventures of Henry Bibb,* 14, 33. Bibb describes his wife as a mulatto slave girl named Malinda, who lived in Oldham County, Kentucky, and who "moved in the highest circle of slaves, and free people of color." To this description, Bibb adds the following footnote: "The distinction among slaves is as marked, as the classes of society are in any aristocratic community. Some refusing to associate with others whom they deem beneath them in point of character, color, condition, or the superior importance of their respective masters." He also explains that his mother-in-law opposed her daughter's marriage to Bibb and hoped that she would instead marry a slave who belonged to a very rich man living nearby and who was well known to be the son of his master. Malinda's mother hoped that the slave's master (and father) might set him free, which, as Bibb writes, "would enable him to do a better part by her daughter than I could!" (39). Bibb offers a number of descriptions of the physical abuse of his wife and his daughter that he was forced to witness. Most painfully, he saw his master's wife slap his daughter's face so brutally that "her little face was bruised black with the whole print of Mrs. Gatewood's hand. This print was plainly to be seen for eight days after it was done." As Bibb writes, "Who can imagine what could be the feelings of a father and mother, when looking upon their infant child whipped and tortured with impunity, and they placed in a situation where they could afford it no protection?" (43).
57. Ibid., 47.
58. Ibid., 50.

59. Ibid., 107.
60. Ibid., 156.
61. Ibid., 164–165.
62. Ibid., 166.
63. Foreman and Sherrard-Johnson, "Racial Recovery, Racial Death," 159–160.
64. Bibb, *Life and Adventures of Henry Bibb,* 183.
65. Still, *Underground Railroad,* 219.
66. Asa J. Davis, "The George Latimer Case: A Benchmark in the Struggle for Freedom," edison.rutgers.edu/latimer/glatcase.htm. Historian Gilbert Osofsky writes: "The escape of three slaves as described by black Garrisonian William Wells Brown to the New England Anti-Slavery Society was a dramatic example of such treachery. One of the three, who was nearly white, had impersonated the master of the other two, but when they had traveled far away from home territory, the white slave claimed the other two as his property and sold them. 'He had not black blood enough in him to make him honest!' Brown said." See Osofsky, *Puttin' On Ole Massa: The Slave Narratives of Henry Bibb, William Wells Brown, and Solomon Northup* (New York: Harper Torchbooks, 1969), 19.
67. Still, *Underground Railroad,* 218–219.
68. Ibid., 310–311.
69. Ibid., 396.
70. Cited in Stevenson, *Life in Black and White,* 306.
71. Still, *Underground Railroad,* 114.
72. Ibid., 538.
73. Newspaper Clippings, 1860–1862, "On Slavery," scrapbook 24-S-4, no. 12, Cromwell Family Papers, MSRC, Howard University.
74. In the preface to Frank Webb's 1858 novel, *The Garies and Their Friends,* Harriet Beecher Stowe described the large class of free blacks in Philadelphia, comprising both fugitive and emancipated slaves, and wrote that they "have increased in numbers, wealth and standing" and that they "constitute a peculiar society

of their own, presenting many social peculiarities worthy of interest and attention." Webb, *The Garies and Their Friends* (repr., BiblioBazaar, 2006). This quotation is taken from the front of the book; the page is unnumbered.

75. Richard Randolph, brother of statesman John Randolph, freed his slaves in his will when he died in 1796. According to historian Melvin Patrick Ely, "Randolph took special care to 'beg[,] *humbly* beg [,] [his slaves'] forgiveness' for his part in the 'infamous practice of usurping the rights of our fellow creatures, equally entitled with ourselves to the enjoyment of Liberty and happiness.'" See Melvin Patrick Ely, *Israel on the Appomattox: A Southern Experiment in Black Freedom from the 1790s through the Civil War* (New York: Vintage Books, 2004), 7. Italics in the original.

76. Peter Williams, "Discourse Delivered in St. Philip's Church for the Benefit of the Coloured Community of Wilberforce, in Upper Canada," July 4, 1830, (microfilm version: reel 1, Black Abolitionist Papers, 1830–1865) (Sanford, N.C.: Microfilming Corp. of America, 1981), (OCoLC)7994795. Instead, he called for better treatment: "We are NATIVES of this country, we ask only to be treated as well as FOREIGNERS. Not a few of our fathers suffered and bled to purchase its independence; we ask only to be treated as well as those who fought against it. We have toiled to cultivate it, and to raise it to its present prosperous condition, we ask only to share equal privileges with those, who come from distant lands, to enjoy the fruits of our labour."

77. Halttunen, *Confidence Men and Painted Women,* 39. Halttunen writes, "The structure of the antebellum American city remained more preindustrial than modern and offered little spatial segregation of activities or of people. Until the introduction of street railways in the 1850s, American cities were predominantly 'walking cities,' without extensive and efficient public transportation that would enable settlement to spread into a larger area and thus become segregated by persons and activities. In antebellum

Philadelphia, most areas were a jumble of occupations and classes, of shops and homes, of immigrants and native-born Americans. Only around 1860 did Philadelphia see the beginning of concentration—a downtown area, a few manufacturing clusters, a small slum, a few blocks dominated by blacks, an occasional class and ethnic enclave—but such spatial segregation was not yet the dominant pattern."

78. Newspaper clippings, 1860–1862, "On Slavery," scrapbook 24-S-4, no. 12, Cromwell Family Papers, MSRC, Howard University.
79. "A Visit to the Colored Upper-Tendom," newspaper clippings, 1860–1862, "On Slavery," scrapbook 24-S-4, no. 12, Cromwell Family Papers, MSRC, Howard University.
80. John Miller, the treasurer of the company, produced the company's printed rules, which stated, "Colored persons will be accommodated on the front platform, except they be nurses in charge of children, in which case they will be carried inside of the car." If Mr. Barrett volunteered to put this man out, he would be guilty as charged. But if the conductor, as the "servant of the company," requested his assistance, his actions would be justifiable, as long as no more force was used than necessary. A passenger testified that the "conduct of the conductor was gentlemanly," and while he did see "some heels flying," he could not tell "whether the colored man was being kicked, or whether he was kicking someone else."

Reporters discussed the absurdity of the railway car politics in the article, "On Colored Inhabitants of this City," and wrote, "We know of several cases where colored men, who are stockholders in certain railways, have been forbidden to ride to the railway terminus to collect the dividends upon their shares." The same reporters also noted, "An intelligent black man lately informed us that he owned a pleasant country residence in the northern suburbs, but that he could not occupy it as it would be impossible to ride over the railways to and from his place of business." See newspaper clippings, 1860–1862, "On Slavery," scrapbook 24-S-4, no. 12, []. Cromwell Family Papers, MSRC, Howard University.

81. See Gross, *What Blood Won't Tell: A History of Race on Trial in America* (Cambridge, Mass.: Harvard University Press, 2008). Gross quotes Judge William Harper who argued, "It may be well and proper, that a man of worth, honesty, industry and respectability, should have the rank of a white man, while a vagabond of the same degree of blood should be confined to the inferior cast. . . . It is hardly necessary to say that a slave cannot be a white man." Harper also argued that it was "very cruel and mischievous" to disturb the racial identity of one "whose caste has never been questioned until now" (164). Gross also describes arguments for a "prescriptive right to whiteness"—"one might acquire a right to property after a *prescribed* number of years by virtue of having used the property and treated it as one's own for those years without challenge" (56). Italics in the original.
82. Quoted in Brenda Stevenson, ed., *The Journals of Charlotte Forten Grimké* (New York: Oxford University Press, 1988), 140. Grimké's emphasis.
83. Ibid., 140, 369–370. Grimké writes that she feels too "thorough a contempt for such people to allow myself to be wounded by them." Born to free parents in Philadelphia in 1838 and the granddaughter of James Forten, a wealthy sailmaker and abolitionist, Charlotte enjoyed an elevated social status and a rarefied life with a "mind stored with recollections of the best authors" and longed for more "intelligent, well-educated people, with good literary tastes. Alas! Among *us* they are too rare" (236). Grimké's emphasis.
84. G. E. Stephens to Jacob C. White, January 8, 1858, box 115-3, folder 129, Jacob C. White Papers, MSRC, Howard University. Commenting on the impact of these kinds of rules, Stephens wrote, "Poor wretches, little do they accomplish by such trivial proscriptions, such miserable oppressions serve not one single dignity? [T]o curb

the spirit of even a crushed and injured African." Stephens was also troubled to find an elderly enslaved woman calling white children "Master or Mistress." Stephens wrote to White, "I could not stand this and reprimanded her." Stevens was even more disturbed by the woman's response: "She was perfectly astonished [and] commenced an argument with me to prove that those children were entitled to this distinction. By way of a caution she told me I must not talk this way—some of the people might overhear me and tell master."

85. Stevenson, *Life in Black and White,* 267.
86. The article, "Arrival of Colored Families," further describes the humiliations that free blacks in Charleston endured: "A law has recently been passed in South Carolina, requiring all free colored persons to wear a badge of distinction. This many of the colored families living in Charleston deem an indignity, and some have left the State in consequence of it. They are generally mulattoes, of varied shades of lightness. . . . Many of them are almost white. Several purchased their own freedom some years ago." Newspaper clippings, 1860–1862, "On Slavery," scrapbook 24-S-4, no. 12, Cromwell Family Papers, MSRC, Howard University.
87. See Melvin Patrick Ely, *Israel on the Appomattox,* 10.
88. See John H. Rapier Jr. to James P. Thomas, August 19, 1862, and John H. Rapier Jr. to James P. Thomas, August 19, 1864, box 84-1, folder 76, Rapier Family Papers, MSRC, Howard University.
89. Joseph A. Boromé, Jacob C. White, Robert B. Ayres, and J. M. McKim, "The Vigilant Committee of Philadelphia, *Pennsylvania Magazine of History and Biography* 92, no. 3 (1968): 321.
90. Quoted in Margaret Hope Bacon, *But One Race: The Life of Robert Purvis* (Albany: State University of New York Press, 2007), 105.
91. Ibid., 106, 111.
92. John H. Rapier Jr. to Sarah Thomas, November 12, 1863, and John H. Rapier Jr. to Sarah Thomas, November 12, 1863, box 84-1, folder 83, Rapier Family Papers, MSRC. Rapier's emphasis.

93. An article published in the *New-York Tribune* announced that Appo was one of three buyers of the Register Publishing Company and the newspaper, *The Sunday Capitol*, in 1889. See "The *Sunday Capitol* Sold," *New-York Tribune* (January 6, 1889), 3. Perhaps he was passing as early as the 1880s despite his mulatto and black census designations. *The New York Times* published an obituary on January 11, 1928 that stated that Appo died at his home in Brooklyn after a career as a newspaper publisher. Appo's obituary lists his survivors as two sons, Reverend Locksley A. Appo, and Garnet Brady, and two daughters, Miss Alice Appo and Miss Martha Appo. Like their father, Garnet, Alice, and Martha are listed as mulatto on the 1880 census. Garnet is listed as black in 1900. Alice and Martha are listed as black on the 1890 census as are Locksley and Garnet on the 1900 census. But in 1920, all of St. John Appo's children are listed as white. Locksley Appo does not appear on the census after 1900, but we can assume that he was white because he is noted as the rector of the Holy Family Church in Brooklyn, New York, in 1928. See "Dedicate Church Today," *The Brooklyn Daily Eagle*, May 6, 1928, 75.
94. Joshua D. Rothman, *Notorious in the Neighborhood: Sex and Families across the Color Line in Virginia, 1787–1861* (Chapel Hill: University of North Carolina Press, 2003), 41–42, 44–46. Beverley, Madison, and Eston were all trained as carpenters when they were teenagers by their uncle John Hemings, and Harriet worked as a spinner and a weaver. Rothman also notes that Madison had to persuade his white children to teach him to read, meaning that Thomas Jefferson did not formally educate his enslaved children. Also see Annette Gordon-Reed, *Thomas Jefferson and Sally Hemings: An American Controversy* (Charlottesville: University of Virginia Press, 1997), 11; *The Hemingses of Monticello: An American Family* (New York: W. W. Norton, 2008).
95. Webb, *The Garies and Their Friends,* 340. Another character is cautioned earlier in the novel, "One thing I must tell you . . . if you

should settle down here, you'll have to be either one thing or other—white or coloured. Either you must live exclusively amongst coloured people, or go to the whites and remain with them. But to do the latter, you must bear in mind that it must never be known that you have a drop of African blood in your veins, or you would be shunned as if you were a pestilence; no matter how fair in complexion or how white you may be." The character further warned, "you are old enough, I presume, to know the difference that exists between the privileges and advantages enjoyed by the whites, and those that are at the command of the coloured people. White boys can go to better schools, and they can enter college and become professional men, lawyers, doctors, &c., or they may be merchants—in fact, they can be anything they please. Coloured people can enjoy none of these advantages; they are shut out of them entirely. Now which of the two would you rather be—coloured or white?" Webb writes, "'I should much rather be white, of course,' answered Clarence, 'but I am coloured, and can't help myself,' said he, innocently" (253).

96. Ibid., 318.
97. Ibid., 17.
98. For more on honor, see Bertram Wyatt-Brown, *Southern Honor: Ethics and Behavior in the Old South* (New York: Oxford University Press, 1983). Also see Orlando Patterson, *Slavery and Social Death: A Comparative Study* (Cambridge, Mass.: Harvard University Press, 1982).
99. Webb, *The Garies and Their Friends,* 18.
100. After Mary (Stevens's daughter who marries into Cogdell family) reads Marcus Rainsford's *An Historical Account of the Black Empire of Hayti* (London, 1805), she recorded the following: "By what strange perversion of reason can it be deemed disgraceful in a white man to marry a black or Mulatto woman, when it is not thought dishonorable in him to be connected with her in the most licentious familiarity? . . . The Laws of a Country are

imperfect allowing such familiarity with impunity, every white man having such connection, should be compell'd by the laws of *humanity* to marry the person, black or Mulatto, with whom such familiaritys have existed, & to have no intercourse with genteel Society or to appear in any public place of amusement on an equality with other Citizens." Mary Ann Elizabeth Stevens Cogdell, Diary and Copy Book, 1805–1823, box 1, Stevens-Cogdell/Sanders-Venning Collection, Library Company of Philadelphia; Phillip S. Lapsansky, "Afro-Americana: Family Values, in Black and White," *The Annual Report of the Library Company of Philadelphia*, 26–27. Mary died in 1827, five years before her son Richard fathered Robert Sanders, the first of his many mulatto children by Sarah Sanders. Mary would become linked to generations of mulattoes who would become part of the black elite.

101. See "Afro-Americana: Family Values, in Black and White," in *The Annual Report of the Library Company of Philadelphia for the Year 1991*, presented at the Annual Meeting, May 1992, Library Company of Philadelphia, Philadelphia, Penn. For more on the extended family, see box 1, Stevens-Cogdell/Sanders-Venning Papers, Library Company of Philadelphia, Philadelphia, Penn.

102. William H. Parham to Jacob C. Cook Jr., September 7, 1862, Cook Family Papers, MSRC, Howard University.

103. Writing from Florence, Alabama, John H. Rapier Sr. asked questions about what the conditions were like for black men in Canada: "When you answer this letter let me know how the man of colour stand in that country for that will be a great country for the white man [and] . . . one who has money that they could do without a few years [would] pay them [well] to lay it out for land and work on a few years they would become rich from the Rise of land you see that large fortune has been made in a few years in Chicago and other places in the northwest—that ought to prompt a man to Save his labour and lay it out for land that will take care of the old man when old what I have wrote you my Son fell [feel]

in my heart." John H. Rapier Sr. to John H. Rapier Jr., October 27, 1856, box 84-1, folder 29, Rapier Family Papers, MSRC, Howard University.

104. William H. Parham to Jacob C. White Jr., August 7, 1863, box 115-2, folder 107, Jacob C. White Collection, MSRC, Howard University.

105. Ibid.

2. WAITING ON A WHITE MAN'S CHANCE

1. Charles Chesnutt, journal entry, July 31, 1875, box 13, folder 1, p. 160, Special Collections, John Hope and Aurelia E. Franklin Library, Fisk University, Nashville, Tenn. (hereafter Chesnutt Collection, Fisk University).
2. W. E. B. Du Bois eulogized Chesnutt, and after Chesnutt's death in 1932, he wrote, "We have lost a fine intellect, a keen sense of humor and a broad tolerant philosophy. Chesnutt was of that group of white folk who because of a more or less remote Negro ancestor identified himself voluntarily with the darker group, studied them, expressed them, defended them, and yet never forgot the absurdity of this artificial position and always refused to admit its logic or its ethical sanction. He was not a Negro; he was a man. But this fact never drove him to the opposite extreme. He did not repudiate persons of Negro blood as social equals and close friends. If his white friends (and he had legion) could not tolerate colored friends, they need not come to Mr. Chesnutt's home. If colored friends demanded racial segregation and hatred, he had no patience with them. Merit and friendship in his broad and tolerant mind knew no lines of color or race, and all men, good, bad and indifferent were simply men. God rest his beautiful memory." "Postscript by W. E. B. Du Bois," box 12, folder 12, Chesnutt Collection, Fisk University. Published in *Crisis* (January 1933): 20.
3. Chesnutt, journal entry, January 3, 1881, box 13, folder 3, Chesnutt Collection, Fisk University.

4. Elsa Barkley Brown, "To Catch a Vision of Freedom: Reconstructing Southern Black Women's Political History, 1865–1880," in *Unequal Sisters: An Inclusive Reader in U.S. Women's History,* ed. Ellen DuBois and Vicki Ruiz (New York: Routledge, 2000).
5. See Eric Foner, "Rights and the Constitution in Black Life during the Civil War and Reconstruction," *Journal of American History* 74, no. 3 (1987): 870.
6. See Kate Masur, "'A Rare Phenomenon of Philological Vegetation': The Word 'Contraband' and the Meanings of Emancipation in the United States," *Journal of American History* 93, no. 4 (2007): 1066. Masur discusses numerous objections to the term "contraband" and writes that some African Americans referred to "so-called contrabands" in an effort to underscore that "'contraband' was not their term, but someone else's."
7. Quoted in Foner, "Rights and the Constitution in Black Life," 866.
8. Minutes from the Central Executive Committee, New Orleans, La., Session of May 23, 1867, box 81-1, folder 54, Pinckney Benton Stewart Pinchback Papers, MSRC (hereafter Pinchback Papers, MSRC, Howard University).
9. Quoted in Foner, "Rights and the Constitution in Black Life," 876. The American Colonization Society (ACS) was founded in 1817. Most blacks voiced strenuous objections to ACS and argued that it was a plot to expel free blacks from the United States and to consolidate the power of slaveholders. Arguments for emigration have ebbed and flowed throughout African American history and gained greater acceptance during the 1850s when race relations worsened and the Fugitive Slave Act made life for runaway slaves and free blacks increasingly insecure.
10. L. W. Ballard to Blanche Bruce, November 2, 1877, box 9-1, folder 10, Blanche Bruce Papers, MSRC, Howard University. Ballard suggested blacks settle in a separate area within the borders of the United States, believing that even the discussion of such a

proposal would bring attention to the plight of blacks. He argued, "It is it true that the colored people can not enjoy their legal rights as citizens, among the white people South, or if they have become so numerous that the two races can not subsist together why not Congress set aside one of the States, or Territories, in the United States, as a Territorial Government for the colored man. This would strengthen our own Government and the money would be spent where it would soon be regained. I believe a Bill of this nature before Congress (whether its passage is possible or impossible) would have a tendency to awaken the public mind to a just consideration of the colored man's rights. . . . All we want is a chance to work out our own fortune and manhood."

11. Quoted in Foner, "Rights and the Constitution in Black Life," 876. The emigration question would be raised again toward the end of Reconstruction, as the hopefulness of the period waned.

Letters from constituents of Blanche Bruce voiced the hope that some type of relocation might offer some relief to blacks. On January 19, 1878, one of Bruce's constituents, who supported Liberian colonization plans, wrote, "Do all you can for our Liberian Colonization [School]. And send me all the information you can get. There are hundreds of colored people here, 'refugees' from the southern part of this State. . . . I hope you will do all you can to help us to Africa as we never can get justice in the U.S. States." See D. D. Bell to Blanche Bruce, January 19, 1878, box 9-1, folder 11, Blanche Bruce Papers, MSRC, Howard University. For Senator Bruce's letter of February 19, 1878, on Liberia in the *Cincinnati Commercial,* see Sadie Daniel St. Clair, "The National Career of Blanche Kelso Bruce," December 1946, box 9-5, folder 139, St. Clair Research—Appendices, pp. 245–311, Blanche Bruce Papers, MSRC, Howard University.

12. Dylan Penningroth, *The Claims of Kinfolk: African American Property and Community in the Nineteenth Century South* (Chapel Hill: University of North Carolina Press, 2003): 409.

13. Penningroth, *Claims of Kinfolk,* 414.
14. Ibid., 431.
15. Ibid.
16. Quoted in Foner, "Rights and the Constitution in Black Life," 868.
17. Quoted in Thomas Holt, *Black over White: Negro Political Leadership During Reconstruction* (Urbana: University of Illinois Press, 1979), 12.
18. P. B. S. Pinchback, untitled speech [Montgomery, Ala., 1865 or 1866], box 81-1, folder 32, Pinchback Papers, MSRC, Howard University.
19. Quoted in Foner, "Rights and the Constitution in Black Life," 876.
20. Ibid.
21. Thomas Holt's *Black over White* discusses the divisions within the Republican Party and the political implications of intraracial conflicts over color. See Holt, *Black over White,* 18.
22. From Laura Foner, "The Free People of Color in Louisiana and St. Domingue: A Comparative Portrait of Two Three-Caste Slave Societies," *Journal of Social History* 3, no. 4 (1970): 406–430. Quoted in Foner, "Rights and the Constitution in Black Life," 867–868.
23. James Lee to Blanche Bruce, November 25, 1879, box 9-2, folder 52, Blanche Bruce Papers, MSRC, Howard University. Emphasis in the original.
24. Albert D. Thompson to Blanche Bruce, December 8, 1875, box 9-3, folder 93, Blanche Bruce Papers, MSRC, Howard University.
25. William D. Frazee to Blanche Bruce, March 23, 1876, box 9-1, folder 25, Blanche Bruce Papers, MSRC, Howard University. Bruce and Lynch had been accused of failing to appoint more Mississippians to lucrative patronage positions. Bruce was guilty of this charge; he staffed his Washington, D.C., office mostly with employees who lived in Washington, D.C. See "Mississippi Politics: The Crusader," *Washington Bee,* February 27, 1892, box 9-4, folder 131, Blanche Bruce Papers, MSRC, Howard University. P. C. Hall of Vicksburg, Mississippi, informed Bruce that Sydney Brooks, also of Vicksburg and who was petitioning for the

position of postmaster, was "opposed to [Bruce's] course . . . he claims that you attempt to ignore the colored men of this country and city in the appointment of Post Master, and attempt to appoint men from other sections of the state, such men as Sydney Brooks are not entitle[d] to respectful consideration at your hands, I write to let you know this fact." See P. C. Hall to Blanche Bruce, March 11, 1879, box 9-1, folder 28, Blanche Bruce Papers, MSRC, Howard University.

26. W. F. Simonton to Blanche Bruce, December 3, 1875, box 9-3, folder 81, Blanche Bruce Papers, MSRC, Howard University. The complete quotation is: "P.S. Any place you can obtain for me that will enable me to live away from this at this time Hell on Earth [illegible word], will be acceptable."

27. On Easter Sunday, April 13, 1873, in Colfax, Louisiana, the White League, a paramilitary group, clashed with Louisiana's nearly all-black state militia. By nightfall, almost one hundred black men had been shot, stabbed, or burned to death, and most were murdered after they had surrendered, in spasms of raw bloodthirst. President Grant sent troops at first; he then feared that the decision to send troops would be unpopular as northern support for Reconstruction waned, and he worried that the Republicans might lose close elections in the North (specifically in Ohio). For more on the Colfax massacre, see Nicholas Lemann, *Redemption: The Last Battle of the Civil War* (New York: Farrar, Straus and Giroux, 2006).

28. "Mississippi Affairs: The Clinton Riot—The Cruelty of the Whites—Vicksburg Adds to Her Long List of Crimes," n.d., box 9-2, folder 70, Blanche Bruce Papers, MSRC, Howard University.

29. For example, see William M. Hancock to Blanche Bruce, August 8, 1876, box 9-1, folder 29, Blanche Bruce Papers, MSRC, Howard University. Hancock continues, "With this kind of protection the Democracy will allow the Colored voters to exercise their right of franchise. . . . If we are going to have protection we ought to know

it *now,* for the Colored voters can not be induced to come out and register unless they know that protection will be afforded them in their right to vote." Emphasis in the original.

30. "The Case Fairly Stated: The Limited Rights of the Colored Race, to Be Protected as Citizens, but Driven from Office," *New Orleans Times,* August 30, 1875, box 81-2, folder 54, Pinchback Papers, MSRC, Howard University.
31. P. B. S. Pinchback, untitled speech [On Effect of Hayes-Tilden Campaign], n.d., box 81-2, folder 45, Pinchback Papers, MSRC, Howard University.
32. See H. C. Bruce to Blanche Bruce, November 14, 1876, box 9-1, folder 3, Blanche Bruce Papers, MSRC, Howard University. The full quote is as follows: "The greatest excitement prevails here among all classes, but more particular among the colored people. They believe that slavery is to be reestablished. They are not alone in this belief. Thousands of Rebels—even up here think the same."
33. H. W. Henley to Blanche Bruce, April 26, 1879, box 9-1, folder 35, Blanche Bruce Papers, MSRC, Howard University.
34. Holt, *Black over White,* 1.
35. Jane Dailey, *Before Jim Crow: The Politics of Race in Postemancipation Virginia* (Chapel Hill: University of North Carolina Press, 2000): 7.
36. Dailey, *Before Jim Crow,* 12.
37. It should be noted that Revels was the first black man to be seated in Congress; J. Willis Menard of Louisiana was elected to the House in 1868, but the House rejected his credentials. Menard did, however, address the House on February 27, 1869. See Elizabeth Lawson, *The Gentleman from Mississippi: Our First Negro Congressman, Hiram Revels* (Author, 1960), 59, f27. Also see William J. Simmons, *Men of Mark: Eminent, Progressive and Rising* (Cleveland, Ohio: Geo. M. Rewell, 1887), 699. One of Bruce's most memorable speeches was on the subject of Chinese immigration. He voted against a measure to restrict Chinese immigration and speaking before the Senate, he argued: "Mr. President, I desire to

submit a single remark. Representing as I do a people who but a few years ago were considered essentially disqualified from enjoying the privileges and immunities of American citizenship, and who have since been so successfully introduced into the body politic, and having a large confidence in the strength and assimilative power of our institutions, I vote against this bill" (701).

38. Lawson, *Gentleman from Mississippi,* 48. By doing so, Revels contradicted every other witness that testified before the Boutwell Committee.
39. See Julius E. Thompson, "Hiram Rhodes Revels, 1827–1901: A Reappraisal," *Journal of Negro History* 79, no. 3 (1994): 299–300. Also see John Hossmer and Joseph Fineman, "Black Congressmen in Reconstruction Historiography," *Phylon* 39, no. 2 (1978): 97–107.
40. George Reasons and Sam Patrick, "They Had a Dream: Blanche Bruce—the 'Silent Senator,'" *Evening Star,* January 9, 1971, box 9-4, folder 132, Blanche Bruce Papers, MSRC, Howard University.
41. "A Most Popular Leader: Position of Ex-Senator Bruce in Washington," *Washington Bee,* September 10, 1891, box 9-4, folder 131, Blanche Bruce Papers, MSRC, Howard University.
42. J.A. Bryson to Blanche Bruce, February 16, 1876, box 9-1, folder 16, Blanche Bruce Papers, MSRC, Howard University.
43. See Lawson, *The Gentleman from Mississippi,* 8.
44. "Senator Bruce Captured," *New York Times,* June 23, 1878, clippings file, Blanche Bruce Papers, Manuscript Division, Library of Congress, Washington, D.C. (hereafter Blanche Bruce Papers, LOC).
45. Blanche Bruce to Josephine Bruce, December 5, 1877, box 9-1, folder 5, Blanche Bruce Papers, MSRC, Howard University.
46. An excerpt from an article reads, "Mr. Bruce, the colored Senator from Mississippi, has brought a bride to the national capital this winter, and the gossips are on the qui vive to know whether the custom will this time be observed. As Don Cameron's bride was the recipient last session of a $700 silver service, it is supposed he

will head the subscription and start the paper on its rounds for the benefit of Mr. Bruce's bride." The article is attached to a letter from D. F. Nelson to Blanche Bruce, December 5, 1878, box 9-2, folder 60, Blanche Bruce Papers, MSRC, Howard University. The attached article, "Not the Place to Draw the Color Line," is dated December 3, but no year is given.

47. "Ought We to Visit Her?," n.d., clippings file, Blanche Bruce Papers, LOC.
48. "How a Colored Senator's Bride Makes Her Way in Washington Society," *The Wilmington Morning Star* (February 1, 1879), 3, clippings file, Blanche Bruce Papers, LOC.
49. "Snobbery," n.d., clippings file, Blanche Bruce Papers, LOC.
50. "Senator Bruce and His Wife: How the Color Line Is Drawn Very Fine by Democratic Politicians," 1879, clippings file, Blanche Bruce Papers, LOC.
51. Ibid. The Bruces insisted that they were "very happy and contented" and found their "treatment in social life in Washington so cordial and considerate that [they] have sometimes thought [their] friends more attentive to [them] than they would have been had not this race prejudice existed among certain classes." Indeed, Blanche Bruce explained that he did not expect Southerners to visit with him or his wife: "We have not asked any person not of our own race to visit us, but we have been surprised and gratified at the number of ladies and gentlemen of both political parties who have called. I know it would be the political ruin of any Southern Democrat to recognize us socially or to have his family do so. And I want it understood that while Mrs. Bruce and I are glad to see all our friends at any time at our house, we would feel very badly if any persons compromised themselves by paying us attention."
52. Untitled article, n.d., *InterOcean,* clippings file, Blanche Bruce Papers, LOC.
53. Joseph Willson, *Sketches of the Higher Classes of Colored Society in Philadelphia* (Philadelphia: Merrihew and Thompson, 1841), quoted in Julie Winch, *The Elite of Our People: Joseph Willson's Sketches of*

Black Upper-Class Life in Antebellum Philadelphia (University Park: Pennsylvania State University Press, 2000), 82–83.

54. Winch, *Elite of Our People,* 60.
55. Ibid., 40–41.
56. Ibid., 40.
57. Ibid., 49. To name a few of the disturbances: in August 1834, the "Flying Horses" riot was ignited by a clash between black and white youths over a carousel on South Street. When a West Indian servant attacked his employer in 1835 and when a white watchman was killed by a mentally ill black man in 1837, the city spiraled into unrest. Another riot began in 1838 when a mob became inflamed by rumors of "race mixing" at an antislavery meeting at Pennsylvania Hall (which was destroyed when the mob set fire to it). Violence erupted in 1842 when an African American temperance parade "encroached" on an Irish neighborhood, whose residents took offense at the parade's banner. The rioters claimed that it pictured "the city burning and slaves running amok," but when it was unveiled in court, it showed "a kneeling slave with his manacles broken and the rising sun in the background, with the motto, 'How grand in age, how fair in truth are holy Friendship, Love, and Truth'" (30).
58. "The Exodus to Europe," clippings file, Blanche Bruce Papers, LOC. For more about Josephine and Blanche Bruce, see Lawrence Otis Graham, *The Senator and the Socialite: The True Story of America's First Black Dynasty* (New York: Harper Perennial, 2006).
59. Calvin Bruce to Blanche Bruce, December 16, 1878, box 9-1, folder 1, Blanche Bruce Papers, MSRC, Howard University. Years later, Josephine Bruce's sister would express distaste for poor, rural blacks in a letter that described the dismal conditions on the family's plantation. On January 12, 1906, she wrote that the plantation had exhausted its credit and was losing money so fast that she "didn't know what to do about getting something to eat for the darkies." She remained disgusted by the behavior of blacks on the plantation and discouraged her sister from alleviating

their plight: "Now in regard to these darkies and the church, *don't you do one thing—they are not suitable to my consideration and not worthy of notice.* They have no regard for moral obligations and let no advantage go by. See what they have done, made you and I lose thousands of dollars here, because they could take the advantage of some infernal law." See ALH [?] to Josephine Bruce, January 12, 1906, box 10-3, folder 58, Roscoe Conkling Bruce Sr. Papers, MSRC (hereafter Roscoe C. Bruce Sr. Papers, MSRC, Howard University). Emphasis in the original.

60. In a letter dated August 28, 1889, Joseph Willson wrote to Josephine Bruce to inform her of the disappearance of Anna Foote, Leonidas Willson's light-skinned wife. Joseph Willson wrote that Leonidas Willson was embarrassed that his wife left him, but his father made efforts to console him because "it is a blessing to him, for she has impoverished him." Perhaps even more egregiously, Anna Foote had not been a good wife. According to Joseph, "[Leonidas'] house is the most desolate-looking I ever saw; she has not done one thing to make it look homelike." But before she left, she was advised by her mother that she could "get away with some money," and she took everything that she could out of the house: "every tidy, the piano cover, the sheets, pillow cases, dishes, glasses, knives & spoons, she has left him absolutely empty." Indeed, she might have made off with more household goods but "the servant seeing what was going on took some lace curtains & a quilt over to the neighbors and left them there until she [left], & this morning she is putting them up in the dining room windows and she is trying to make things look nice." See Joseph Willson to Josephine Bruce, August 28, 1889, box 10-2, folder 40, Blanche Bruce Papers, MSRC, Howard University.

61. "Pinchback's Case," *New York Commercial Advertiser,* February 23, n.d., clippings, box 81-2, folder 54, Pinchback Papers, MSRC, Howard University. James F. Casey stated that Pinchback "has no chance of getting his seat in the Senate, as Northern Senators are a

little particular who they associate with." See "Louisiana Politics," July 6, 1875, clippings, box 81-2, folder 55, Pinchback Papers, MSRC, Howard University.

62. P. B. S. Pinchback to Blanche Bruce, June 17, 1878, box 9-2, folder 67, Blanche Bruce Papers, MSRC, Howard University.
63. Simmons, *Men of Mark,* 761.
64. "Mr. Pinchback's Letter," n.d., clippings, box 81-2, folder 54, Pinchback Papers, MSRC, Howard University.
65. "Pinchback's Case," *New York Commercial Advertiser,* February 23, n.d., clippings, box 81-2, folder 54, Pinchback Papers, MSRC, Howard University.
66. "Sawing Themselves Off," n.d., clippings, box 81-2, folder 53, Pinchback Papers, MSRC, Howard University. In "An Open Letter of Ex-Gov Pinchback" [April 20, 1884], Pinchback responded to accusations made by the editor of the *New Orleans Times Democrat* that he had been "inciting Negroes" and acting in a way that was "unfriendly to the white people of the State." An untitled and undated article spoke of his rowdy past: "But the reckless life he has led, from cabin boy on a Mississippi steamer to a first-class gambler, makes him naturally without the checks and restraints of good society; unscrupulous, determined to carry, at all hazards, any point which he starts out for, and, on the whole, has a kind of guerilla disposition, which has some of the character of the true soldier in it, while at the same time it is associated with a desperation and fearlessness which in an emergency would know no restraints." See clippings, box 81-2, folder 52, Pinchback Papers, MSRC, Howard University.
67. "Senator P. B. S. Pinchback, His Frank Criticism upon a Late Personal Attack," February 12, 1876, clippings, box 81-2, folder 53, Pinchback Papers, MSRC, Howard University.
68. P. B. S. Pinchback, untitled speech [Concerning Louisiana Case, etc. 9-4-1873], September 4, 1873, box 81-1, folder 36, Pinchback Papers, MSRC, Howard University. In a letter to Blanche Bruce

dated December 14, 1878, Pinchback spoke candidly about his insistence to be seated in the Senate: "One thing is certain, the Republicans must either do the proper thing by me, or I will make them rue the day they *forced* me to take up arms against them. I know just enough of Southern Republican management to be a formidable opponent upon the Northern stump in 1880 and they had better not *drive* me to desperation. I am as true a republican as treads the earth, and you know it well, but by the eternal, I will have recognition, or *revenge*. The time for play has passed forever with me." Emphasis in the original. See Pinchback, general correspondence, June 1878–June 20, 1879, box 9-2, folder 67, Blanche Bruce Papers, MSRC, Howard University.

In an address to a convention of black editors, Pinchback voiced his disgust and rejected the obsequious role that he believed that white politicians expected him to play: "This rolling in the dust—this knuckling to power, whether wrapped up in an individual or a party, I have long since abandoned. I strike out boldly, as if born in a desert, and looking for civilization; I am groping about through this American forest of prejudice and proscription, determined to find some form of civilization where all men will be accepted for what they are worth. I demand nothing for our race because they are black. Even the wrongs of two hundred years I will overlook, although they entitle us to some consideration. Still I hope the future will present no necessity for frequent reference to this matter." See "Colored Editors Convention: Project to Make the Colored People a Reading People," August 5, 1875, clippings, box 81-2, folder 53, Pinchback Papers, MSRC, Howard University.

69. P. B. S. Pinchback, untitled speech [On Thirteenth Amendment], January 4, 1869, box 81-1, folder 34, Pinchback Papers, MSRC, Howard University.

70. "Senator P. B. S. Pinchback, His Frank Criticism upon a Late Personal Attack," February 12, 1876, clippings, box 81-2, folder 53, Pinchback Papers, MSRC, Howard University.

71. P. B. S. Pinchback to Blanche Bruce, June 25, 1879, clippings, box 9-2, folder 68, Blanche Bruce Papers, MSRC, Howard University.
72. "Personal. Senator Pinchback Rises to Explain," February 7, 1875, box 81-2, folder 54, Pinchback Papers, MSRC, Howard University. Emphasis in the original.
73. P. B. S. Pinchback, untitled speech [On equal rights], June 1874, box 81-1, folder 38, Pinchback Papers, MSRC, Howard University.
74. James W. Gordon, "Did the First Justice Harlan Have a Black Brother?," in *Critical White Studies: Looking Behind the Mirror,* ed. Richard Delgado and Jean Stefancic (Philadelphia: Temple University Press, 1997), 444. This assumption was supported by the similarly ruddy complexion of James, John Marshall, and Robert Harlan.
75. It was not illegal to teach a slave (or a "servant," as slaves were called in the Harlan household) to read and write in Kentucky as it was in other southern states, but it was still frowned upon. James Harlan may have had some ambivalent feelings about slavery, but he was hardly an abolitionist. Harlan's tax records demonstrate that he bought and sold slaves throughout his life, and census reports show that he held between 12 and 14 slaves between the years of 1850 and 1860, which was typical given the lack of large plantations in Kentucky. With the exception of Robert Harlan, James Harlan was not known to educate or to emancipate his slaves. See Gordon, "Did the First Justice Harlan?" Linda Przybyszewski, author of *The Republic According to John Marshall Harlan* (Chapel Hill: University of North Carolina Press, 1999), writes that James Harlan may have expressed contempt for the brutality of slavery; his thinking was the result of his confidence in paternalism, not racial egalitarianism (18–27).
76. See Alan F. Westin, "John Marshall Harlan and the Constitutional Rights of Negroes: The Transformation of a Southerner," *Yale Law Journal* 66, no. 5 (1957): 652.
77. Przybyszewski, *Republic According to John Marshall Harlan,* 23.
78. Simmons, *Men of Mark,* 613–616.

79. Ibid. Very little is known about Robert Harlan's life. He married a free woman of color in the 1840s and had five daughters between the years of 1842 and 1848. Robert, similar to James Harlan, sent his son to Woodward High School, a white school where William Howard Taft was one of his classmates. This choice of schools raises questions about Robert Jr.'s racial identity and whether his father assumed that he would pass as white to attend the school.

80. For a discussion of John Marshall Harlan's political development, see Westin, "J. M. Harlan and the Constitutional Rights of Negroes." The rough outline is as follows: he moved from the Whigs to the Know-Nothings to the Opposition (Whig-American) Party and tried to walk a middle road, against secession but for southern property rights in slaves. He joined the Conservative Union Party in 1865 but eventually became a Republican, a choice that was described as one that "he drifted to rather than made freely." Given the frequency of Harlan's switches, he was dogged by accusations that he was a "political weathercock," to which he replied that he would "rather be right than consistent" (650–655, 662). During 1875, Democrats posed "some ugly questions" to Harlan, including one about whether he "sat by the side of a negro at a dinner table in Maine a few years ago." The question referred to a dinner in 1872 hosted by Senator James Blaine of Maine where Harlan sat between Frederick Douglass and Benjamin Butler. Harlan responded, "I ate my dinner in entire comfort, eating neither more nor less because of Douglass' presence near me. Why fellow-citizens, I not only ate by the side of Douglass at Blaine's house, but during the campaign sat at the same table with him in public hotels and spoke from the same platform with him. And here let me say that there is no man of any party in Kentucky who can make an abler address before a public audience than can Frederick Douglass. . . . I not only do not apologize for what I did, but frankly say that I would rather eat dinner any day

by the side of Douglass than to eat with the fellow across the way who sought to entrap me by a question which has nothing to do with the contest" (665).

81. "The Republicans," *New Orleans Times Democrat,* January 24, 1888, clippings, box 81-2, folder 54, Pinchback Papers, MSRC, Howard University.

82. Gordon, "Did the First Justice Harlan?," 450.

83. Harlan's dissent in *Plessy:* "In respect of civil rights, common to all citizens, the Constitution of the United States does not . . . permit any public authority to know the race of those entitled to be protected in the enjoyment of such rights." On the Civil War Amendments, John Marshall Harlan wrote: "There cannot be, in this republic, any class of human beings in practical subjection to another class, with power in the latter to dole out to the former just such privileges as they choose to grant. The supreme law of the land has decreed that no authority shall be exercised in this country upon the basis of discrimination, in respect of civil rights, against [free men] and citizens because of their race, color, or previous condition of servitude." Perhaps the most famous part of the dissent was: "In view of the Constitution, in the eyes of the law, there is in this country no superior, dominant, ruling class of citizens. There is no caste here. Our Constitution is color-blind, an neither knows nor tolerates classes among citizens. In respect of civil rights, all citizens are equal before the law." For more on the case, see Charles A. Lofgren, *The Plessy Case: A Legal-Historical Interpretation* (New York: Oxford University Press, 1987).

84. Westin, "J. M. Harlan and the Constitutional Rights of Negroes," 656.

85. Ibid., 660.

86. Ibid., 666. Harlan attracted national attention and was championed as a nominee for the presidential election of 1884. The Democrats "lashed out at Harlan the chameleon." The *Louisville*

Courier-Journal remarked that "no one can laugh off inconsistency better than he, for his youth, the passions of the time, for which he was not responsible, are always at hand to excuse positions that to his present view are incorrect." And Senator George Edmunds, the chairman of the committee, wrote in opposition to Harlan's nomination to the Supreme Court, "As sure as you and I live, we will both see the hour when he will be the sycophantic friend and suppliant tool of the Democratic party. He *was that* when he thought it was to his interest to be so. He *will be* so again when he believes that his interests require it" (667, 669). Emphasis in the original.

87. Przybyszewski, *Republic According to John Marshall Harlan,* 85. Later cases also demonstrate Harlan's efforts "to uplift and evangelize blacks while maintaining a clear social separation from them" (87).
88. Westin, "J. M. Harlan and the Constitutional Rights of Negroes," 663.
89. Lofgren, *The Plessy Case,* 201.
90. Westin, "J. M. Harlan and the Constitutional Rights of Negroes," 637.
91. Lofgren, *The Plessy Case,* 192. Lofgren explained the problem at the heart of laws that discriminated against blacks: "The separate car law worked 'a distinct disparagement' of a group whose members, because of their color, had mostly been within 'the line of the late institution of slavery.' . . . The statute 'amount[ed] to a *taunt by law* of that previous condition of their class'—a taunt by the State, to be administered with perpetually repeated like taunts *in word* by railroad employees. . . . Everyone must concede . . . that within society whites as a class occupied the position of Sir Walter Scott's Rob Roy: *'wherever he sate* [*sic*], *was the head of the table.'*" Emphasis in the original.
92. Ibid., 194.
93. Benno Schmidt, quoted in Lofgren, *The Plessy Case,* 197.

94. Richard Brodhead, ed., *The Journals of Charles W. Chesnutt* (Durham, N.C.: Duke University Press, 1993), 9.
95. Charles Chesnutt, journal entry, January 21, 1881, box 13, folder 3, Chesnutt Collection, Fisk University. Chesnutt's journals also reveal that in Fayetteville, he met a number of liberal, sympathetic whites including a doctor, a bookseller who opened his store to Chesnutt, and a German Jewish merchant who offered Chesnutt language instruction, despite the objections of other whites in the town.
96. Chesnutt, journal entry, June 7, 1875, box 13, folder 1, Chesnutt Collection, Fisk University.
97. Chesnutt smarted at the casual manners and informality of the rural folk: "Last Friday, a high-headed young gentleman of considerable color accosted me by the venerable title of 'Uncle Chess.' I, in a most graceful and polite manner informed him that I was unaware of sustaining that relationship to him, so he dropped down to Mr. Chess." Charles Chesnutt, journal entry, July 28, 1875, box 13, folder 1, Chesnutt Collection, Fisk University.
98. Chesnutt, journal entry, June 7, 1875, box 13, folder 1, Chesnutt Collection, Fisk University.
99. Chesnutt, journal entry, August 13, 1875, box 13, folder 1, Chesnutt Collection, Fisk University. Around June 1875, Chesnutt wrote that the parents "are a very trifling, shiftless set of people up there, and their children are following in their footsteps."
100. Chesnutt, journal entry, March 7, 1882, box 13, folder 3, Chesnutt Collection, Fisk University.
101. Chesnutt, journal entry, April 23, 1879, box 13, folder 2, Chesnutt Collection, Fisk University.
102. Chesnutt, journal entry, n.d., box 13, folder 2, Chesnutt Collection, Fisk University. Years later, sociologist E. Franklin Frazier would excoriate this status-oriented black society that he claimed lived in "a world of make-believe" in *Black Bourgeoisie* (New York:

Collier Books, 1957). See esp. Part Two: The World of Make-Believe, 127–191.

103. "Noted Author in High Praises of Chesnutt," *Chicago Defender,* January 21, 1933, clippings, box 15, folder 1, Chesnutt Collection, Fisk University.

104. Ibid.

105. Charles Chesnutt, *The House Behind the Cedars* (New York: Penguin, 1993), 57.

106. Chesnutt, *House Behind the Cedars,* 122–123.

107. Frank Webb, *The Garies and Their Friends* (Baltimore: Johns Hopkins University Press, 1997), 302.

108. John Lynch to Blanche Bruce, October 27, 1877, box 9-2, folder 58, Blanche Bruce Papers, MSRC, Howard University. On September 13, 1889, Chesnutt received a letter with a similarly dismal outlook from the editor of the *Progressive Educator:* "I am sorry that I cannot say that the relations between the races in this state are improving. I am sorry that I cannot say that they have grown no worse since you were here. . . . There has not been such bitterness in N.C. since emancipation barring the years immediately succeeding Reconstruction, the Ku Klux era. Nor is this feeling confined to the Democrats. White republicans are showing a bitter proscription of Negro citizens. Thinking colored citizens now have under advisement plans by which the race may be placed in an attitude that will command the just judgment of just men and women every where regardless of party." See Editor of the *Progressive Educator* to Charles Chesnutt, box 4, folder 31, Chesnutt Collection, Fisk University.

109. John Lynch to Blanche Bruce, September 21, 1877, box 9-2, folder 58, Blanche Bruce Papers, MSRC, Howard University.

110. See Richard Kluger, *Simple Justice: The History of* Brown v. Board of Education *and Black America's Struggle for Equality* (New York: Vintage Books, 1975), 62. George H. White of North Carolina would be the last black politician to leave office during the period, in 1901.

111. Colonel A. K. McClure, "Coming and Overthrow of the Negro in Congress: Random Recollections of Half a Century," *Washington Post,* January 5, 1902.
112. Speech on State Constitution Amendments, n.d., box 81-2, folder 43, Pinchback Papers, MSRC, Howard University.
113. Editor of the *Progressive Educator* to Charles Chesnutt, September 13, 1889, box 4, folder 31, Chesnutt Collection, Fisk University.
114. "An Estimate of the National Career of Blanche Kelso Bruce," box 9-5, folder 143, St. Clair Research, chap. 10, p. 256, Blanche Bruce Papers, MSRC, Howard University. Reiterating some of the themes that led Bruce to be labeled the "Silent Senator," the author adds, "Bruce's unquestioning acceptance of and firm adherence to the 'status quo' caused his career to be less meaningful to his race today than it would have been had he appreciated the fact that the solution of the political problems of the Negro is dependent upon an evolving concept of democracy."
115. Pinchback would seek shelter in the colored society of Washington, D.C. One biographical account described his domestic life as "one of happiness and cultured refinement in the splendid home he has recently erected in Washington." See "Hon. P. B. S. Pinchback," box 81-1, folder 1, Pinchback Papers, MSRC, Howard University. For more on Roscoe Conkling Bruce Jr., see "Harvard Draws Color Line on Son of Graduate," January 11, 1923, and "Harvard's Policy Is to Bar Colored Students," January 12, 1923, clippings, box 10-4, folder 96, Roscoe C. Bruce Sr. Papers, MSRC, Howard University. For more on Barrington Guy and Clara Bruce Jr., see letters dated October–November 1922 between Barrington Guy's father, Nathaniel Guy, and Roscoe Conkling Bruce Sr. that discuss the parents' discovery of and disappointment with the couple's elopement, box 10-3, folders 65, 66, and 68, Roscoe C. Bruce Sr. Papers, MSRC, Howard University. For more on Barrington Guy, see "Did You Happen to See—Barrington Sharma?" and "'High Yaller' Proves as Big a Barrier to Theatre Progress as

Ebony Color Skin," Barrington Guy clippings, box 10-4, folder 98, Roscoe C. Bruce Sr. Papers, MSRC, Howard University.

3. LOST KIN

1. Caroline Bond Day, "The Pink Hat," *Opportunity* (December 1926): 379–380. Day won third place in the *Opportunity* fiction contest for this story.
2. C. Vann Woodward, *The Strange Career of Jim Crow* (New York: Oxford University Press, 2002), 82.
3. Ibid., 84. Woodward explains that these clauses enabled the disenfranchisement of blacks while granting lower-class whites the right to vote.
4. Neil R. McMillen, *Dark Journey: Black Mississippians in the Age of Jim Crow* (Urbana: University of Illinois Press, 1989), 38.
5. Constitutional Rights Foundation, *Bill of Rights in Action*, "Voting and Discrimination: Race and Voting in the Segregated South," June 2000, www.crf-usa.org/bill-of-rights-in-action/bria-12-2-b-race-and-voting-in-the-segregated-south
6. Eric Foner, "Rooted in Reconstruction: The First Wave of Black Congressmen," *Nation,* November 3, 2008. Not until 1972 did black political representation increase significantly, beginning with the elections of Andrew Young in Georgia and Barbara Jordan in Texas.
7. Leon F. Litwack, *Trouble in Mind* (New York: Knopf, 1998), 284. Also see Glenda Gilmore, *Gender and Jim Crow: Women and the Politics of White Supremacy in North Carolina, 1896–1920* (Chapel Hill: The University of North Carolina Press, 1996), 91–118.
8. James Weldon Johnson, *The Autobiography of an Ex-Colored Man* (New York: Dover Thrift Publications, 1995), 88.
9. Jacqueline Goldsby, *A Spectacular Secret: Lynching in American Life* (Chicago: University of Chicago Press, 2006), 173.
10. I borrow the expression "the cheapness of black life" from Leon Litwack, *Trouble in Mind,* 284. See Johnson, *Autobiography,* 90, 100.

11. Charles B. Davenport, the most preeminent eugenicist in America and founder of the United States' first research center in genetics at Cold Spring Harbor, New York, quoted in John Higham, *Strangers in the Land: Patterns of American Nativism, 1860–1925* (New Brunswick, N.J.: Rutgers University Press, 1955), 151.
12. Chinese immigrants were already prohibited through the Chinese Exclusion Acts of 1883. Congress allowed approximately 287,000 immigrants per year to enter the country, but this number included immigrants from Canada and Latin American countries that were exempt from the quota system. Higham, *Strangers in the Land,* 324.
13. W. A. Plecker to the Editor of *Survey Graphic,* March 13, 1925, box 41, folder 35. Series IV. Eugenics and Racial Integrity. Subseries C: Correspondence concerning Eugenics: Plecker. The Papers of John Powell, 1888–1978, N. D. Albert and Shirley Small Special Collections Library, University of Virginia, Charlottesville, Virginia (hereafter Powell Papers, Small Library, UVA). My thanks to Steven Porter for bringing this collection to my attention.
14. W. A. Plecker to the Honorable Stone Deavours, Mississippi, April 15, 1925, box 41, folder 39, Powell Papers, Small Library, UVA.
15. W. A. Plecker to the Editor of *Survey Graphic,* March 13, 1925, box 41, folder 35, Powell Papers, Small Library, UVA.
16. Paul A. Lombardo, "Miscegenation, Eugenics, and Racism: Historical Footnotes to *Loving v. Virginia,*" *UC Davis Law Review* 21 (Winter 1987–1988): 434.
17. W. A. Plecker to Honorable W. M. Steuart, Director of the U.S. Bureau of the Census, August 4, 1931, box 41, folder 53, Powell Papers, Small Library, UVA.
18. W. A. Plecker to Miss Aileen Hartless, March 9, 1944, box 42, folder 51. Powell Papers, Small Library, UVA.
19. W. A. Plecker to Miss Blanche Cunningham, June 11, 1940, box 41, folder 78, Powell Papers, Small Library, UVA.

20. W. A. Plecker to the Superintendent, Riverview Cemetery, August 1, 1940, box 41, folder 88, Powell Papers, Small Library, UVA.
21. W. A. Plecker to W. G. Muncy, Secretary, Riverview Cemetery Company, August 3, 1940, box 41, folder 89, Powell Papers, Small Library, UVA.
22. W. A. Plecker to Dr. R. R. Kason, May 8, 1943, box 42, folder 39, Powell Papers, Small Library, UVA.
23. W. A. Plecker to Mrs. Robert Cheatham, and Mrs. Mary Gildon (two letters typed on the same page), April 30, 1924, box 41, folder 7, Powell Papers, Small Library, UVA.
24. W. A. Plecker to Mrs. Robert Cheatham, and Mrs. Mary Gildon (two letters typed on the same page), April 30, 1924, box 41, folder 7, Powell Papers, Small Library, UVA.
25. W. A. Plecker to the Editor of *Survey Graphic,* March 13, 1925, box 41, folder 35, Powell Papers, Small Library, UVA.
26. Thomas C. Holt, "Marking: Race, Race-making and the Writing of History," *American Historical Review* 100 (1995): 2.
27. Elmer A. Carter, "Crossing Over," *Opportunity* (December 1926): 376.
28. Ray Stannard Baker, *Following the Color Line: American Negro Citizenship in the Progressive Era* (New York: Harper & Row, 1964), 160.
29. Gilmore, *Gender and Jim Crow,* 280, fn 79.
30. Ray Stannard Baker, "Wanted: A Mudsill: Why Many Whites Hate to See the Negro Rise," *New-York Tribune,* June 23, 1907, C5.
31. See Isabel Wilkerson, *The Warmth of Other Suns: The Epic Story of America's Great Migration* (New York: Random House, 2010).
32. Richard B. Baker, "The Great Migration's Impact on the Education of Southern-born African Americans" (paper presented at Harvard University, Cambridge, MA, March 2011). Isabel Wilkerson, *The Warmth of Other Suns: The Epic Story of America's Great Migration* (New York: Random House, 2010), 11.
33. Frederick Brown, "The Northward Movement of the Colored Population: A Statistical Study" (Baltimore: Cushing, 1897), box 93,

subseries 5.9.2.6–5.9.3, Myrdal Study, folder 1426, series 5.9.2.6, Migration, no. 3826, Guy Benton Johnston Papers, Southern Historical Collection, Wilson Library, University of North Carolina, Chapel Hill (hereafter Guy Benton Johnston Papers, Wilson Library, UNC).

34. Cheryl Harris, "Whiteness as Property," *Harvard Law Review* 106 (1993): 1711.

35. "Negro Girl at Vassar," Anita Hemmings clippings file, Special Collections, Catherine Pelton Durrell '25 Archives and Special Collections Library, Vassar College, Poughkeepsie, N.Y.

36. Roscoe C. Bruce Sr. to Clara Burrill, March 10, 1903, box 10-2, folder 29, Roscoe Conkling Bruce Sr. Papers, MSRC, Howard University. Bruce's emphasis.

37. "Not Even His Wife Knew Birth Secret of Claimant to Negro's Rich Fortune," n.d., *Buffalo New York Courier Express*, "Wall St. Lawyer Asking Fortune, Silent on Race," "Establishes Kinship to Negro: Attorney Accepted as White Clinches Claim to Estate," and "Wall St. Lawyer Claims He Is Negro's Kin, Heir," clippings, Theophilus John McKee Sr. Papers, Special Collections, The Watkinson Library, Trinity College, Hartford, Conn. (hereafter McKee Papers, Trinity College).

38. Taliaferro, Mary [wife of Elsie Roxborough's father's law partner]. Interview by Kathleen A. Hauke [author], Unpublished interview. August 27, 1982. Oral History Transcripts and Interviews, R-W, box 2, folder 6, Roxborough Family Papers, Burton Historical Collection, Detroit Public Library, Detroit, Michigan (hereafter Roxborough Family Papers, Burton Historical Collection). Kathleen A. Hauke conducted extensive research on the Roxborough family and published the article, "The 'Passing' of Elsie Roxborough," *Michigan Quarterly Review* 23, no. 2 (Spring 1984): 155–170.

39. Lewis Walker and Ben C. Wilson, *Black Eden: The Idlewild Community* (East Lansing: Michigan State University Press, 2002).

40. Julia Bradby. Interview by Kathleen A. Hauke. Unpublished Interview. October 9, 1982. Oral History Transcripts and Interviews, B-N, box 2, folder 4, Roxborough Family Papers, Burton Historical Collection.
41. Enoch P. Waters, Jr. "Play By Detroit Girl is Called Poor By Chicagoan," *The Chicago Defender*, March 28, 1936, 4.
42. Dr. Benjamin Brownley [Elsie Roxborough's brother-in-law]. Interview by Kathleen A. Hauke. Unpublished Interview. September 16, 1982. Oral History Transcripts and Interviews, Dr. Ben Brownley, 1982, box 2, folder 5, Roxborough Family Papers, Burton Historical Collection.
43. Langston Hughes, *I Wonder As I Wander* (New York: Hill and Wang, 1956), 328.
44. Quoted in Kathleen Hauke to Marshall D. Solomon, December 29, 1982, box 1, folder 4, Correspondence, 1931–1984, Roxborough Family Papers, Burton Historical Collection.
45. Hughes, *I Wonder As I Wander,* 328.
46. "Elsie Roxborough Dies," *Michigan Chronicle* (October 8, 1949), box 1, folder 2, Roxborough Family Papers, Burton Historical Collection.
47. William Smallwood, "Elsie Roxborough Reported Living Incognito in Gotham," *Baltimore Afro-American,* December 25, 1937, 9.
48. "Elsie Roxborough Dies," *Michigan Chronicle* (October 8, 1949), box 1, folder 2, Roxborough Family Papers, Burton Historical Collection.
49. Sonny Roxborough [Elsie Roxborough's brother]. Interview by Kathleen A. Hauke. Unpublished Interview. January 9, 1983, box 1, folder 11, Charles A. Roxborough Jr. ("Sonny"), Letters and Interviews, 1982–1983, Roxborough Family Papers, Burton Historical Collection.
50. Lisa Henry [?] to Virginia Brownley, October 4, 1949, box 1, folder 4, Correspondence, 1931–1984, Roxborough Family Papers, Burton Historical Collection.

51. Ernest Lehman to Virginia Brownley, October 4, 1949, box 1, folder 4, Correspondence, 1931–1984, Roxborough Family Papers, Burton Historical Collection.
52. Carol Roxborough. Interview by Kathleen A. Hauke. Unpublished Interview. December 12, 1982. Oral History Transcripts and Interviews, R-W, box 2, folder 6, Burton Historical Collection, Detroit Public Library.
53. Sonny Roxborough [Elsie Roxborough's brother]. Interview by Kathleen A. Hauke. Unpublished Interview. November 19, 1982, box 1, folder 11, Charles A. Roxborough Jr. ("Sonny"), Letters and Interviews, 1982–1983, Roxborough Family Papers, Burton Historical Collection.
54. Kermit Bailer. Interview by Kathleen A. Hauke. Unpublished Interview. Oral History Transcripts and Interviews, B-N, box 2, folder 4, Roxborough Family Papers, Burton Historical Collection.
55. Dr. Benjamin Brownley [Elsie Roxborough's brother-in-law]. Interview by Kathleen A. Hauke. Unpublished Interview. September 16, 1982. Oral History Transcripts and Interviews, Dr. Ben Brownley, 1982, box 2, folder 5, Roxborough Family Papers, Burton Historical Collection.
56. Carol Roxborough to Dr. Benjamin Brownley, November 13, 1982. Correspondence, 1931–1984, box 1, folder 5, Roxborough Family Papers, Burton Historical Collection.
57. Carter, "Crossing Over," 376.
58. Harry B. Anderson, "Meet Your Neighbor," *Baltimore Afro-American,* July 16, 1938, 24.
59. Caroline Bond Day to Mrs. Judea [Judia ?] J. Harris, July 21, 1927, box 1, Caroline Bond Day Papers, Peabody Museum Archives, Harvard University (hereafter Caroline Bond Day Papers, Peabody Museum Archives, Harvard University).
60. See Caroline Bond Day to Mrs. Elizabeth Abel Cook, March 30, 1927, box 1, Caroline Bond Day Papers, Peabody Museum Archives, Harvard University.

61. Anastasia C. Curwood, "Caroline Bond Day (1889–1948): A Black Woman Outsider within Physical Anthropology," *Transforming Anthropology* 20, no. 1 (2012): 83.
62. Heidi Ardizzone, "'Such Fine Families': Photography and Race in the Work of Caroline Bond Day," *Visual Studies* (October 2006): 113. Day included her own racial makeup and photograph on one of the family charts. See Curwood, "Caroline Bond Day," 80.
63. "Harvard University Anthropologist Makes Preliminary Report of Study: Several Theories Upset as to Types of Individuals That Result from Mixture of White and Colored Races," *New York Amsterdam News,* June 11, 1930, 14; "Blood Study Report Made," *New Journal and Guide,* June 7, 1930, 16.
64. "Harvard University Anthropologist Makes Preliminary Report of Study: Several Theories Upset as to Types of Individuals That Result from Mixture of White and Colored Races," *New York Amsterdam News,* June 11, 1930, 4.
65. Curwood, "Caroline Bond Day," 85.
66. Ibid.
67. Jonathan Scott Hollaway, *Confronting the Veil: Abram Harris Jr., E. Franklin Frazier, and Ralph Bunche, 1919–1941* (Chapel Hill: University of North Carolina Press, 2002), 131.
68. Hollaway, *Confronting the Veil,* 127. Melville Herskovits and Frazier debated the question of whether or not black Americans retained African cultural patterns. Frazier argued that they did not, and thus the only cultural traditions that blacks could lay claim to developed during slavery. Herskovits argued that black Americans' cultural traditions were far more enduring and reached back to Africa.
69. "Dr. E. Franklin Frazier," *Pittsburgh Courier,* June 2, 1962, 12.
70. "Dr. Frazier Heads World UN Group," *New Journal and Guide,* December 31, 1949, D5.
71. E. Franklin Frazier, *Black Bourgeoisie* (New York: Simon and Schuster, 1957), 201.

72. Robert M. Ratcliffe, "Behind the Headlines!: *'Black Bourgeoisie,'"* *Pittsburgh Courier,* January 18, 1958, A3.
73. Edgar A. Toppin, "E. Franklin Frazier: Sociologist," *Baltimore Afro-American,* November 18, 1972, A1.
74. "Death of a Great Scholar," *Chicago Defender,* May 23, 1962, 11.
75. Holloway, *Confronting the Veil,* 137–140.
76. Ibid., 152.
77. "E. Franklin Frazier," *Washington Post,* May 21, 1962, A18.
78. "A Study of the Negro Family," undated, no. 2513, E. Franklin Frazier Papers, MSRC (hereafter E. Franklin Frazier Papers, MSRC, Howard University).
79. Caroline Bond Day, "A Study of Some Negro-White Families in the United States," (master's thesis, Harvard University, 1932), 6.
80. "Interview with Squire Clemens and Wife," n.d., research projects, box 131-92, folder 9, p. 3, E. Franklin Frazier Papers, MSRC, Howard University.
81. Leona Glover, "My Family History," March 13, 1944, research projects, box 131-86, folder 29, p. 1, E. Franklin Frazier Papers, MSRC, Howard University.
82. Autobiographical Sketch: Lloyd Harding Bailer, box 93, subseries 5.9.2.6–5.9.3, Myrdal Study, folder 1441, no. 3826, Guy Benton Johnston Papers, Wilson Library, UNC.
83. "William Smalley," correspondence, box 1, Caroline Bond Day Papers, Peabody Museum Archives, Harvard University.
84. "1. Some Odd Scraps of Family Histories Secured by Miss Fisher. 2. Family Histories of High School Students Secured in Birmingham," n.d., research projects, box 131-92, folder 5, pp. 2–3, E. Franklin Frazier Papers, MSRC, Howard University.
85. "Interview with Rev. and Mrs. J. A. Bass," n.d., research projects, box 131-92, folder 9, p. 4, E. Franklin Frazier Papers, MSRC, Howard University.
86. Ibid., 10.

87. Langston Hughes, "Passing," in *The Ways of White Folks* (New York: Random House, 1969), 51–52.
88. Mary Church Terrell, "Why, How, When, and Where Black Becomes White," writings, box 102-3, folder 128, pp. 1–11, Mary Church Terrell Papers, MSRC, Howard University.
89. Willard B. Gatewood, *Aristocrats of Color: The Black Elite, 1880–1920* (Bloomington: Indiana University Press, 1990), 181.
90. "A Study of the Negro Family," William Jefferson, n.d., research projects, family questionnaires, box 131-102, folder 6, E. Franklin Frazier Papers, MSRC, Howard University. This quotation is taken from the first of three pages of handwritten notes inserted in the middle of the questionnaire. Jefferson's questionnaire appears to be faintly numbered in the upper right corner as "[3001]."
91. Gatewood, *Aristocrats of Color,* 340. Two years later, however, in 1941, Guy changed his stage name to Barrington Sharma and claimed that his father "came from India." See Nathaniel Guy to Roscoe Conkling Bruce Sr., October 24, 1922, box 10-3, folder 68, Roscoe Conkling Bruce Sr. Papers, MSRC, Howard University.
92. "Interview with Rev. and Mrs. J. A. Bass," research projects, box 131-92, folder 9, pp. 15–16, E. Franklin Frazier Papers, MSRC, Howard University.
93. Langston Hughes, "Fooling Our White Folks," *Negro Digest,* April 1950, 41.
94. Helen Chesnutt, *Charles Waddell Chesnutt: Pioneer of the Color Line* (Chapel Hill: University of North Carolina Press, 1952), 273–274.
95. Nella Larsen, *Passing* (New Brunswick: Rutgers University Press, 1986), 157–158.
96. The question also presumed that the person inquiring might have relatives in common or might know members of the larger family network. Ronne Hartfield, *Another Way Home: The Tangled Roots of Race in One Chicago Family* (Chicago: University of Chicago Press, 2004), 88. Also see Chapter 1, "Now, Who Are Your People?:

Norfolk, Virginia, and Littleton, North Carolina, 1903–1918," in Barbara Ransby, *Ella Baker and the Black Freedom Movement: A Radical Democratic Vision* (Chapel Hill: The University of North Carolina Press, 2003), 12–45.

97. Hartfield, *Another Way Home,* 91–92.
98. Ibid., 52.
99. Ibid., 42.
100. Ibid., 41–42.
101. "Questionnaire—Negro and Mulatto Families," 1927–28 Bureau of International Research, Harvard University and Radcliffe College, box 3, tables, questionnaires and guides, Caroline Bond Day Papers, Peabody Museum Archives, Harvard University.
102. Annie Sims Lewis to Caroline Bond Day, February 3, 1927, box 1, Caroline Bond Day Papers, Peabody Museum Archives, Harvard University.
103. Alice McNeill to Caroline Bond Day, June 11, 1928, box 1, Caroline Bond Day Papers, Peabody Museum Archives, Harvard University. Poet and political activist Alice Dunbar-Nelson wrote a humorous response to Day: "What on earth are you doing with all this rigid questionnaire business? The only thing it doesn't ask is if your grandmother's aunt had epizootic in the left hind toe." See Alice Dunbar-Nelson to Caroline Bond Day, July 8, 1927, box 1, Caroline Bond Day Papers, Peabody Museum Archives, Harvard University.
104. Emma L. Milliston [?] to Caroline Bond Day, April 6, 1928, box 1, Caroline Bond Day Papers, Peabody Museum Archives, Harvard University.
105. Mrs. Edgar J. Penney to Caroline Bond Day, August 8, 1927, box 1, Caroline Bond Day Papers, Peabody Museum Archives, Harvard University.
106. Caroline Bond Day to Mrs. Corrie Percival, July 26, 1927, box 1, Caroline Bond Day Papers, Peabody Museum Archives, Harvard University. Day knew that it would be difficult to get her friends

to donate photographs, but she hoped that given their personal relationships, she could persuade them to trust her.

107. Mrs. Corrie Percival to Caroline Bond Day, January 31, 1928, box 1, Caroline Bond Day Papers, Peabody Museum Archives, Harvard University.
108. "Interview with Rev. and Mrs. J. A. Bass," n.d., research projects, box 131-92, folder 9, p. 16, E. Franklin Frazier Papers, MSRC, Howard University.
109. "I'm Through with Passing," *Ebony,* March 1951, 22.
110. "Case # 2: An Old Louisiana Mulatto Family," in "Documents on Higher Class Families in Chicago," research projects, box 131-81, folder 13, p. 3, E. Franklin Frazier Papers, MSRC, Howard University.
111. Bazoline Usher to Caroline Bond Day, n.d., box 1, Caroline Bond Day Papers, Peabody Museum Archives, Harvard University.
112. Quoted in Nathan Huggins, *Harlem Renaissance* (New York: Oxford University Press, 1971), 159. Similarly, the narrator in *The Autobiography of an Ex-Colored Man* feels "possessed by a strange longing" for his mother's people.
113. Larsen, *Passing,* 145.
114. Baker, *Following the Color Line,* 161.
115. Ibid., 162.
116. "Case # 15: Young Woman Divorced from West Indian," in "Documents on Higher Class Families in Chicago," research projects, box 131-81, folder 13, p. 3, E. Franklin Frazier Papers, MSRC, Howard University.
117. Research Projects, *The Negro Family in the U.S.,* Family Histories, Gene Thompson, box 131-90, folder 19, E. Franklin Frazier Papers, MSRC, Howard University.
118. Ralph Ellison, "The World and the Jug," in *Shadow and Act* (New York: Random House, 1964), 124.
119. Gatewood, *Aristocrats of Color,* 175.
120. "Case #19, A Family of West Indian and American Negro Origin, Mulatto," in "Documents on Higher Class Families in Chicago,"

research projects, box 131-81, folder 13, p. 4, E. Franklin Frazier Papers, MSRC, Howard University.

121. Also see Daniel J. Sharfstein, "The Secret History of Race in the United States," *Yale Law Journal* 112, no. 1473 (2003): 1473–1509.

122. Kenneth C. Field, "'Passing' No Passing Fad with Lawyer, Background Indicates," *Los Angeles Sentinel,* January 31, 1957, A1.

123. "Claims Dad Passed for White 45 Years: Widow Seeking $275,000 Estate," *Chicago Defender,* January 19, 1957, 1.

124. "Judge Throw Torregano Case out of Court: Mrs. Stevens Loses 3½ G Will Contest," *Los Angeles Sentinel,* May 30, 1957.

125. DeWreatha Valores Green, "The History of My Family," n.d., research projects, box 131-86, folder 31, E. Franklin Frazier Papers, MSRC, Howard University.

126. Thelma M. Dale, "A History of the Dale-Patterson Family," January 16, 1935, research projects, box 131-86, folder 11, pp. 7, 11, E. Franklin Frazier Papers, MSRC, Howard University.

127. "A Study of the Negro Family," Merthilda C. Duhe, research projects, questionnaires, box 131-102, folder 1, no. 2534, E. Franklin Frazier Papers, MSRC, Howard University.

128. "A Study of the Negro Family," Clyde DeHoughley, research projects, questionnaires, box 131-102, folder 1, no. 2535, E. Franklin Frazier Papers, MSRC, Howard University.

129. "Interview with Mr. and Mrs. Haywood Clemens," n.d., research projects, box 131-92, folder 8, p. 1, E. Franklin Frazier Papers, MSRC, Howard University.

130. Raymond A. Brownbow, "Family History," n.d., research projects, box 131-85, folder 23, p. 3, E. Franklin Frazier Papers, MSRC, Howard University.

131. Anthony Driver Chase, "My Family History," May 1942, research projects, box 131-85, folder 30, pp. 31–32, E. Franklin Frazier Papers, MSRC, Howard University.

132. "Case # 2: An Old Louisiana Mulatto Family," in "Documents on Higher Class Families in Chicago," research projects, box 131-81,

folder 13, p. 5, E. Franklin Frazier Papers, MSRC, Howard University.

133. T. S. Inborden to E. Franklin Frazier, July 5, 1932, research projects, questionnaires, box 131-102, folder 3, no. 2609, E. Franklin Frazier Papers, MSRC, Howard University. The letter is attached to Inborden's family questionnaire (no. 2609).

134. "A Study of the Negro Family," Helen Yancey, research projects, questionnaires, box 131-102, folder 5, no. 2705, E. Franklin Frazier Papers, MSRC, Howard University.

135. Pearle Foreman, "Family History," research projects, box 131-86, folder 26, p. 12, E. Franklin Frazier Papers, MSRC, Howard University.

136. "Go Along to See," review of *Imitation of Life,* January 1935, scrapbook, box 3, folder 4, Fredi Washington Papers, Schomburg Center for Research in Black Culture, New York Public Library (hereafter Fredi Washington Papers, Schomburg Center, NYPL).

137. "'Imitation of Life Leads Film Grosses,'" *Baltimore Afro-American,* May 25, 1935, 8.

138. Lou Layne, "Moon Over Harlem," July 6, 1936, clippings, box 3, folder 3, Fredi Washington Papers, Schomburg Center, NYPL.

139. Interview of Miss Washington by Mr. Blasco for the Met Theater, February 10, 1934, box 1, folder 1, Fredi Washington Papers, Schomburg Center, NYPL.

140. "Washington Refuses to Be Anyone but Fredi," December 14, 1949, box 1, folder 6, Fredi Washington Papers, Schomburg Center, NYPL.

141. Ibid.

142. Sheila Rule, "Fredi Washington, 90, Actress; Broke Ground for Black Artists," *New York Times,* June 30, 1994.

143. "Our Four Star Washington Gal," August 14, 1943, box 3, folder 1, Fredi Washington Papers, Library of Congress, Washington, D.C.

144. Yvonne Gregory, "Who Passes for White?," *Color* (April 1947): 11–14.

145. Langston Hughes, "Passing for White, Passing for Colored, Passing for Negroes Plus," *Chicago Defender,* October 11, 1952, newspaper columns, series 8, folder 8656, Beinecke Manuscript and Rare Books Library, Yale University.

4. SEARCHING FOR A NEW SOUL IN HARLEM

1. Nella Larsen to Carl Van Vechten, May 1, 1932, box Huh-I, folder 4, Carl Van Vechten Papers, James Weldon Johnson Collection, Beinecke Rare Books and Manuscripts Library, Yale University, New Haven, Conn. (hereafter Carl Van Vechten Papers, Beinecke Rare Books and Manuscripts Library). Larsen's emphasis. My thanks to Nancy Kuhl for guiding me to this letter.
2. Nella Larsen, *Passing* (New Brunswick: Rutgers University Press, 1986), 147.
3. Quoted in George Hutchinson, "Jean Toomer and the 'New Negroes' of Washington," *American Literature* 63, no. 4 (1991), 688.
4. Cheryl A. Wall, *Women of the Harlem Renaissance* (Bloomington: Indiana University Press, 1995), 131, 138.
5. Alain Locke, ed., *The New Negro: Voices of the Harlem Renaissance* (1925; repr., New York: Simon & Schuster, 1997), xxvii. *The New Negro* was originally published by Albert & Charles Boni.
6. Jessie Fauset to Langston Hughes, June 24, 1924, box 61, folder 1164, Langston Hughes Papers, James Weldon Johnson Collection, Beinecke Rare Books and Manuscripts Library (hereafter Langston Hughes Papers, Beinecke Rare Books and Manuscripts Library).
7. A few of the major works include David Levering Lewis, *When Harlem Was in Vogue* (New York: Penguin Books, 1980); Ann Douglas, *Terrible Honesty: Mongrel Manhattan in the 1920s* (New York: Farrar, Straus and Giroux, 1995); Wall, *Women of the Harlem Renaissance*; Thadious Davis, *Nella Larsen: Novelist of the Harlem Renaissance: A Woman's Life Unveiled* (Baton Rouge, LA: LSU Press, 1996); Charles R. Larson, *Invisible Darkness: Nella Larsen and Jean Toomer* (Iowa City, IA: University of Iowa Press, 1993); Caroline

Goeser, *Picturing the New Negro: Harlem Renaissance Print Culture and Modern Black Identity* (Lawrence: University Press of Kansas, 2007); George Hutchinson, *The Harlem Renaissance in Black and White* (Cambridge, Mass.: Harvard University Press, 1995).

8. Hutchinson, "Jean Toomer and the 'New Negroes,'" 240.
9. Claude Barnett to Jean Toomer, April 23, 1923, box 1, folder 10, Jean Toomer Papers, James Weldon Johnson Collection, Beinecke Rare Books and Manuscripts Library (hereafter Jean Toomer Papers, Beinecke Rare Books and Manuscripts Library).
10. Jean Toomer to Claude Barnett, April 29, 1923, box 1, folder 10, Jean Toomer Papers, Beinecke Rare Books and Manuscripts Library.
11. Jean Toomer to Sherwood Anderson, December 18, 1922, box 1, folder 5, Jean Toomer Papers, Beinecke Rare Books and Manuscripts Library.
12. Jean Toomer to Claude Barnett, April 19, 1923, Jean Toomer Papers, Beinecke Rare Books and Manuscripts Library.
13. James T. Campbell, *Middle Passages: African American Journeys to Africa, 1787–2005* (New York: Penguin Press, 2006), 196.
14. Jean Toomer to Waldo Frank, n.d. [Summer 1923?], box 3, folder 84, Jean Toomer Papers, Beinecke Rare Books and Manuscripts Library.
15. Jean Toomer to Waldo Frank, n.d. [Summer 1923?], box 3, folder 84, Jean Toomer Papers, Beinecke Rare Books and Manuscripts Library.
16. Jean Toomer, "Song of the Son," in Toomer, *Cane* (1923; repr., New York: W. W. Norton & Company, 1975), 12.
17. Jean Toomer to Lola Ridge, August 20, 1922, box 1, folder 18, Jean Toomer Papers, Beinecke Rare Books and Manuscripts Library.
18. Darwin T. Turner, ed., *The Wayward and the Seeking: A Collection of Writings by Jean Toomer* (Washington, D.C.: Howard University Press, 1980), 123.
19. As Toomer explained, "I was in Georgia, I believe it was the fall of 1929, for several months. When I went there, I had no intention of

writing about life there, or, as it is said, gathering material. It just happened that certain aspects of life there, particularly Negroes singing spirituals and work songs as they went about their daily work, touched me deeply; and I was certainly thinking of that, or rather feeling that, when I wrote a number of the sketches that first appeared in the Little Magazines and then in Cane." See Jean Toomer to Miss Freeman, August 10, 1949, box 3, folder 78, Jean Toomer Papers, Beinecke Rare Books and Manuscripts Library.

20. Quoted in Siobhan Somerville, *Queering the Color Line: Race and the Invention of Homosexuality in American Culture* (Durham, N.C.: Duke University Press, 2000), 131.
21. Countee Cullen to Jean Toomer, September 29, 1923, box 1, folder 38, Jean Toomer Papers, Beinecke Rare Books and Manuscripts Library.
22. Sherwood Anderson to Jean Toomer, December 22 [1922?], box 1, folder 5, Jean Toomer Papers, Beinecke Rare Books and Manuscripts Library.
23. Jean Toomer to James Weldon Johnson, July 11, 1930, box 4, folder 119, Jean Toomer Papers, Beinecke Rare Books and Manuscripts Library.
24. Ibid.
25. Jean Toomer to Sherwood Anderson, December 18, 1922, box 1, folder 5, Jean Toomer Papers, Beinecke Rare Books and Manuscripts Library.
26. Jean Toomer to Sherwood Anderson, December 22, 1922, box 1, folder 5, Jean Toomer Papers, Beinecke Rare Books and Manuscripts Library.
27. Ibid.
28. Jean Toomer to Waldo Frank, n.d., box 3, folder 83, Jean Toomer Papers, Beinecke Rare Books and Manuscripts Library. The date of this letter is likely 1922, given the letters that come before and after. It is somewhat surprising that Toomer would share this with Waldo Frank, given Frank's naivete about race relations and

about Toomer's racial identity: "The important thing which has at length released you to the creating of literature is that you do not write as a Negro." Sherwood Anderson winced at a black woman who he believed "was inclined to overestimate everything done by a negro because a negro had done it." Anderson respected Toomer's work because of its "inner humbleness"; unlike other blacks, Toomer was not "too negro" in Anderson's estimation. See Somerville, *Queering the Color Line,* 159.

29. Horace Liveright to Jean Toomer, August 29, 1923, box 1, folder 16, Jean Toomer Papers, Beinecke Rare Books and Manuscripts Library.
30. Jean Toomer to Horace Liveright, September 5, 1923, box 1, folder 16, Jean Toomer Papers, Beinecke Rare Books and Manuscripts Library.
31. Jean Toomer to Waldo Frank, n.d., box 3, folder 83, Jean Toomer Papers, Beinecke Rare Books and Manuscripts Library.
32. Somerville, *Queering the Color Line,* 163. But it is difficult, as Siobhan Somerville points out, "to extricate 'American' from a history of racialization and imperialism."
33. Jean Toomer to Jack McClure, June 30, 1922, box 2, folder 46, Jean Toomer Papers, Beinecke Rare Books and Manuscripts Library.
34. As Somerville writes, "like the conventional figure of the tragic mulatto, he appears caught in an unresolvable dilemma, alienated from either white or black identity. Invoking this narrative of passing also has the effect of containing the ambiguity of racial categories within a model that posits 'black' and 'white' as the only possible authentic identities, a model that Toomer rejected." See Somerville, *Queering the Color Line*, 134. As Somerville explains, this pairing of racial and gender categories renders Toomer inauthentic and compromised, both as black and as male. Somerville argues that "compulsory heterosexuality in the twentieth century United States has drawn much of its ideological power from the ways in which it buttresses as well as depends on naturalized categories of racial difference."

35. Henry Louis Gates, Jr., *Figures in Black: Words, Signs, and the "Racial" Self* (New York: Oxford University Press, 1987), 206.
36. James Weldon Johnson, *Along This Way: The Autobiography of James Weldon Johnson* (1933; repr., New York: Da Capo Press, 2000), 375.
37. See chap. 5, "'Queer to Myself as I Am to You': Jean Toomer, Racial Disidentification, and Queer Reading," in Somerville, *Queering the Color Line,* 131–165.
38. Quoted in Somerville, *Queering the Color Line*, 132. Years later in 1951, Toomer wrote a letter to Ralph Rose, a member of a committee on race relations who was investigating life in Washington, D.C. Toomer expressed a particular interest in this study because, as he explained, he "was born in that city, grew up in the white world there, and then, during [his] high school years, lived in the colored world." For these reasons, Toomer explained that he knew "both worlds from the inside," that he knew "something of the prejudice, etc., that is rife in the nation's capital." Given his grandfather's political connections and stature, it is not unsurprising that Toomer would have been part of the white world of Washington and would describe himself as growing up in the white world.
39. See William M. Ramsey, "Jean Toomer's Eternal South," *Southern Literary Journal* (Fall 2003): 74–89 and Michael J. Krasny, "Jean Toomer's Life Prior to *Cane*: A Brief Sketch of the Emergence of a Black Writer," in Therman B. O'Daniel, ed., *Jean Toomer: A Critical Evaluation* (Washington, D.C.: Howard University Press, 1988), 41–45.
40. Jean Toomer to Waldo Frank, n.d., box 3, folder 83, Jean Toomer Papers, Beinecke Rare Books and Manuscripts Library.
41. Elizabeth Alexander, "Toomer," *American Scholar* (September 2010), 51. Similarly, Zora Neale Hurston wrote, "At certain times, I am no race, I am *me*." See Zora Neale Hurston, "How It Feels to Be Colored Me," *World Tomorrow* (May 1928): 215–216.
42. Jean Toomer to Jack McClure, June 30, 1922, box 2, folder 46, Jean Toomer Papers, Beinecke Rare Books and Manuscripts Library.

43. Jean Toomer to Sherwood Anderson, December 22, 1922, box 1, folder 5, Jean Toomer Papers, Beinecke Rare Books and Manuscripts Library.
44. Turner, *The Wayward and the Seeking,* 5. Georges Gurdjieff, the founder of the Institute of Man's Harmonious Development, believed that modern man needed a new education to restore inner harmony.
45. Nella Larsen to Carl Van Vechten, n.d. [dated "Tuesday, 19th," probably July 1927, given the earlier letter that she mentions], box 1, folder 26, Carl Van Vecten Papers, Beinecke Rare Books and Manuscripts Library.
46. The epithet "mystery woman" is quoted in Hutchinson, *In Search of Nella Larsen: A Biography of the Color Line* (Cambridge, Mass.: Harvard University Press), 1; the description was also used by Mary Helen Washington in an article in *Ms.* magazine in 1980. More recent scholarship has questioned whether or not Peter Walker considered himself Negro since he was from the Danish West Indies. Perhaps some of the secrecy had more to do with Nella's embarrassment about the fact that her parents were not married (20).
47. Ibid., 25.
48. Hutchinson, *In Search of Nella Larsen,* 30.
49. Wall, *Women of the Harlem Renaissance,* 92.
50. "Dicty" is a term used to describe a pretentious person or a social climber.
51. Nella Larsen to Carl Van Vechten, May 1, 1928, box Huh-I, folder 2, Carl Van Vechten Papers, Beinecke Rare Books and Manuscripts Library.
52. Nella Larsen to Dorothy Peterson, n.d. [dated "Saturday"], box 1, folder 26, Dorothy Peterson Collection, James Weldon Johnson Collection, Beinecke Rare Books and Manuscripts Library (hereafter, Dorothy Peterson Collection, Beinecke Rare Books and Manuscripts Library). Larsen wrote to Dorothy

Peterson, "I divorced Elmer last Wednesday very easily quickly and quietly. He is getting married tomorrow in Wellington, Ohio. The new Mrs. Imes (or shall I say the second) will live in the North while he works in the South. It won't be so much different from last year. . . . So much for that! Oh! Yes! Elmer expects to be a father along with February or March of next year. Isn't that swell!"

53. "Fisk Professor Is Divorced by N.Y. Novelist," *Baltimore Afro-American* (October 7, 1933), 1.
54. Nella Larsen to Carl Van Vechten, July 1, 1926, box Huh-I, folder 1, Carl Van Vechten Papers, Beinecke Rare Books and Manuscripts Library. Larsen's emphasis.
55. Nella Larsen to Carl Van Vechten, March 19, 1928, box Huh-I, folder 2, Carl Van Vechten Papers, Beinecke Rare Books and Manuscripts Library.
56. Nella Larsen to Carl Van Vechten, June 14, 1929, box Huh-I, folder 2, Carl Van Vechten Papers, Beinecke Rare Books and Manuscripts Library. A "fay" is a colloquial term for white person.
57. Nella Larsen to Carl Van Vechten, July 28, 1929, box Huh-I, folder 2, Carl Van Vechten Papers, Beinecke Rare Books and Manuscripts Library.
58. Wall, *Women of the Harlem Renaissance,* 88–89. As Wall explains, "As several critics have noted, 'quicksand' is not merely a title, but a unifying metaphor supported throughout by concrete images of suffocation, asphyxiation, and claustrophobia" (113).
59. Nella Larsen, *Quicksand & Passing* (New Brunswick, NJ: Rutgers University Press, 1986), 47, 122.
60. Ibid., 176.
61. Ibid., 94.
62. Ibid., 238–239.
63. Ibid., 222.
64. Ibid., 252.
65. Ibid., 183.

66. Ibid., 192.
67. Ibid., 135.
68. Ibid., 103.
69. Dorothy Peterson to Carl Van Vechten, September 27, 1940; Dorothy Peterson to Carl Van Vechten, February 22, 1944, box PET, Carl Van Vechten Papers, James Weldon Johnson Collection, Beinecke Rare Books and Manuscripts Library.
70. Roark Bedford, "*Quicksand*," box L-LEDZ, folder Larsen, Nella, James Weldon Johnson Collection Clippings, Beinecke Rare Books and Manuscripts Library.
71. Langston Hughes, *The Big Sea: An Autobiography* (New York: Hill and Wang, 1963), 103. Hughes is also prevented from attending the JuJu ritual because he is a "white man."
72. Ibid. Hughes's emphasis.
73. Ibid., 303–304.
74. Ibid., 54.
75. Langston Hughes to Carl Van Vechten, November 8, 1941. Emily Bernard, ed., *Remember Me to Harlem: The Letters of Langston Hughes and Carl Van Vechten, 1925–1962* (New York: Alfred A. Knopf, 2001), 198–199.
76. Langston Hughes, "Passing," box 389, folder 7198, Langston Hughes Papers, Beinecke Rare Books and Manuscripts Library.
77. Hughes, *The Big Sea,* 39.
78. Ibid., xxii.
79. Ibid., xxi. As Hughes explains: "My father hated Negroes. I think he hated himself, too, for being a Negro. He disliked all of his family because they were Negroes and remained in the United States, where none of them had a chance to be much of anything but servants—like my mother, who started out with a good education at the University of Kansas, he said, but had sunk to working in a restaurant, waiting on niggers, when she wasn't in some white woman's kitchen. My father said he wanted me to leave the United States as soon as I finished high school, and

never return—unless I wanted to be a porter or a red cap all my life" (40).

80. Langston Hughes, "Who's Passing for Who?," in *Langston Hughes Short Stories,* ed. Akiba Sullivan Harper (New York: Hill and Wang, 1996), 170–174.
81. Ibid., 173–174.
82. Ibid. Hughes's emphasis.
83. Langston Hughes to Carl Van Vechten, October 30, 1941. Emily Bernard, ed., *Remember Me to Harlem: The Letters of Langston Hughes and Carl Van Vechten, 1925–1962* (New York: Alfred A. Knopf, 2001), 193.
84. Langston Hughes, "Fooling Our White Folks," *Negro Digest,* April 1950, 41.
85. Langston Hughes, "Passing," in *The Ways of White Folks* (New York: Knopf, 1969), 51–52.
86. Ibid., 54.
87. Quoted in Emily Bernard, ed., *Remember Me to Harlem: The Letters of Langston Hughes and Carl Van Vechten* (New York: Vintage, 2001), 310.

5. COMING HOME

1. "Army Man's Suicide Reveals He Is Negro," *New York Times,* January 4, 1932, 1. Also see "Black or White," *Atlanta World,* January 20, 1932, 1.
2. Albert Johnston to Chief of Naval Personnel, January 11, 1943, Johnston scrapbook, series 1, box 2, Johnston Family Papers, Archive Center of the Historical Society of Cheshire County, Keene, N.H. (hereafter Johnston Family Papers, HSCC).
3. Albert Johnston Jr., "Synopsis of Johnston Family's Story," *Lost Boundaries* scrapbook, series 2, box 3, Johnston Family Papers, HSCC. Albert Johnston Jr. sent this essay to Louis de Rochemont, the producer of *Lost Boundaries,* on May 26, 1947. Albert Johnston Jr. wrote that in 1941, there were approximately

2,000 to 2,500 accredited radiologists in the United States; a large percentage were elderly, disabled, or essential to the home front.

4. The Commandant, First Naval District, Navy Department, Bureau of Navigation, to Albert Johnston, August 4, 1941, Johnston scrapbook, series 1, box 2, Johnston Family Papers, HSCC. At this time, the Navy was segregated; there were no black officers, and blacks served mostly as mess attendants. See James T. Patterson, *Grand Expectations: The United States, 1945–1974* (New York: Oxford University Press, 1996), 22. Also see Howard Mansfield, "Prejudice and a Fraction of Success: The Albert Johnston Story and a 'Lost Boundaries' Reunion," *Washington Post,* July 25, 1989, clippings, *Lost Boundaries* scrapbook, series 2, box 4, folder 18, Johnston Family Papers, HSCC. Johnston also applied for a position in the Army's Medical Corps for Negro medical officers but was informed that there were no openings. See M. O. Bousfield, Lt. Col., Medical Corps, to Albert Johnston, September 23, 1942, Johnston scrapbook, series 1, box 1, folder 15, Johnston Family Papers, HSCC.
5. In Albert Johnston Jr.'s essay to Louis de Rochemont, he identified his father as "one-sixth colored" and described his mother as "less than one-eighth" colored. See Johnston Jr., "Synopsis of Johnston Family's Story," Johnston Family Papers, HSCC.
6. "Why 'Passing' Is Passing Out," *Jet,* July 17, 1952, 12–13.
7. See Michael Klarman, *From Jim Crow to Civil Rights: The Supreme Court and the Struggle for Racial Equality* (New York: Oxford University Press, 2004), 3–4.
8. Hanes Walton Jr., Donald R. Deskins Jr., and Sherman Puckett, *The African American Electorate: A Statistical History,* vol. 1 (Thousand Oaks, CA: CQ Press/Sage, 2012).
9. Lani Guinier, "From Racial Liberalism to Racial Literacy: *Brown v. Board of Education* and the Interest-Divergence Dilemma," *Journal of American History* (June 2004): 100.

10. Steve Fraser, "The Good War and the Workers," *American Prospect,* October 2009, A18–A20.
11. Historian Adam Green provides these statistics: "The national median income for urban blacks increased between 1940 and 1950 from $700 to $1,263, and went up again to $2,911 by 1960. Black unemployment between 1948 and 1955 remained under 6 percent for half of the eight years, reaching as low as 4.5% in 1953. Specific occupations showed dramatic increase in the number of African Americans, in particular for men. Black male clerical and sales workers nationwide rose from 58,000 in 1940 to 145,000 in 1950, and to 261,000 in 1960." See Adam Green, *Selling the Race: Culture, Community, and Black Chicago, 1940–1955* (Chicago: University of Chicago Press, 2007), 10.
12. Fraser, "The Good War and the Workers," A18–A20.
13. On the director of *Lost Boundaries,* Louis de Rochemont, see Eugene Lyons, "Louis de Rochemont: Maverick of the Movies," *Reader's Digest,* July 1949, 23–27.
14. The decision to cast whites in black roles was a way of getting around film censors who would not allow even the suggestion of an "interracial" romance, the ease of promoting and marketing films with white stars, and the belief that audiences would feel more compassion for white characters. See Gayle Wald, *Crossing the Color Line: Racial Passing in Twentieth-Century U.S. Literature and Culture* (Durham, N.C.: Duke University Press, 2000), 91.
15. Quoted in Arnold Hirsch, "Massive Resistance in the Urban North: Trumbull Park, Chicago, 1953–1966," *Journal of American History* 82, no. 2 (1995): 523. For more on the Howards' case and the violence that followed, see Chicago Commission on Human Relations, *The Trumbull Park Home Disturbances: A Chronological Report, August 5, 1953 to June 30, 1955* (Chicago: Mayor's Commission on Human Relations, 1955).
16. "Riot Victim," *Ebony,* June 1954, 17–24.

17. W. L. White, *Lost Boundaries* (New York: Harcourt, Brace & World, 1947, 1948), 15. Albert Johnston Jr. told the family's story to film producer Louis de Rochemont, who lived near Keene in Newingtown, New Hampshire. Louis de Rochemont asked author W. L. White to write the family's story that also appeared in *Reader's Digest.* The film was based on the book as told to White by Albert Johnston Jr. See "Lost Boundaries Paved the Way to Understanding," *Kentucky New Era,* July 24, 1989, 7B.
18. Kathleen Wolgemuth, "Woodrow Wilson and Federal Segregation," *Journal of Negro History* 44, no. 2 (1959): 158–159.
19. White, *Lost Boundaries,* 12.
20. *Topsy and Eva,* Act 1, utc.iath.virginia.edu/onstage/duncanhp.html.
21. "Rosetta Bathes Herself in Black," *Sunday Advertiser,* May 31, 1925. Four years after Albert and Thyra saw the play, D. W. Griffith, the infamous director of the racist epic, *The Birth of a Nation* (1915), would direct a combination of the stage show as an eighty-minute movie.
22. White, *Lost Boundaries,* 18.
23. Ibid., 21.
24. "What Happened to the 'Lost Boundaries' Family?," *Ebony,* August 1952, 56.
25. White, *Lost Boundaries,* 23.
26. David W. Blight, *Race and Reunion: The Civil War in American Memory* (Cambridge, Mass.: Harvard University Press, 2001), 110–122.
27. White, *Lost Boundaries,* 23.
28. Ibid., 26.
29. Ibid., 25.
30. Ibid., 5.
31. Ibid., 25–26.
32. Ibid., 35.
33. Ibid., 28.

34. Howard Mansfield, "Prejudice and a Fraction of Success: The Albert Johnston Story and a 'Lost Boundaries' Reunion," *Washington Post,* July 25, 1989.
35. Johnston Jr., "Synopsis of Johnston Family's Story," Johnson Family Papers, HSCC.
36. "Lost Boundaries," *Showmen's Trade Review,* July 2, 1949, *Lost Boundaries* scrapbook, series 2, box 3, Johnston Family Papers, HSCC. Emphasis in the original.
37. White, *Lost Boundaries,* 7–8.
38. Ibid., 8.
39. Ibid.
40. Johnston Jr., "Synopsis of Johnston Family's Story," Johnston Family Papers, HSCC.
41. White, *Lost Boundaries,* 55–56.
42. Erika Doss, ed., *Looking at* Life *Magazine* (Washington, D.C.: Smithsonian Institution Press, 2001), 42.
43. "Henry Luce, 68, Dies in Phoenix; Started a Publishing Empire with *Time,*" *New York Times,* March 1, 1967. Also see Wendy Kozol, "Gazing at Race in the Pages of *Life:* Picturing Segregation through Theory and History," in Doss, *Looking at* Life *Magazine.*
44. Wald, *Crossing the Color Line,* 126.
45. William Houseman to Albert Johnston Jr., December 1, 1948, *Lost Boundaries* scrapbook, series 2, box 3, Johnston Family Papers, HSCC.
46. "What Happened to the 'Lost Boundaries' Family?," *Ebony,* August 1952, 52–66; "Movie of the Week: *Lost Boundaries,*" *Life,* July 4, 1949, 64, *Lost Boundaries* scrapbook, series 2, box 3, Johnston Family Papers, HSCC. For more on *Life*'s representations of postwar America, see Wendy Kozol, *Life's America: Family and Nation in Postwar Photojournalism* (Philadelphia: Temple University Press, 1994).
47. Wald makes this observation in her discussion of *Lost Boundaries.* Wald, *Crossing the Color Line,* 85.

48. "N.H. Neighborliness Crosses the Color Line," *New Hampshire Sunday News,* November 30, 1947, clippings, *Lost Boundaries* scrapbook, series 2, box 4, folder 18, Johnston Family Papers, HSCC.
49. Ibid.
50. Sprague W. Drenan, "'Lost Boundaries' Makes Deep Impression on Keene Audience," *Keene Sentinel,* July 25, 1949.
51. "Democracy at Work in 'Lost Boundaries,'" *Boston Record,* July 16, 1949, *Lost Boundaries* scrapbook, series 2, box 3, Johnston Family Papers, HSCC.
52. Quoted in Walter A. Jackson, *Gunnar Myrdal and America's Conscience: Social Engineering and Racial Liberalism, 1938–1987* (Chapel Hill: University of North Carolina Press, 1990), 190.
53. "Lost Boundaries," *Ebony,* May 1948, 45.
54. "What Happened to the 'Lost Boundaries' Family?" *Ebony,* August 1952, 58.
55. *Ebony* cited Keene's population as 13,832 in the article, "Lost Boundaries," May 1948, 45.
56. "What Happened to the 'Lost Boundaries' Family?" *Ebony,* August 1952, 58.
57. Thyra Johnston quoted in Dorothy Dunbar Bromley, untitled article, n.d., *Lost Boundaries* scrapbook, series 2, box 3, Johnston Family Papers, HSCC.
58. "This Family Was White for Twenty Years," *Look,* February 1, 1949, 38.
59. Bromley, untitled article. This article states that Johnston increased the radiology department's annual income from $9,000 to $35,000 during his thirteen-year tenure.
60. Thyra Johnston to Louis de Rochemont, July 11, 1949, *Lost Boundaries* scrapbook, series 2, box 3, Johnston Family Papers, HSCC.
61. Thyra Johnston to Albert Johnston Jr., n.d., *Lost Boundaries* scrapbook, series 2, box 3, Johnston Family Papers, HSCC.
62. Thyra Johnston to Louis de Rochemont, July 11, 1949, *Lost Boundaries* scrapbook, series 2, box 3, Johnston Family Papers, HSCC.

63. Lillie Jackson to Thyra Johnston, October 17, 1949, personal papers, Speaking Tour as a Result of "Lost Boundaries," series 1, box 1, folder 4, Johnston Family Papers, HSCC. At the time of Johnston's speech to the Baltimore branch, the branch was the largest in the country, with more than 20,000 members.
64. Ibid.
65. "Family of 'Lost Boundaries' Promotes Interracial Understanding," *Baltimore Afro-American,* November 26, 1949.
66. Albert Johnston, untitled speech to Camden NAACP, n.d., personal papers, series 1, box 1, folder 5, Johnston Family Papers, HSCC.
67. Ibid. All quotations are from Johnston's speech to the Camden NAACP. Although the title of the folder links this speech to Dr. Johnston's appearance before the Camden NAACP, it appears that he gave the same speech to other branches of the NAACP.
68. "Move to Oust Dr. A. C. Johnston from Hospital Staff Reported," *Keene Sentinel,* November 21, 1949.
69. "Negro Doctor Says He Accepts Ouster: Asserts Keene, N.H., Hospital's Attitude Changed After He Bared Race—Board Differs," n.d., *Lost Boundaries* clippings file, Billy Rose Theatre Collection, New York Public Library for the Performing Arts, New York (hereafter Billy Rose Theatre Collection, NYPL).
70. "Dr. Johnston Dropped—Hospital Trustees Claim that X-Ray Department Neglected," *Keene Sentinel,* June 12, 1953.
71. Ibid.
72. Ibid.
73. Ralph Ellison, *Shadow and Act* (New York: Vintage Books, 1953, 1964), 275.
74. The Johnstons were renamed the Carters in the film; *Lost Boundaries* photographs, series 2, box 4, folder 22, Johnston Family Papers, HSCC.
75. Ellison, *Shadow and Act,* 277. In 1949 alone, three "message movies" were released: *Home of the Brave, Lost Boundaries,* and *Pinky.* For

further discussion of "message movies," see Cripps, *Making Movies Black.*

76. Johnston Jr., "Synopsis of Johnston Family's Story." Johnston Family Papers, HSCC.
77. Thyra Johnston to Louis de Rochemont, n.d., *Lost Boundaries* scrapbook, series 2, box 3, Johnston Family Papers, HSCC.
78. See Al Sweeney, "Lee Shows 'Coolness' on Racial Discussions," *Baltimore Afro-American,* November 5, 1949. Lee told the *Afro-American* that he thought that *Lost Boundaries* was the best of the films dealing with racial issues because the film did not stereotype blacks.
79. Al Sweeney, "Lee Shows 'Coolness' on Racial Discussions," *Baltimore Afro-American* (November 5, 1949).
80. Dowdal H. Davis, "Movie Industry Progresses: Interracial Films Prove Beneficial," *Baltimore Afro-American,* January 7, 1950.
81. Alvin E. White, "'Lost Boundaries' Movie, A 'Must,'" *Atlanta Daily World,* July 21, 1949, 3.
82. "Needed: A Negro Legion of Decency," *Ebony,* February 1947, 36.
83. Eugene Lyons, "Louis de Rochemont: Maverick of the Movies," *Reader's Digest,* July 1949, 27.
84. "Lost Boundaries," *Variety,* June 29, 1949, *Lost Boundaries* clippings file, Billy Rose Theatre Collection, NYPL.
85. Howard Mansfield, "Prejudice and a Fraction of Success: The Albert Johnston Story and a 'Lost Boundaries' Reunion," *Washington Post,* July 25, 1989.
86. "Atlanta, Memphis Ban 'Lost Boundaries,'" *Pittsburgh Courier,* August 27, 1949.
87. Laurie Beth Green, 1999, "Battling the Plantation Mentality: Consciousness, Culture and the Politics of Race, Class and Gender in Memphis, 1940–1968," The University of Chicago, 210, 241, citing the Memphis Municipal Code, Article XIV, and Board of Censors Resolution. Green writes that in 1947, Binford banned the film *Curley* solely because it showed black and white children playing together.

88. Walter White, "On the Tragedy of the Color Line; 'Lost Boundaries,'" *New York Times,* March 28, 1948.
89. Lloyd Binford quoted in Billy Rowe, "Dixie TV Refuses to Sell Air Time for Film Showing," *Pittsburgh Courier,* n.d., *Lost Boundaries* clippings, series 2, box 4, folder 18, Johnston Family Papers, HSCC.
90. Eileen Boris uses this term in her article "'You Wouldn't Want One of 'Em Dancing with Your Wife': Racialized Bodies on the Job in World War II," *American Quarterly* 50 (March 1998): 77–108.
91. President's Committee on Fair Employment Practice, "The Birmingham Hearing," *Press Clippings Digest,* July 6, 1942, Fair Employment Practices Commission, box 3, p. 15, Franklin D. Roosevelt Presidential Library and Museum, Hyde Park, New York (hereafter FDR Library).
92. Eugene 'Bull' Connor to President Franklin D. Roosevelt, August 7, 1942 [attached to memorandum from Dr. MacLean, August 18, 1942], Fair Employment Practices Commission, box 3, FDR Library.
93. "Bilbo Warns White Woman: 'Don't Entertain Negroes,'" *Chicago Defender,* December 18, 1943. In 1930, the state of Mississippi enacted a criminal statute that made punishable the "publishing, printing, or circulating of any literature in favor of or urging interracial marriage or social equality." Quoted in Werner Sollors, *Neither Black nor White yet Both* (New York: Oxford University Press, 1997), 4.
94. The Dixiecrat revolt ultimately failed. The Dixiecrat appeal was essentially confined to the Deep South, and the Dixiecrats carried only four states: Mississippi, Alabama, South Carolina, and Louisiana. The New Deal coalition remained strong in metropolitan areas of the South. See Michael J. Klarman, "How Brown Changed Race Relations: The Backlash Thesis," *Journal of American History* 81 (June 1994): 92–93. Despite the six million followers who heard Strom Thurmond's stump speeches, the votes of blacks in key states such as California, Illinois, and Ohio led to Truman's reelection. Also see Patterson, *Grand Expectations,* 150–151.

95. Original transcript, IRD-DR Corporation, et al. v. Christine Smith, et al., no. 373889 F. Supp. 596 (March 1950) at 50. Surprisingly, Smith approved three other films on racial tolerance (*Home of the Brave, Pinky,* and *Intruder in the Dust*). The day that the suit was filed in Atlanta against *Lost Boundaries, Pinky* opened without incident, to packed houses and good press. See Thomas M. Pryor, "Censorship Issues: Atlanta Ban on 'Lost Boundaries' Goes Before Federal Court Tomorrow," *Lost Boundaries* clippings, series 2, box 4, folder 13, Johnston Family Papers, HSCC.
96. Lester Coleman, "Not 'Anti-Segregation': Censor Tells Why She Approved 'Home of the Brave' for Showing Here," *Atlanta Constitution,* October 2, 1949.
97. Alexander F. Miller, Director of the Atlanta Anti-Defamation League, to Donald Oberdorfer Jr., October 6, 1949, *Lost Boundaries* scrapbook, series 2, box 3, Johnston Family Papers, HSCC.
98. "A Negro Doctor: LOST BOUNDARIES," *Washington Post,* April 4, 1948, B7.
99. "His Is a Personal Interest," letter to the editor, *Atlanta Constitution,* October 25, 1949.
100. "Story of Former Gorham Residents Told in New Film," n.d., *Lost Boundaries* clippings, series 2, box 4, folder 18, Johnston Family Papers, HSCC.
101. Pryor, "Censorship Issues: Atlanta Ban on 'Lost Boundaries' Goes Before Federal Court Tomorrow."
102. James L. Hicks, "'Never Again,' Says Man Who 'Passed' 20 Years: Doctor Would Tell Race if He Could Start Over Subject of Play 'Lost Boundaries,'" *Baltimore Afro-American,* July 16, 1949, C8, and "Doctor 'Passed' 20 Years, Turns Colored Again," *New Journal and Guide,* July 16, 1949, D4.
103. "Physician Feels Sense of Relief," n.d., *Lost Boundaries* clippings, series 2, box 4, folder 18, Johnston Family Papers, HSCC.

104. See Nathan Irvin Huggins and Brenda Smith Huggins, eds., in *Revelations: American History, American Myths* (New York: Oxford University Press, 1995), 246. For more on the rising levels of economic well-being among blacks in the postwar period, see Gerald David Jaynes and Robin M. Williams Jr., eds., *A Common Destiny: Blacks and American Society* (Washington, D.C.: National Academy Press, 1989).
105. Janice Kingslow, "I Refuse to Pass," *Negro Digest,* May 1950, 23.
106. Ibid., 26.
107. Ibid., 30.
108. Ibid.
109. Richard L. Williams, "He Wouldn't Cross the Line: Herb Jeffries Cheerfully Pays the Price of Choosing His Race," *Life,* September 3, 1951, 90.
110. Ibid., 82.
111. Ibid., 81.
112. *Jet* also noted that progress on economic and civil rights fronts also negated the need for "situational" or temporary passing. Although many light-skinned blacks opted to pass to enjoy access to better traveling accommodations or entertainment in white night clubs, *Jet* noted that "federal rulings on restrictive covenants and inter-state travel, equal rights statutes, etc., are all helping to decrease the number of Negroes who find it 'convenient' to 'pass.'" See *Jet* "Why 'Passing' Is Passing Out," July 17, 1952, 12–16.
113. See "How Negroes Are Gaining in the U.S.," *U.S. News & World Report,* June 28, 1957, 105–106; "Negroes: Big Advances in Jobs, Wealth and Status," *U.S. News & World Report,* November 28, 1958, 90–92.
114. "Negroes: Big Advances in Jobs, Wealth, Status," 91.
115. "Medicine Found Most Biased Profession," *Chicago Defender,* August 5, 1944, 1. Information on the American Medical Association's resolutions is printed in "Louisiana Medical Association

Calls for Dropping of Racial Bars," *Journal of the National Medical Association* (July 1953): 289. In addition to this article, this issue includes an article regarding the integration of an Orange, New Jersey, hospital and the article "Alabama Medical Association Votes to Admit Negroes" (289–291).

116. Quoted in Wald, *Crossing the Line*, 123.
117. Quoted in Adam Green, *Selling the Race,* 141.
118. "Why 'Passing' Is Passing Out," 15.
119. Film scholar J. Ronald Green uses the concept of "false uplift" in a discussion of Oscar Micheaux's films in *Straight Lick: The Cinema of Oscar Micheaux* (Bloomington: Indiana University Press, 2000), 174–182.
120. "I'm Through with Passing," *Ebony,* March 1951, 22.
121. N. Huggins and B. Huggins, eds., *Revelations,* 245. Black strategies would continue to change as the militancy of black protest increased through the 1950s and into the 1960s. Describing the struggles of the 1960s, Nathan Huggins wrote, "The [Black] Revolution's insistence on race identity, race consciousness, race pride, and race beauty has made anachronistic the game of hide-and-seek traditionally played by whites and blacks in America."
122. Joe Cooper, "Black Pride, Black Unity, Black Progress," *Sacramento Observer,* June 3, 1971, B3.
123. Don Quinn Kelley, "How to Build Black Pride," *Chicago Defender,* July 24, 1968, 4.
124. J. R. Green, *Straight Lick,* 183–192.
125. J. R. Green, *Straight Lick,* 192.

6. EPILOGUE

Epigraph: "A Family History," n.d., research projects, *The Negro Family in the U.S.,* family histories, box 131-91, folder 24, p.1, E. Franklin Frazier Papers, MSRC, Howard University. This chapter draws on a series of family histories that sociologist E. Franklin Frazier collected while teaching at Howard University during the 1930s and 1940s. My thanks to the late

Donna Wells at the Moorland-Spingarn Research Center for guiding me to this collection.

1. Ibid.
2. Ibid., 24–25.
3. Ibid., 24.
4. Ibid., 28–29.
5. Ralph Ellison, "The World and the Jug," in *Shadow and Act* (New York: Vintage Books, 1964), 124
6. For more on the complex history of Brer Rabbit, the trickster figure, and African American folklore, see Lawrence Levine, *Black Culture and Black Consciousness* (New York: Oxford University Press, 1977), esp. chap. 2, "The Meaning of Slave Tales," and chap. 6, "A Pantheon of Heroes."
7. James Clifford, *The Predicament of Culture: Twentieth-Century Ethnography, Literature, and Art* (Cambridge, Mass.: Harvard University Press, 1988), 344.
8. *Le retour de Martin Guerre* [The return of Martin Guerre], directed by Daniel Vigne (Dussault, France 3: Société Française de Production, 1982), DVD.
9. Natalie Zemon Davis, *The Return of Martin Guerre* (Cambridge, Mass., 1983). See esp. chap. 4, "The Masks of Arnaud du Tilh," 35–41.
10. "The Republicans," *New Orleans Times Democrat,* January 24, 1888, clippings, box 81-2, folder 54, Pinchback Papers, MSRC, Howard University.
11. Harlan is quoted in "The Republicans," *New Orleans Times Democrat,* January 24, 1888, clippings, box 81-2, folder 54, Pinchback Papers, MSRC. Lenore Drew is quoted in Spencie Love, *One Blood: The Death and Resurrection of Charles R. Drew* (Chapel Hill: University of North Carolina Press, 1996), 22.
12. J. Ronald Green, *Straight Lick: The Cinema of Oscar Micheaux* (Bloomington: Indiana University Press, 2000), 190–191.
13. Ronne Hartfield, *Another Way Home: The Tangled Roots of Race in One Chicago Family,* 81, 41–42.

14. For more on the plasticity and reproduction of racial ideologies, see Thomas Holt, *The Problem of Race in the 21st Century* (Cambridge, Mass.: Harvard University Press, 2002).
15. Jean Toomer to Waldo Frank, n.d., box 3, folder 83, Jean Toomer Papers, Beinecke Rare Books and Manuscripts Library. The date of this letter is likely 1922, given the letters that come before and after.
16. Ibid.
17. Political scientist Melissa Harris-Perry describes Obama as functioning as a "green screen" or a "blank screen onto which Americans could project their own identities, political goals, and national hopes." See Melissa Harris-Perry, *Sister Citizen: Shame Stereotypes, and Black Women in America* (New Haven, Conn.: Yale University Press, 2011), 271–272.
18. Barack Obama, *Dreams From My Father: A Story of Race and Inheritance* (1995, repr., New York: Three Rivers Press, 2004), 305.
19. Kimberly McClain DaCosta, *Making Multiracials: State, Family, and Market in the Redrawing of the Color Line* (Stanford, Calif.: Stanford University Press, 2007), 1–4.
20. Ruth La Ferla, "Generation E. A.," *New York Times,* December 28, 2003.
21. Ibid.
22. DaCosta, *Making Multiracials,* 7.
23. Danzy Senna, "The Mulatto Millenium," *Utne Reader,* September–October 1998. This article is an excerpt from Claudine C. O'Hearn, *Half and Half: Writers on Growing Up Biracial and Bicultural* (New York: Pantheon Books, 1998). Senna's first book, *Caucasia,* was about two mixed-race daughters who are separated by their parents. The darker-skinned daughter moves to Brazil with her militant African American father, and the lighter-skinned daughter passes as white with her white mother in New Hampshire. See Senna, *Caucasia* (New York: Riverhead/Penguin, 1999). For more on representations of mixed-race people in literature

and art, see Michele Elam, *The Souls of Mixed Folk: Race, Politics, and Aesthetics in the New Milennium* (Stanford, Calif.: Stanford University Press, 2011).

There has been an explosion of memoirs written on this subject since the mid-1990s. See James McBride, *The Color of Water: A Black Man's Tribute to His White Mother* (New York: Riverhead/Penguin Books, 1996); Essie Mae Washington-Williams and William Stadiem, *Dear Senator: A Memoir by the Daughter of Strom Thurmond* (New York: HarperCollins, 2005); June Cross, *Secret Daughter: A Mixed Race Daughter and the Mother Who Gave Her Away* (New York: Viking, 2006); Victoria Rowell, *The Woman Who Raised Me: A Memoir* (New York: HarperCollins, 2007); Bliss Broyard, *One Drop: My Father's Hidden Lie—A Story of Race and Family Secrets* (New York: Little, Brown and Company, 2007).

24. For an argument about the importance of marking only one census category, see Michele Elam, "2010 Census: Think Twice, Check Once," http://www.huffingtonpost.com/michele-elam/2010-census-think-twice-c_b_490164.html.

Acknowledgments

I have had a lifetime of extraordinary teachers. It is my pleasure to thank the teachers and the institutions that made this book possible.

Thomas Holt taught me the craft of history. My debts to him are beyond measure. Through his teaching and his scholarship, Tom broadened my imagination of what American and African American history might be. His equanimity, keen advice, steady guidance, and illuminating comments were indispensable to this book.

A wide circle of professors, mentors, students, and friends at the University of Chicago encouraged my intellectual growth. Jacqueline Stewart taught me how to use rich literary and film sources to understand history in new ways. George Chauncey's work offered an exceptional model of how to write a long history about a seemingly hidden world. For their careful readings, insightful questions, and thoughtful comments, I am grateful to Melissa Barton, Dain Borges, Kornel Chang, Mike Czaplicki, Michael Flug, Mollie

Godfrey, Jacqueline Goldsby, Jim Grossman, Melissa Harris-Perry, Moira Hinderer, Gwennan Ickes, Tracye Matthews, Deborah Nelson, Mae Ngai, Adolph Reed, Julie Saville, David Spatz, Amy Dru Stanley, Ken Warren, and the members of the Social History Workshop, the Workshop on Race and the Reproduction of Racial Ideologies, the American Cultures Workshop, and the Mellon Dissertation Seminar in the Humanities.

In Chicago I found a vibrant intellectual community and camaraderie with many people whom I feel lucky to call my friends. Chris Freeburg, Matt Millikan, and Mike Wakeford have been generous sounding boards and sources of constant support. I thank Gabby Cavagnaro, Beth Cooper, Dave Ferguson, Jessica Graham, José Angel Hernández, Quincy Mills, Arissa Oh, Sarah Potter, Alison Lefkowitz, Jon Levy, Sheldon Lyke, Carl Nash, Meredith Oda, Mihir Pandya, Laurel Spindel, Kyle Volk, and Ellen Wu for their friendship and intellectual engagement. I am grateful for the enthusiasm that Ryan Sandrock showed for this project in its earliest stages.

Historians owe a tremendous debt of gratitude to the archivists who provide invaluable direction. This project required guidance through numerous archives, and I am deeply appreciative to the indispensable assistance provided by archivists and staff members who helped me locate materials in their own collections and steered me toward collections that I otherwise would not have found. I am thankful to the archivists at the following libraries: the Moorland-Spingarn Research Center at Howard University (and especially to the late Donna Wells for pointing me to the E. Franklin Frazier collection); the Beinecke Rare Book and Manuscript Library at Yale University; the John Hope and Aurelia E. Franklin Library at Fisk University; the Archives of the Peabody Museum at Harvard University; the Archive Center of the Historical Society of Cheshire

County in Keene, New Hampshire; the Library Company of Philadelphia; the Library of Congress in Washington, D.C.; the Southern Historical Collection at the Wilson Library at the University of North Carolina, Chapel Hill; the Schomburg Center for Research in Black Culture in New York; the Watkinson Library at Trinity College; the Catherine Pelton Durrell '25 Archives and Special Collections Library at Vassar College; the Burton Historical Collection in Detroit, Michigan; the Albert and Shirley Small Special Collections Library at the University of Virginia; and the Bentley Historical Library at the University of Michigan.

I am grateful to the faculty fellows at the Clayman Institute for Gender Research at Stanford University and to the comments of discussants and the responses from audiences at the meetings of the Organization for American Historians, the American Studies Association, the Southern Association for Women Historians, and the Berkshires Conference on American Women. The comments and questions raised at these conferences helped me to put the pieces of this puzzle together. I am especially thankful to Martha Sandweiss and Martha Jones for their close readings, acute observations, and criticisms.

As I faced the daunting task of writing this book, many generous scholars provided clarity and direction. I am grateful to Estelle Freedman for graciously reading this manuscript several times and for her razor-sharp criticism. Jim Campbell could not have been more giving with the time he spent to help me refine and focus the book. I thank Richard White for providing an exemplary model of gifted storytelling and for thinking through my major arguments with me. The comments and interventions of the anonymous readers at Harvard University Press were especially rich, enlightening, and inspiring.

I completed much of the work of this project while I had fellowships from the Ford Foundation, the Clayman Institute for Gender Research at Stanford, and the Center for the Comparative Study of Race and Ethnicity at Stanford. I am grateful to each of these institutions for giving me the luxury of time to think and to write. I am thankful to Tom Holt for connecting me to Rebecca Scott. I thank her for being a fantastic mentor and a stunning example of exemplary scholarship and committed teaching and mentoring.

I am deeply grateful to the team at Harvard University Press. Joyce Seltzer is the consummate editor. I am thankful for her belief in this book and for her expert editorial direction. I am grateful to Brian Distelberg for his equanimity, for keeping me on schedule, and for adeptly shepherding the book through the publication process. I thank Pat Cattani, Maggie Smith-Beehler, and Hannah Hayes for putting the polish on my manuscript through their skillful copyediting and proofreading. I am grateful to Jennifer Bossert for her patience and for expertly coordinating the production of this book.

Supportive and encouraging colleagues at Stanford—H. Samy Alim, Jennifer Brody, Cheryl Brown, Jennifer Burns, Al Camarillo, Clay Carson, Gordon Chang, Bob Crews, Michele Elam, Shelley Fisher Fishkin, Zephyr Frank, Sean Hanretta, Yumi Moon, Vaughn Rasberry, Richard Roberts, Priya Satia, Laura Stokes, Kären Wigen, Mikael Wolfe, and Caroline Winterer—were more important to this book's completion than they may know. I am grateful to David Como, my mentor at Stanford, for being a model for my scholarship and teaching. For endless emotional support and friendship, I give special thanks to Prudence Carter, Andrea Rees Davies, J. P. Daughton, Carol McKibben, Ana Minian, Edith Sheffer, and Jun Uchida.

I am deeply appreciative to my talented research assistants, Bianca Dang, April Gregory, and Maya Humes. Bianca, April, and Maya put their extraordinary creativity, deep engagement with history, and boundless energy into making this book the best it could be. Maya Humes deserves special mention for her hard work, incisive research skills, and sharp-eyed reading of the manuscript.

Without the hospitality and friendship of Nikia Bergan and Cormac Miller, I would have not been able to explore the archive at Moorland-Spingarn, and I would not have had the time or the space to develop the key arguments of this book. Nikia and Cormac let me stay in their guest room for weeks on end. Words fail to express how grateful I am for Nikia and Cormac and how much this book benefited from their kindness and generosity.

The love and constant support of my childhood friends—Margot Kenaston, Liz Krieger, Jane Manners, Ben Peyser, and Becky Prentice—have made my life much, much richer. The wonderful friendship and brilliant, curious minds of many others—Nikia Bergan, Warren Chain, Iris Choi, Jennifer Chung, Caroline Cromwell, Chris-Tia Donaldson, Jim Downs, Salem Fisseha, Margo Flug, Sarah Glass, Cheryl Goodrich, Janna Hansen, Ellen Klutznick, Kristy Johnson, Melissa LaSalle, Jaime Lester, Amy Millikan, Crescent Muhammad, Florencia Polite, Jennifer Rhodes, and Leslie Wakeford—mean the world to me.

For encouragement and emotional support, I am truly grateful for my family, whose love has sustained me. I am especially thankful for my grandmother, Vieran Parish; my aunts, Elaine Govan, Sedette Ward, and Gwen Parish; my cousins, Tory Dunson, Kevan Fareed, Evan Fareed, Norman Parish, and Lecretia Johnson; and my immediate family, Greg and Debra Hobbs and Lloyd Dirkson.

My sister, Verinda Hobbs, has generously encouraged and lovingly supported me at every turn.

My best teachers have been my parents, Joyce and Al Hobbs. To date, there has not been one paper that I have written that has not been improved by their care. They are, without a doubt, the most generous and compassionate people I know. I am deeply appreciative of the unconditional love, endless enthusiasm, and tender support that they have given me in this as in every endeavor. For this and so much more, this book is dedicated to them.

This book is about loss. Maybe that is because loss in its sometimes sudden, sometimes anticipated, but always painful iterations has been a constant theme in my adult life. Maybe that is why I saw it in the lives of the people whom I studied. Loss reminds us of just how much we have and how deeply we love. Loss is not easy to articulate. Words fail us even when the feelings are the most acute. My aim in this book has been to find the sounds, the scenes, and the stories to put words to loss to show that it is a constant and defining aspect of living.

I wrote this book with a heavy heart. I lost many of my most enthusiastic cheerleaders and most loving supporters while I was writing. I grieve the loss of my dear friend Myrna Robinson, who offered me an unexpected sanctuary when I needed it the most. She became the kind of friend that one is lucky to have just once in a lifetime. Her dedication to her work made me more committed to mine. I am so very grateful for the time that I had with her.

My uncle, Norman Parish Jr., taught me to appreciate art. He would have loved this book's cover, as he was a gifted artist himself, and had graduated from the Art Institute in Chicago several years after Archibald Motley Jr. I also lost my aunt Shirley Kitching, the magnificent storyteller who inspired this book by sharing the story of a family member who passed as white. We cried tears of joy when I gave her my completed dissertation. She couldn't believe that her name was in it. I could not have written it without her. I am so grateful for the vital connection that she gave me to my family's history. Joan Didion has written that one can grieve only one loss at a time. So for now, I will grieve the loss of Shirley. At some point, I will have to face the loss of my cousins Cynthia, Valerie, and Mark, who were like sisters and brothers to me and who inherited their mother's gift of rich storytelling.

The most wrenching loss came just a year after I graduated from college, when my sister, Sharon, died at the age of thirty-one after a courageous five-year battle with breast cancer. She would have gotten a real kick out of the idea that her little sister had written a book. One of our favorite jokes was that I had been admitted to Harvard by a complete fluke: I had won a raffle at our local grocery store.

When Sharon died, we had to share the tragic news with her friends. Sharon's friends did not cry. They screamed. Some sobbed and yelled for what seemed like hours before they could gather themselves together to write down the arrangements. As exhausting as this work was, it was profoundly moving to feel just how deeply my sister was loved. One of Sharon's most bereaved friends surprised me by immediately asking about me. In words that were barely intelligible, she asked, "What about Allyson?" I said, "I'm Allyson." She stuttered and repeated over and over, "She was so proud of you."

This book is for you, Sharon. I hope that your dear friend was right. I hope that you are proud.

Index

Page numbers in italics refer to figures.

INDEX